Womanhood
Revisited

As a woman, wife and mother I found tremendous encouragement and challenge in this book. Anne traces God's intentions for women through Scripture, outlines the changing expectations of women through the course of history, and thus presents the present-day dilemma for women in its wider context. The book is thus a valuable tool to help every woman to 'learn to apply Biblical truth to their life in such a way that they are not swayed by a secular society.' I am constantly aware of media and society pressure on women to be discontented with the 'traditional' roles for women. It is thus refreshing to be affirmed in our equality of value with men in God's sight, yet also in our unique and complementary differences.

Joyce Gledhill

Womanhood Revisited is a very carefully researched and well thought-through book. As well as presenting an overview of the role of women through Biblical times and in more recent history, it makes practical applications for a way forward in the third millennium. The question of how men and women should relate in the home, society and the church has been notoriously difficult to answer. Anne has some brave and refreshing things to say about how she understands what the Bible says. *Womanhood Revisited* deserves to be read by people on both 'sides' of the role of women debate. Even if you disagree with Anne's conclusions, it will make you think again about what you do believe.

Janet Gaukroger

I am grateful to Anne for the hours she has struggled and agonized over the writing of this book. It is only when it has been read from cover to cover that the reader will discover that it provides a holistic view of the role women have played in society over the years. Her efforts have been well worthwhile and will, I'm sure, be a challenge and encouragement to all who read it.

Fiona Castle

Womanhood Revisited

Anne Graham

Christian Focus

ISBN 1-85792-685-4

© Copyright Anne Graham 2002

Published in 2002
by
Christian Focus Publications Ltd
Geanies House, Fearn, Tain,
Ross-shire, IV20 1TW, Great Britain
www.christianfocus.com

Printed in Great Britain by Guernsey Press

Cover Design by Alister MacInnes

Contents

Acknowledgments

Thank you:
— to Jim, my husband, who has loved me (warts and all) and who has been my best friend on earth for more than half a century; who has not only taught God's Word faithfully from the pulpit but has also lived out what he has taught as husband and father; who has patiently read my handwritten manuscript, has endured my pre-occupation when words wouldn't come, has been my Greek lexicon and has prayed for me and with me.
— to Alex Brooks (Formerly President of Bethany Missionary Fellowship and now of the relief organization Charis International), who, over many years, has stimulated my brain cells with earnest conversation and discussion; has kept me supplied with magazine articles and books from the USA, who introduced me to the many faceted collection of essays and papers which makes up 'Recovering Biblical Manhood and Womanhood' at a time when I was beginning to wonder if I had really heard God speak.
— to Derek Bingham, who introduced me to William MacKenzie and Christian Focus Publications
— to Di Naden of Wycliffe Bible Translators, who has stimulated my thinking, has been a patient listener and an encourager ever since we were involved in Bible Studies with young mums nearly twenty years ago.
— to Lyn Vernon and other members of my spiritual family at Gold Hill who have prayed for me since I began writing almost three years ago.
— to those who have allowed me to use personal material in this book.
— and lastly, but certainly not least, to Anne Falconer, who has spent long hours and endless sheets of paper transforming my pencil scribbles into a typed manuscript.

Why Womanhood Revisited?

For many months I had tried to find a clever title for this book. Some made suggestions but nothing seemed right. Eventually I decided to stop trying and to believe that if He had really put it in my heart to write this book, God would also provide me with a title. One morning, many months later, I woke up quite early and suddenly (not a common occurrence for me!) with the words 'Womanhood Revisited' running through my head.

The purpose of this book is to challenge the political correctness which regards me as a person rather than a woman; to explore the unchanging nature of God's plans and purpose in regard to womanhood; and to explore how Scriptural principles can be worked out against the tide of a secular, unbelieving society.

I am writing as a wife and a mother and so much of what I have written is from that perspective. However, all women enter womanhood single and most women end life single. Those who are single have a unique opportunity to impact the 'working world' outside the home in a way in which those of us who have taken on marriage and family cannot do.

Womanhood needs to be celebrated as God intended it to be – not competing with manhood but rather complementing it. Christian women need to demonstrate a different spirit from that of those around them.

Foreword

Womanhood Revisited is an unbiased appraisal of men and women throughout the Old and New Testament times and right up to the present day. Anne has brought the roles of men and women under severe scrutiny as she examines the Word of God. She has skilfully combined personal anecdotes drawn from life's experiences with many characters from the Bible, to illustrate God's plan and purpose for our lives.

Society, fashions and technology may change and advance, but God's Word remains relevant. Anne highlights the consequences of the behaviour of those who seek to obey God and those who don't and the effects these have on society. This book has been a long time in the making. It is borne out of Anne's yearning for women to be proud of the role they play in God's order for living.

I first met Anne twenty-five years ago as wife of the senior pastor of Gold Hill Baptist Church, Jim Graham. But she was much more than that, she was the mother of three lively young sons and one daughter who were a little older than my four children. Anne would not have known at the time the influence she exerted on my own management of family and home, not to mention marriage. She was a role model of quiet, godly contentment, and fulfilment in the circumstances in which God had placed her. I have heard her speak to roomfuls of young mothers to quietly encourage them in their roles, and I have also watched her live out her teaching in her own life. As this book will reveal, she gave up career opportunities in order to fulfil her role as a wife and mother, and looking back at her now adult family, I'm sure she has no regrets.

Since becoming a Christian, I have also been a champion of mothers who, through choosing to sacrifice career in favour of raising their families, so often suffer from low self-esteem as they are denigrated by society. Therefore it is wonderful to find a book which affirms mothers and encourages them to look to God, rather than society, for their guidelines.

I am grateful to Anne for the hours she has struggled and agonized over the writing of this book. It is only when it has been read from cover to cover that the reader will discover that it provides a holistic view of the role women have played in society over the years. Her efforts have been well worthwhile and will, I'm sure, be a challenge and encouragement to all who read it.

Fiona Castle

Prologue

Charles Dickens begins his novel *The Tale of Two Cities*, set at the time of the French Revolution, with these words:

> It was the best of times, it was the worst of times.
> It was the age of wisdom, it was the age of foolishness.
> It was the epoch of belief, it was the epoch of incredulity.
> It was the season of light, it was the season of darkness.
> It was the spring of hope, it was the winter of despair.
> We had everything before us, we had nothing before us.
> We were all going direct to heaven, we were all going direct the other way.[1]

It often happens that words written long ago have an uncanny relevance to the present time. At the start of a new millennium, some feel that the best is yet to be, while others look forward with apprehension. Some find the rapidly expanding world of information technology exhilarating and challenging, while others feel that they live in a society that no longer speaks the same language. Some look back to the 'best of times', while others remember them as 'the worst of times'. In fact both perceptions are true! It is not possible to live in present time on memories of past glories, but it is possible to learn from the past and avoid making the same mistakes! That society worldwide is changing rapidly is a reality that needs to be accepted. There are opportunities to be grasped as well as dangers to be faced. That God does not change is also a reality that needs to be accepted. There are truths and certainties that need to be re-affirmed.

It was the epoch of belief

When Dickens wrote these lines, the church had a powerful influence in setting standards of behaviour not only in Britain but throughout Europe. According to the historian William Leckie the spiritual awakening which came in response to the travelling ministry of John and Charles Wesley, saved Britain from the same bloodbath of revolution as happened in France. Anyone who has read or watched portrayals of Dickens' books will know the grinding poverty and social injustice that were the lot of most people in Britain in the early nineteenth century. This was a time when many committed Christians in places of power got their hands dirty in order to bring social and political change. William Wilberforce, Lord Shaftesbury, Elizabeth Fry, are all well-known reformers, but there were many others who were involved in caring for the homeless, the orphans, setting up schools (the original Sunday School was established in 1780 to provide education for the poor). This was an era when belief in God led to action on behalf of those with no voice and no power. Their willingness to speak out and to act were an important factor in building the form of government that we take for granted today.

It was the epoch of incredulity

Other contemporaries of Dickens have also had an effect on society today. Charles Darwin, a clergyman, produced the first theories of evolution which focused on changes in plants and animals from generation to generation – a theory which later took a giant leap in suggesting an evolutionary link between the higher apes and human beings. Soren Kierkegaard was a Danish theologian who introduced the philosophy of existentialism, which questioned the absolutes of Christian doctrine. The Oxford English Reference Dictionary defines existentialism as a belief 'that the individual person is a free and responsible agent determining his or her own development through acts of will'. In the beginning this philosophy was contained to the sphere of the academics, but gradually, through the years, has made deep inroads into theological and secular institutions, eventually filtering down into the thinking of ordinary people.

The twentieth century saw a snowballing of this and other anti-God 'isms' such as humanism – a belief in the essential goodness of human beings which enables them to solve problems in a rational way without any need to acknowledge a power outside themselves. The great social/political upheavals of two world wars further contributed to a discarding of traditional certainties based on Judaeo/Christian teaching. Twentieth century society gradually ceased to look to the Christian church for guidance. The new gods of science and technology were poised to capture the minds of people. That's where all the answers lay. We were becoming a post-Christian society.

A new epoch of credulity

But during the last forty years of the twentieth century a new interest in spirituality began to emerge. There was a revival of old pre-Christian beliefs and an importing of Eastern forms of spirituality. New Age religion spread like wildfire amongst people who had turned away from their own biblically inaccurate perception of God but knew that there was a void which science and technology could not satisfy. But belief can now be in anything that suits the individual – a popular form of existentialism. If it feels good, do it or believe it. Belief in the God of the Bible may be all right for you but not for me. Right and wrong now depend on circumstances and popular opinion. On radio and TV, soaps, dramas and even serious discussion programmes all endorse a mixture of humanist and existentialist thought. Anyone who tries to introduce Judaeo/ Christian absolutes is made to look foolish.

The sad thing is that many Christians have been influenced by these thought patterns without realizing it. An attempt has been made to make the Bible fit in to what is now known as post-modern society. It's a bit like the effect of passive smoking. For years non-smokers sat in smoke-filled rooms completely unaware that their physical health was being damaged by other people's cigarettes. Now we know differently. There is a great deal of concern about atmospheric pollution, and rightly so, but much more subtle is the pollution of our thinking by philosophies which are not in accordance with scriptural principles. Wrong thinking leads to wrong behaving. For the first time since the signing of the Magna Carta *circa* one thousand years ago, the moral and ethical fibre of our nation is not based on Judaeo/ Christian absolutes, but on what seems right at the time.

In sharp contrast are the words spoken by William Penn, the famous Quaker, who once said, 'Right is right even if everyone is against it and wrong is wrong even if everyone is for it.'

Nothing new under the sun

If Dickens' words seem apt for the present time, how much more are the timeless words from Ecclesiastes: 'What has been will be again, and what has been done will be done again: there is nothing new under the sun. Is there anything of which any one can say, 'Look! this is something new'? It was already here long ago, it was here before our time.' (Ecc. 1:9-10, NIV)

All over the world since the beginning of time great civilizations have risen, prospered and then declined. Each one has been marked with some aspect of greatness in the arts – poetry, music, drama, literature, philosophy, in architecture, in exploration of the world, in advancing the science and technology of their time. Each one of them has disintegrated not because their poets and authors have stopped writing, their artists have stopped painting, their musicians have stopped composing, their explorers have stopped exploring, but because the moral and ethical fibre of these societies fell apart, leading to a breakdown in marriage and family structure. Historians who have written of the fall of two of the best known civilizations – Rome and Greece – have written of corruption, teenage rebellion and sexual permissiveness of both men and women, blurring of gender differences and a rise in homosexual practice. (Fourteen out of fifteen Roman Emperors were homosexual.) Paul's letter to the church in Rome is almost a prophetic word to the great Roman

Empire of his day. He gives an accurate picture of the symptoms of a disintegrating civilization.

But God's angry displeasure erupts as acts of human mistrust and wrongdoing and lying accumulate, as people try to put a shroud over truth. But the basic reality of God is plain enough. Open your eyes and there it is! By taking a long and thoughtful look at what God has created, people have always been able to see what their eyes as such can't see: eternal power, for instance, and the mystery of his divine being. So nobody has a good excuse. What happened was this: People knew God perfectly well, but when they didn't treat him like God, refusing to worship him, they trivialized themselves into silliness and confusion so that there was neither sense nor direction left in their lives. They pretended to know it all, but were illiterate regarding life. They traded the glory of God who holds the whole world in his hands for cheap figurines you can buy at any roadside stand.

So God said, in effect, 'If that's what you want, that's what you get.' It wasn't long before they were living in a pigpen, smeared with filth, filthy inside and out. And all this because they traded the true God for a fake god, and worshipped the god they made instead of the God who made them – the God we bless, the God who blesses us. Oh, yes!

Worse followed. Refusing to know God, they soon didn't know how to be human either – women didn't know how to be women, men didn't know how to be men. Sexually confused, they abused and defiled one another, women with women, men with men – all lust, no love. And then they paid for it, oh, how they paid for it – emptied of God and love, godless and loveless wretches.

Since they didn't bother to acknowledge God, God quit bothering them and let them run loose. And then all hell broke loose: rampant evil, grabbing and grasping, vicious

15

backstabbing. They made life hell on earth with their envy, wanton killing, bickering, and cheating. Look at them: mean-spirited, venomous, fork-tongued God-bashers. Bullies, swaggerers, insufferable windbags! They keep inventing new ways of wrecking lives. They ditch their parents when they get in the way. Stupid, slimy, cruel, coldblooded. And it's not as if they don't know better. They know perfectly well they're spitting in God's face. And they don't care – worse, they hand out prizes to those who do the worst things best! (Romans 1:18-32 *The Message*)

This is an ever-repeating consequence when people replace God with gods of their own making and God's rules for living are rejected. Paul says that these people have no excuse because God's blueprint has been written into every human being since the time of creation. This is particularly true as far as the creational ordinance of marriage is concerned – the God-given building block of every society the world over.

The best of times?
At the beginning of the twentieth century few people moved away from the locality in which they were born. Children at school were still using slates and slate pencils. Anything beyond basic education was still the privilege of the few. Members of parliament were elected by 40 per cent of men and 0 per cent of women. Science and technology were still very basic. As the century passed, the rate of the development of knowledge increased with meteoric speed. People are becoming more and more expert in ever narrowing fields of research and development. Continuous study has become a necessity to keep abreast. Children use computers with ease and many are well travelled by the time they start school. Young teenagers are learning things that their parents only learned at university.

Women's lives have changed radically in social, political, professional, economic and moral spheres. Many of these changes have come about by confronting and correcting injustices. Many have come about by the invasion of our homes by modern technology which has freed women from the hard work of housekeeping which our mothers and grandmothers took for granted.

But is it a coincidence that the breakdown in marriage and family life has run parallel with the move from dealing with injustices to the demand for equal opportunities and the desire to live independent lives?

As Christian women we need to stop and think. We are living now in a secular society. Should that society dictate to us the way in which we live out our womanhood?

In the book of the prophet Isaiah we read these words: 'For my thoughts are not your thoughts, neither are your ways my ways,' declares the Lord. 'As the heavens are higher than the earth so are my ways higher than your ways, and my thoughts than your thoughts.' (Isaiah 55:8-9)

Through the prophet God is calling His people to repent and return to Him, to live by His standards and not by the standards of the people around them. He is calling them to turn away from the worship of false gods and get back to obeying His commandments.

Scripture applies to all people at all times. This same challenge comes to us at the beginning of the twenty-first century. We need to distinguish clearly between human justice and human wisdom – both often based on expediency – and the justice and wisdom of God based on His unchanging absolutes. For hundreds of years these two concepts ran in parallel lines and often merged into one. In the moral mess and ethical chaos of our post-Christian society, this is no longer true.

Part One –
Our Ways

1

Our Ways in Twentieth Century Britain - A Brief Overview[2]

Queen Victoria was still on the throne when the bells pealed out to welcome the twentieth century. She ruled over an Empire on which the sun never set – an Empire which had become a Commonwealth of Nations by the time Elizabeth became queen. It is interesting that the century that has brought such profound change to women's lives has had a queen and not a king as sovereign at the beginning and end, and for almost half of that century.

In 1900 women were allowed to participate for the first time in the Olympic Games (but only in tennis and golf). A British woman won the first Gold Medal. It's hard for us to imagine that this was a major breakthrough. But there were much more serious issues to be tackled in those early years of the twentieth century.

In 1903 Emmeline Pankhurst, having been frustrated by the constant refusal of politicians to take the idea of women's suffrage seriously, formed her 'Women's Social and Political Union'. The motto of this group was 'Deeds not Words'. It was a declaration of war on the sexism and male chauvinism which pervaded all spheres of political and social life – a war which continued throughout the twentieth century – another '100 years' war'.

Women in Wartime

The twentieth century saw many wars – wars among nations, strife between ethnic groups within nations. No sooner was one situation settled than another arose. The great discoveries of science and technology have not brought peace, but have merely made bloodshed and destruction more widespread and horrendous.

The two World Wars have acted as catalysts for change in the lives of many women and their daughters. Women responded with enthusiasm when the call came in 1915 to work in trade, industry, agriculture, and in the making of armaments. Factory foremen who were at first sceptical about their usefulness eventually commended the women for their energy, punctuality, willingness and level of productivity. Other women went to the battle zones to nurse the wounded. They saw many gory and shocking sights. In her book *Testament of Youth*, Vera Brittain records very movingly the appalling conditions she and others experienced when working in the field hospitals of Italy and France. Her brother and his three friends, one of whom was her fiancé, were all killed in action. It is hardly surprising that she spent most of the rest of her life working for peace through the League of Nations.

Women responded in a similar way at the beginning of the Second World War. This time they were conscripted to women's branches of the army, navy and air force, as well as to work on the land, and in munitions factories. In both wars they held the fort at home, scrimping and saving, and learning to make a little food go a long way, often doing without themselves for the benefit of their children. Those whose husbands were in the forces had full responsibility for every aspect of home and family life. Many women gave their skills on a voluntary basis, knitting, sewing, manning forces' canteens, in caring for the sick and the elderly, and in helping young mothers who were coping on their own.

Down through history women all over the world have responded to the departure of their men in this way. What was new was the reluctance to return to the status quo afterwards.

Many husbands and fiancés did not return. Many who did return were disabled in mind and/or body. Readjusting to family life was sometimes quite difficult. Some five year old children found it hard to accept a man they had only heard about, and who had suddenly taken over their mother's attention, and the ordering of the household. Some wives had formed other relationships. Some husbands had been unfaithful as they travelled the world. For many young women marriage prospects had gone, while some of those returning from the forces could not settle into expected patterns of marriage and homemaking. Against the background of a nation turning its back on God, marriage and family life came increasingly under strain.

It is interesting to note that during both world wars, when both men and women were focused on defeating a common foe, the battle of the sexes quietened down, only to be resumed when peace was restored.

Women at War in Peacetime

Emmeline Pankhurst's 'Women's Social and Political Union' lived up to its motto of 'Deeds not Words'. In the years leading up to World War I they caused endless public disorder. They threw stones at the Lord Mayor's banquet; they smashed shop windows in the West End of London. They exploded a bomb in the Prime Minister's country house. They planted a bomb, which was fortunately discovered, in St Paul's Cathedral. They burned down a church and two mansion houses in Scotland. They sent a letter bomb to a magistrate. They disrupted church services.

In March 1917 – before the end of World War I – a bill came before parliament to enfranchise married women thirty years old and over. In December 1918 just one month after Armistice had been signed, women voted for the first time in a parliamentary election and the first woman M.P. was elected. The first battle of the 100 years' war was coming to an end. It is, however, interesting to note that only 40 per cent of men had been enfranchised before this same election! In 1928 all women (and men) over the age of 21 years were enfranchised and in May 1929 the number of women M.P.s grew to thirteen.

Since democracy is a system of Government involving the whole population, it would seem just that the outcome of this long battle would be that every adult would be entitled to vote. It is sad, though, that so much terrorism was used to achieve this result, and women constantly portray a one-sided picture of the actual state of franchise early in the twentieth century.

Franchise was only one battleground – at the beginning of the century a husband could divorce an unfaithful wife, but a wife could not divorce an unfaithful husband. In 1900 a suffragette confronted the commission, set up to consider the divorce laws, with the injustice of this fact. It was 1923 before the law was altered so that a wife could divorce her husband for adultery.

By 1919 all professions were open to women, but access to them was still a struggle until the passing of the Equal Opportunities Act in 1975. Many professions denied women the opportunity to continue after marriage, e.g. women teachers were not allowed to go on teaching until after 1944. This seems strange in a profession that is probably the one most compatible with family life.

Married women could not enter into financial and legal contracts in their own right until 1969. In 1980 the United Nations passed a resolution for the Elimination of All Forms of Discrimination against Women, in law, education and franchise. This was ratified in 1986 by the UK government led by Margaret Thatcher.

Resurgence of feminism in the twentieth century

One would have thought that the 1986 legislation would have brought about an end to the hostilities. But in actual fact the terms of warfare had long since changed from being a desire to right wrongs to a rising militant disparaging of men and a desire to take over completely. All men were tarred as male chauvinists by this new breed of female chauvinists. Chauvinism, be it male or female, is wrong and needs to be challenged whenever it is detected in either men towards women or women towards men.

Feminism is not the invention of the twentieth century. It has been strongest when civilizations were in decline. Throughout history, inside and outside the church, there have been feminist movements. Modern feminism probably had its roots in the egalitarian outcry of the French Revolution and is a thread running through communism, Zionism and most modern secular democracies.

The original exponent of twentieth century radical feminism was a French woman called Simone de Beauvoir who was the mistress of Jean-Paul Sartre, the eminent existentialist. 'One is not born a woman but becomes one,' was acclaimed the most famous quote of the year in 1949. It comes from her book *The Second Sex*, which is regarded as the key textbook of radical feminism. Although the book was written in 1949 it wasn't until the 1960s that its effects exploded around the world. It was at this time that the women's movement, which had been gaining momentum through the century, changed from a reasonable aim of correcting injustices to an aggressive crusade to suppress and belittle manhood. The USA was the main breeding ground of this form of feminism. Unisex became the cry of these days, with much bra-burning, cutting of hair (while young men grew theirs!) and blue jeans wearing. Anything which, in any way, depicted femininity was out. Not only was this breed of feminism anti-men, but it was also anti-family. Many emotive phrases were used to denigrate the role of home-making. Home was described by one woman as 'a comfortable concentration camp' – surely a contradiction in terms! Another called for the abolition of the family because it stood for the very foundations of a patriarchal society.

In fairness it has to be recorded that some of these 60s and 70s women have retreated from their entrenched positions – usually when they had children themselves – but the bitterness and hatred which their writings fed into our society has remained and has had a profound effect on many of the women who are in education and are shaping the minds of girls and young women today.

Men – 'warts and all'

Media, magazines, newspapers, and book coverage about the plight of women and the struggle for justice would all suggest that all women have always been downtrodden baby-producing sex objects, while all men have always lived trouble free lives and had the best of everything. It would probably be truer to say that some men have treated other men and most women in a way which is demeaning, discourteous and dismissive, while other men have treated both men and women in a way which is affirming and appropriate to their varying relationships.

In the early twentieth century men were also struggling in the political and social arena. Boys ten years old and younger were still working in mining until 1900 when the age was raised to thirteen. But the employment of women and girls in mines had become illegal more than fifty years before. Working conditions in coal and tin mines were little short of slavery. A relatively small number of men held all the rest of the people in their power. Until the trade unions began to flex their muscles there was little anyone could do about it. Free secondary education was no more available to boys than it was to girls. In 1919, when women finally gained access to all the professions, a very small proportion of men were able to aspire to professional life.

Attitudes towards the opposite sex are birthed and developed at home. The way in which a father treats a mother or a mother treats a father is the starting point. Many men are violent towards their spouse and/or children because this is the behaviour which has been modelled in their growing-up years. But although this may be understandable, it is always inexcusable. Some men have had no such violent background but only seem to respond to conflict with physical abuse. This is neither understandable or excusable. The liberalizing of the divorce laws and the abandonment of the institution of marriage by many couples does not seem to have brought about a decrease in violence in the home. It is a sad fact that many women seem drawn to exchange one violent relationship for another. Although the vast majority of home violence is perpetrated by men towards women, there is a growing number of situations in which the violence is perpetrated by women. But most of the abuse perpetrated by women in the home is not physical. Wounds inflicted by the tongue in public or in private are just as culpable and often take longer to heal.

Men in the workplace have increasingly come under fire because of their attitudes to women. Some women have been patronized and excluded, while others have suffered inexcusable sexual harassment. Whatever some men may feel about the presence of women at the top of the business or professional tree does not alter the fact that they have earned their place there and are protected by the law of the land since 1975. On the other hand many men feel that their masculinity is constantly under attack by the constraints of political correctness. If a man compliments a woman on a piece of work she has done, he is accused of patronizing her. If he offers legitimate criticism, he is being sexist. The law of the land does not alter the fact that women have babies and men do not. Entering into motherhood brings all kinds of additional pressures into a woman's life – physical, emotional, mental – which fatherhood does not. These are not all dealt with by even the best substitute child-care arrangements. Men do not need paternity leave, even though it is being thrust upon them. Generations of good fathers did not enjoy such luxury. It may be this fact, and not necessarily male chauvinism which may influence top job decisions that are made at boardroom level.

The poem learned in early childhood about what little boys and little girls are made of is nothing short of female chauvinism. Men aren't all horrible and women aren't all angels!

...meanwhile at Westminster other laws were passed

In 1950 an act which had been on the statute books for hundreds of years was repealed. It was an act that had forbidden the practice of witchcraft in Britain. At the time its repeal passed by unnoticed, but it led to an explosion of occult practices which has been mushrooming ever since. It was the opening of the door to all kinds of pagan influences which are now focused around the New Age movement. This may not seem to have a direct bearing on the subject under discussion, but it is a fact that women are more spiritually aware than men, and are very vulnerable to all kinds of spiritual influence. Is there a woman's magazine today that has not replaced the 'God slot' with horoscopes? Articles on all kinds of therapies and aids to relaxation and meditation (of a non-Biblical kind) abound in even the most sophisticated ones.

In 1961 the contraceptive pill became available on the NHS. There is no denying that the introduction of this form of contraception, used wisely, was of benefit to many married women for whom another pregnancy was not advisable. However, it was seen by many as the liberation from the fear of pregnancy which held them back from entering into extra-marital sex. It was regarded as another area of equality with men, who from time immemorial had had this so-called freedom. It opened the door to promiscuity on a new scale among young unmarried people, some of them barely out of childhood. In 1968 Malcolm Muggeridge resigned from the Rectorship of Edinburgh University when it was decided that 'the pill' would be given free of charge to women students.

1967 – The Abortion Act [3]

The act of terminating a pregnancy has long been an area of medical and social controversy. No changes had been made in the laws concerning abortion since 1837. In the 1930s a group of women formed the Abortion Law Reform Association. It's membership remained small until the tragedy of thalidomide in 1958. With much campaigning their numbers grew to 1,000. It was the campaigning of this group which succeeded, where others had failed, to bring pressure on parliament. They won the support of David Steele (son of a Presbyterian minister). One of the leading members of ALRA (74 per cent of whom were either atheist or agnostic) said, 'Most of the early ALRA committee were free thinkers who saw organized religion as the main obstacle to the full emancipation of women'. Some argued that improved contraception would limit the demand for legal abortion. The contraceptive pill had already been available free for six years before this act was passed and yet the legal abortion rate had increased from 2,040 in 1960 to 6,380 in 1966. The death rate from criminal abortion had been falling steadily since 1930 when it was 432 to 62 in 1960. In the first few weeks after the act was passed abortions were being performed at a rate equivalent to 25,000 per annum. In 1971 it was 90,000 per annum. By 1995 4,212,193 legal abortions had been carried out in England and Wales.[4]

More Acts passed

In 1967 another act was passed in the same year for which there had been campaigning since 1957. It was the act that made homosexual acts between consenting adults legal. Lesbianism became a legitimate addition to the agenda of some feminists.

In 1969 a human egg was fertilized *in vitro,* but it wasn't until 1978 that the first test-tube baby was born. The positive side of this is that it has enabled women whose Fallopian tubes have been blocked by disease to become pregnant, bringing joy to many otherwise childless couples. With every discovery of this kind, benefit is brought to some, but it opens up the door to abuse by others. Husbands are no longer necessary – only a donor sperm from a sperm bank.

In October 1969 breakdown of marriage became the only necessary reason for divorce, followed in June 1984 by a further bill making divorce possible after one year of marriage.

All of these acts of parliament have had a profound effect on the morality of our society. All were perceived to bring greater freedom to people's lives, and especially to the lives of women, so that they could enjoy a much better life than those lived by their mothers and grandmothers. Perhaps it has for a few.

So how much better is it?

The following statistics have been compiled from a publication 'Social Focus on Women' available in reference sections of public libraries.[5] There are 24 million women in Britain aged 16+.

Relationships

1 in 4 women aged 18-49 are cohabiting each year

There are 338,000 marriages each year

There are 137,000 divorces

Average age of women when first child is born is 27.4 years

1 in 5 conceptions ends in abortion

7 million women have children of school age (under 16 years)

Work, education, financial commitment

More than 50 per cent of women are in full time work

70 per cent of women are in some form of paid employment

17 per cent of all mortgages are held by women

Women in further education has increased by 49 per cent in 10 years

Health

1 in 5 women suffer from some form of neurotic disorder – fatigue, sleep problems, irritability, anxiety, depression, phobias

Injury or poison-induced suicide is the most common cause of death of women under 35 years

Women are worried about being mugged, burgled or raped

Major cause of stress is balancing work, home and family

Leisure pursuits

Most popular is watching TV (least popular are gardening, sewing, knitting, DIY)

Favourite TV channel is ITV

Favourite programmes are soaps

Favourite female author is Catherine Cookson

Favourite newspaper is *The Sun*

Most popular magazine – Weight Watchers!

Exercise and sport
60 per cent do some form of exercise or sport
Walking, keep fit/yoga are the most popular

At a Christian Viewpoint Speakers conference a group of women were studying the above statistics. At the end of the time one of them produced the following parody of Proverbs 31:

Ways of communicating with modern woman who can find?
She is more complex than many microchips.
Her husband lost confidence in himself after his third redundancy and the man she liveth with now is not her husband.
She bringeth to this relationship limited expectations, two children from an earlier marriage, and one born out of wedlock.
Knitting needles she used to employ now act as props for her house plants, and her sewing machine has gone to the Charity Shop.
Many clothes she buyeth from mail order catalogues.
She stays up late at night watching videos of soaps she has missed while at work during the day.
The family no longer eateth together but putteth instant snacks into the microwave.
She is not interested in buying a field but the publicity pertaining to a timeshare in Lanzarote tempteth her.
Her arms are strong as twice a week she pumpeth iron at the leisure centre.
Her charitable giving is an emotional response to a visual appeal.
She needeth tranquillizers to deal with the stress of juggling all the parts of her life.

Her teenagers rarely rise before noon at the weekends and in spite of all her sacrifices for them her children call her.....all sorts of names.

And their bedrooms resembleth pigsties.

She laugheth rarely and the fears of losing her current man are very real.

She considereth suicide and rape, mugging, cancer and loneliness are a constant fear.

The name of Jesus is often on her lips, as a swear word.

This woman really needs to meet Him.[6]

Is this caricature a complete exaggeration? – The previously recorded statistics certainly don't suggest that this is so for a large number of women. A survey carried out more recently by the magazine *Top Sauté* (reported in *Daily Telegraph* June 2001) found that 93 per cent of women who participated said that they were frequently under stress. Only 1 in 11 would choose to work full time. 75 per cent attribute marriage breakdown to the fact that both partners were in full-time work. The magazine's editor says, 'The Government wants to encourage as many women as possible into full-time work, but this survey clearly shows this is blatantly not what most women want especially those with families.' Is this freedom?

2

Our Ways in the Twentieth Century – A personal perspective

Writing from a personal perspective is always dangerous. On the one hand there can be a desire by the writer to prove a point by using one's own experience. Oswald Chambers warns against this when he says, 'Never make a principle out of your own experience, let God be as original with other people as He is with you.' On the other hand our own thought processes can be stimulated by the reality of life as experienced by other people. This is my hope as I share a short history of my family.

The twentieth century spans five generations of the female line in my family. My mother was eight years old when the twentieth century began. One of my granddaughters was seven years of age when the twenty-first century began. One hundred years and fifty-one weeks separate their births. The contrast in prospects for these two little girls is enormous. The only common factor is that both were born to loving parents in homes where God's standards were, and are, upheld.

A Mother's Story
Early years in a mining village
My grandfather and his brothers owned two coalmines in the village of Greengairs in Lanarkshire, Scotland. It was here that my mother was born – third child and oldest daughter in a family of ten. All her formal education – which ended when she was

fourteen – took place at the local village school. The other pupils, apart from the children of the miners and local farmers, were her brothers and cousins. There was one village schoolmaster and two lady assistants. The pupils were well drilled in 'the three R's', history, geography, and little else. The schoolmaster would have liked my mother to continue her education at secondary school. However, the nearest secondary school was five miles away in Airdrie. There was no public transport. Her brothers transferred there at the age of twelve, walking there in the morning, and back in the evening. Even more significant, however, was the social custom that the oldest daughter became her mother's right hand woman at home – and this is what my mother did.

Home economics training – the hard way

Long before she left school my mother had begun her apprenticeship in housekeeping and child-rearing. By the time she left school she had two younger brothers and four younger sisters – one of whom suffered from cerebral palsy. She died at the age of twelve – a very deep grief for my mum, who loved her sister dearly. The only other help in the home was a woman who came weekly to help with the family laundry. This was a whole day's work, which took place in the washhouse outside in the yard. Fires had to be lit, water boiled. Washing took place in washtubs, with much rubbing and scrubbing with bars of green soap, followed by rinsing and wringing and hanging out to dry. Sheets and pillowcases were mangled to remove the creases. Flat irons were heated at the kitchen fire and ironing was done on the kitchen table. Mod. cons. were non-existent. Every day mum swept and dusted and cleaned and polished. Every day she helped bake the girdle scones and pancakes for the family tea. Cooking was done on the kitchen range – an early precursor of the Aga – which was coal fired. It had to be lit at crack of dawn and polished with black lead once a week to keep it bright and shining. With the birth of each child my grandmother's health declined, with the result that more and more responsibility fell on mum's young shoulders.

All work and no play?

By today's standards I suppose it sounds as though this young woman lived a life of drudgery. However, the only alternatives for her on leaving school would have been to work in the village shop, or to leave home and go into some form of domestic service. Most of the boys in the village left school and went straight to the coalface or the farm, before they were fourteen. Although her formal education had finished, her learning did not. She learned to play the piano. She read books and newspapers. She loved a good discussion on current affairs and was well aware of the activities of the suffragettes. All that I know about my mother's life came from her own lips. She was a wonderful storyteller and often entertained my sister, brother and me on winter evenings when our homework was completed. Her recollections went back to the turn of the century, the Boer War, and the death of Queen Victoria. Her tales of childhood escapades with her brothers, sisters and cousins in that small close-knit village community – where unusual characters seemed to abound – are a precious childhood memory. I never sensed that she viewed her own life during those growing-up years in a negative way.

The family attended the local Presbyterian Church every Sunday. She had a personal faith in God that had been nurtured there. She taught in Sunday School and played the piano for worship in the Bible class. Social life amongst the young people in the village seemed to issue from the church. Well-chaperoned dances, held in the village hall, were very popular. There was a great deal of fun in my mother's life in the home, and out of it. She had a very close relationship with her father, who affirmed her and was very proud of his eldest daughter. This may have been a very significant factor in her positive attitude.

Clouds of War 1914-18

Many of the young men of the village, including two of my mother's brothers and several cousins, enlisted in response to Lord Kitchener's appeal for volunteers. Her older brother – against his will – stayed at home because, by this time, he was a mine manager and his job was regarded as essential in wartime. My mother's war effort was also based at home because of circumstances. I have a feeling that, if circumstances had been different, she might well have wanted to train to nurse the wounded, as Vera Brittain did. There were many anxious months when both brothers were involved in the battle zone around Gallipoli. They returned safely, however, at the end of the war, but her favourite cousin, a pilot in the Royal Flying Corps, did not. The victory of the suffragettes in 1918 brought no new status to my mother, who was still single and not yet thirty! She did, however, become engaged to a newly demobbed schoolteacher, and when she married in April 1919 she became mistress of her own home.

Marriage and motherhood

My mother's circumstances were no different from hundreds of young women the length and breadth of the land. Most of them, like my mother, did what was expected of them, some happily and others with growing resentment. Could it be that those who were caught up in the heart of the suffragette movement were young women from wealthier homes whose days were filled with trivialities, marking time until an appropriate husband was found for them? It is understandable that young women of intelligence found this life intolerable. Many of them were denied educational opportunities because their fathers felt that it would be a waste of time and money.

The early years of marriage must have seemed very different for my mother after the hectic years in her family home. They hadn't been married for long, however, when, for several months, they gave a home to one of her brothers, his wife and young baby. My grandfather's mining business was wound up after a disaster in which several miners were killed. His health declined and he died a few months before my sister was born. Many businesses were going through difficult times. These were years of growing industrial unrest and unemployment. Most of my father's family and three of the younger members of my mother's family emigrated to the USA and Canada. My mother considered herself to be very privileged – she had a husband who had worked his way through university and had a secure job. Moreover, unlike many women, she did not need to find employment to supplement the family income. Her many years of training in home management bore fruit at this time.

My brother was born on the 12 May 1926 – the day on which the General Strike ended. This was wonderful timing. My mother thought she would have to walk to hospital! The departure of my aunt, who lived with my grandmother, to Canada, resulted in the selling of the family home and my grandmother came to live with her oldest daughter! From time to time my father's unmarried aunt also joined the family circle. My grandmother was physically delicate, and the aunt was emotionally delicate. My mother's life had not really changed much after all!

Some would see my mother's life as the story of a woman who was educationally disadvantaged and who spent her whole life being put upon by others. Others would see her as a woman who built on the few educational opportunities she had, by developing her numerous home-making skills and God given gifts of hospitality and caring, which made others – family and strangers – feel secure and at home.

My mother was a strong and energetic character – a person who had very definite ideas on dress, social behaviour, manners, moral standards, and politics! She found it hard to tolerate those who saw things differently and could be quite critical of those who did not conform. She never found it easy to demonstrate affection in public. Instead she demonstrated her love in action. Her neighbours knew she was to be trusted with a confidence. She gave wise counsel. In physical stature she was small and slim – but when she died in 1976 she left a huge gap in the lives of many people.

A Daughter's Story 1931 -
The 1930s were years of political, social, and economic unrest not only in Britain but throughout the Western world. Two million people (mostly men) in this country were unemployed. Policemen, teachers, and the armed forces had salary cuts of 10 per cent as Britain teetered on the edge of bankruptcy. The National Coalition Government replaced the Labour Government and remained in power until 1945.

In Europe Hitler's rise to power accelerated, with all the accompanying horrors of his desire to eliminate people with physical or mental disability, the Jewish race, and anyone else who disagreed with him. His aggression towards neighbouring nations caused a growing disquiet throughout Europe. In Britain a king died, a king abdicated, and a new king was crowned.

All of these factors created a climate of anxiety and uncertainty in ordinary people which was sensed by those of us who were children in these years.

A surprise late addition
My mother had no desire to follow her mother's example in childbearing. Perhaps the most powerful effect that the women's movement had in the early thirties was to bring about, by one means or another, a reduction in the number of children in families. My mother was very content with her daughter and son. I was, I am fairly sure, a surprise, but not unwelcome addition!

My earliest memories are not of my mother but of my granny, whom I adored. Because she lived with us and because my mother was fully occupied with the time-consuming realities of early 1930s housekeeping (without electricity), I spent most of my time with my grandmother. She read books with me, and took me with her in the afternoons when she went visiting friends and family. It was a kind of role reversal between my mother and grandmother – the opposite of what had happened in the previous generation when my mother had almost taken over as mother to her younger sisters and brother. In 1937 granny went to live in Canada. My heart was broken. I never saw her again although she lived until 1967.

Education – early school years

My educational opportunities were as different from my mother's as chalk is from cheese. My parents were committed to giving their children every opportunity possible. To this end my father taught mathematics to apprentices in evening classes on three evenings every week. The money he earned was saved for our further education. I knew this from an early age, and grew up with the expectancy of going to university.

All my schooling was under the auspices of Lanark County Council. The ethos and moral stance of these schools was according to Judaeo-Christian principles. Every morning school began with the Lord's prayer and then it was straight into reciting multiplication tables! I don't regret the strong foundations in the three R's and grammar. I loved mental arithmetic and problem solving. History and geography as they were taught were totally uninspiring. Arts and crafts were taught without any imagination. The early years were spent in the school which topped the educational league tables for places in the 'A' stream in Airdrie Academy. Its pupils were drawn from one of the wealthiest and from the poorest areas in the town. Daily I saw evidences of social and economic deprivation in some of my classmates who were ill-clad and undernourished. It was in these early years that I experienced the rising desire in young women teachers to encourage the girls of the class to aspire to higher things. Test situations were preceded by a challenge to do better than the boys! This may seem a trivial thing, but it embedded in me a determination to succeed and was probably part of the motivation in choosing to go for physics and chemistry rather than a language option in later years at the Academy. My middle years at school were during the Second World War.

Family Life in Wartime

I can remember very clearly on Sunday 3 September 1939 when Britain declared war on Germany. We were all dressed in our Sunday clothes ready to go to church. My parents were very solemn. There had been a growing atmosphere of gloom and apprehension everywhere. Suddenly the waiting was over. We were at war.

I had no clear idea of what this would mean for our family. I was relieved that my father was too old to be conscripted and that my brother was too young. The immediate effect was that we had to carry our gas masks – issued some months before – everywhere we went. Gas mask drill and air raid drill became a routine part of school life. Street lamps were extinguished. The windows of our home were covered with strips of sticky brown paper to protect us from shattering glass. Black blinds and thick curtains kept any chink of light from showing outside. Food gradually became scarcer. As a family regular exciting food parcels from our relatives across the Atlantic supplemented our meagre rations.

From the start I was very fearful about the prospect of bombs dropping on our house. When London began to be bombed this fear increased. The fear became a reality in March 1941 when the shipbuilding and industrial areas of Clydeside were devastated. All night for three nights German bombers flew overhead, chased by R.A.F. fighter planes. Very few bombs actually fell near our town – none of them on houses – but the noise of anti-aircraft guns was constant. We huddled in our coal cellar, cleared for the purpose, dressed in several layers of clothing to keep us warm. I can still remember shaking with fear, while my mother – cool, calm and collected – did everything she could to entertain and reassure us. My father was on Home Guard duty. Later I discovered that she was just as scared as we were!

My mother was no different from many others in this respect. It was as though an added inner strength and energy was given to cope with all the additional stresses of family life in wartime. She, like many others, developed new skills and took on responsibilities never required of her before. For a full day every week she led a team of women from our church, who helped to prepare and serve food in an army canteen in a barracks ten miles from our home. She sewed pyjamas for the wounded to wear and knitted helmets and gloves to keep men in the Front Line warm. Our meagre rations were often shared by off duty soldiers billeted in our church hall. Several Canadian service men, including two cousins, spent their leaves with us.

My father went out nearly every evening, teaching, on Home Guard duty or fire-watching in the school where he taught. (Two or three employees occupied every school and public building every night to be prepared for attack by incendiary bombs.) He cultivated an allotment, where he grew many of the vegetables that we ate summer and autumn.

Education in wartime

Many male teachers joined the armed forces when war began. Education was another area where there was greater dependence on women. Classes were larger (40+!). School hours were adjusted to take account of the blackout in the winter. An extra holiday was introduced in the autumn so that older children could help with the potato harvest. That the same amount of work had to be covered in less time brought added stress to teachers and pupils.

My sister's university education took place during the second half of the war. If she hadn't gone to university she would have had to enlist in one of the women's branches of Army, Navy or Air Force, as two of my cousins had already done. She travelled daily to Glasgow, which, at the time of the Clydebank raids, was a source of anxiety to my parents. During her summer vacations she was required to do something towards the war effort. She chose to work on a farm. It was student life with no frills. Financially however, the scarcity of food and clothes, and the fact that we never went on family holidays during the war, made it easier for my parents to cope with fees and books and travelling expenses.

My brother, like many other lads of his age, could not wait to be old enough to join the R.A.F. He had been in the Air Training Corps since the age of fourteen. His dream was realized just before the war in Europe ended. He spent two and a half years in the Far East. I think these were more difficult than the war years for my mother!

Years in the senior school
By the time I had reached senior school many of the male teachers had returned from the forces. The upper school staff, with the exception of the modern language and English departments, was male. I had a high regard for many of the women who taught me in earlier years, but I found that the male teachers were more academically challenging. I can never remember receiving anything other than encouragement to succeed from these men. I owe a great deal to one English teacher. He was an agnostic with strong socialist tendencies. He never tried to indoctrinate us with his own views, but made sure that we thought through for ourselves many things relating to social issues and religious belief. It was at this point that I first encountered existential philosophy (although unaware of it at the time) and the theory of evolution. There was a very embryonic but real feminist ethos emerging amongst the girls, with which I became infected. It was for me a separate issue from my Christian beliefs – just the way a modern young woman with educational opportunities before her should think.

When the time came to move on to university four females and no males applied and were accepted to study medicine. Two of us completed the course. One dropped out after one year and the other was tragically killed in a road accident in the fourth year of her very successful studies.

Why medicine?
God sometimes allows circumstances to come into our lives which we would not choose but which He uses to get our attention. It is often in hindsight that we are able to understand

why. Very early in my life I learned to talk to God about things that I found difficult, but somehow I was so occupied at school with getting results that it never really occurred to me that God might have plans for my future life.

Four months before I was due to sit the Scottish Higher Leaving Certificate Exams, for which I was entered at a higher-grade level in more subjects than anyone else in my year, I became seriously ill with rheumatic fever. My mother did not want me to be admitted to hospital. For weeks she tended me day and night, giving care that I certainly would not have had in hospital. Our G.P. came two or three times a day for several weeks. I owe a great deal to both of them. I was one of the first people in our town to be given penicillin.

On the day that our doctor told me that there was not the remotest possibility of me sitting the exams, I felt two opposite emotions. On the one hand I thought that the bottom had fallen out of my world, and on the other hand I felt a sense of relief. The slightest effort caused my heart to do very strange things. Studying was out of the question. At this point God began to get my attention. I began to think beyond the exams and what I would do at university. I became quite perplexed. I knew that I didn't want to teach, nor did I want to go into pure science. I had thought about physiotherapy and nursing – but I did want to go to university. One day, lying flat on my back, I began to talk to God about my future. A strange warmth went through my body and a deep sense of well-being and peace came into my heart. It was as though God was saying that He had it already planned. Until that point I was physically weak and emotionally low.

From that time on I wanted to get up and get on with life. I had had a similar experience two years before when I was baptized as a believer in the Baptist church where my father was a deacon and where we worshipped as a family every Sunday. On neither occasion did I tell anyone. I felt that no one would understand. In hindsight I believe that both of these occasions were touches of the Holy Spirit on my life. I believe that on the second occasion, God touched my whole being, body, soul, and spirit, although I had no realization at the time that this was so. Within six months of this experience I had resumed a full active life – cycling to school up several hills and playing hockey in the First XI team – and I began to know what I would study at university. I can only believe that the increasing sense that I should study medicine was a direct result of the experience I had had some months before. It was both scary and exciting.

As I looked back to childhood, I remembered how often my dolls were lined up as though in hospital. Some even had 'surgical' scars! But – and I knew it was a big 'but' – my parents would never be able to afford the cost of a medical degree. Moreover my father had cataract in both eyes and early retirement was more than a possibility. Competitive scholarships were not a feature of educational provision in Scotland as they were in other parts of the UK. When I finally plucked up the courage to share my thinking with my parents, they did not respond very positively. Finance was certainly a big barrier, but they were more concerned about my physical ability to cope. When consulted, our G.P. was not very encouraging either – but then he hadn't been too keen about me cycling to school or playing hockey either! He did concede that my heart had made an excellent recovery and agreed that I should apply. The financial issue was eased when later that year local education authority grants became available for the first time. If I had done my exams at the time I should have done this would not have been there. However, there was still a big gap between the amount needed and the amount available. Fees were paid out of the grant and took about one third of the total. My parents, with my sister's help, paid for board and lodging and clothes, while I paid travel and books and daily expenses from the remaining part of the grant.

Student years

In October 1950 – just at the time Simone de Beavoir's book *The Second Sex* was beginning to hit the headlines – I entered the Medical Faculty of Edinburgh University. I was one of a class of forty women and 120 men. It came as quite a shock to discover that a large proportion of my fellow students came from south of the border and others from Commonwealth countries. The latter I could cope with, but the former offended my Scottish Nationalist leanings! Very few of the women were, as I was, products of Scottish state schools; most came either from the independent sector or English grammar schools. They had a great deal more self-assurance than I had. The thing that united us was a determination to resist any unfair treatment because we were women. There was a definite tendency for the women to have a much heavier schedule leading up to professional examinations. There was one very famous anatomist who refused to acknowledge our existence in the anatomy laboratory! The other main source of discrimination as we went through into clinical years were those ward sisters who did not like medical students in general and women medical students in particular. There were also one or two lecturers with whom we women made sure that we were never left alone!

My national prejudice against those from the south was dispelled very quickly as friendships developed. My dearest friend, Mary, with whom I shared a room for three years, was from Surrey. She was an Anglican Christian whose generosity of spirit was a constant challenge to my narrow Baptist perspective on things. Sadly she died of cancer in her early thirties – my first real experience of bereavement.

Another challenge in the spiritual realm came in our year Bible study group from two young men who were members of the Christian Brethren. This challenge was to my increasingly feminist attitudes. For the first time I realized that the Bible had something to say on the subject – but my life was still very definitely in two compartments, secular and sacred, and I was not prepared to listen to them!

After each professional examination I felt that there had been a point where it was only by God's help that I had survived. So often things sprang into my mind in the middle of oral and clinical

examinations that I had completely forgotten until that point.
This happened particularly in the gruelling three weeks of Final
Examinations. Most of the male students had completed clinical
examinations in Child Life and Health and Obstetrics and
Gynaecology at the end of the previous two terms. We women
had heavy case loads in these subjects to write up as well as the
three weeks of clinical and written exams to contend with. This
happened every year in spite of protests. We survived, and a
higher proportion of women students passed the Finals than men!

'They have taken their medicine like men'

At our graduation ceremony in the MacEwan Hall in Edinburgh,
Sir Walter Mercer, an eminent orthopaedic surgeon, congratulated
the women graduates who had 'taken their medicine like men'.
In a sense this summed up the attitude that we had encountered
throughout the six years of study. We had chosen to enter into
what was still regarded as a male domain more than seventy-five
years after the first woman had fought her way in! It was in
1869, in fact, that five women, led by Sophia Jex-Blake, finally
gained admission as medical students to Edinburgh University.
One of them, Edith Pechey, was the daughter of a Baptist
minister at Langham near Colchester in Essex. In spite of her
success in her studies, she (along with the others) was not allowed
to graduate. She was denied the chemistry prize because she
was a woman. She finally gained her M.D. in Switzerland and
L.R.C.P. in Ireland in 1877.[8] It was difficult to understand why
gaining the knowledge necessary to bring help to sick people
should be regarded as a male prerogative. I was later to discover
that it was relatively easy to gain professional qualifications, but
more difficult for a woman to use them in a profession which
was still totally structured to the pattern of a man's working life.

Less than two weeks after graduation, Mary and I presented
ourselves at Law Hospital in Lanarkshire to begin six months as
House Surgeons. We were full of head knowledge but short on
experience – as many Scottish medical graduates of that era were.
Four of us (three females and one male) were responsible for six

general surgery wards, each with thirty-two beds. We also covered for paediatrics and gynaecology after six each evening. We were told that although we were never officially off-duty, we could work out a reasonable number of evenings and weekends off amongst ourselves as long as two of us were always available. The other two were both married (not to each other). Compulsory live-in accommodation consisted of a very basic bedroom (iron hospital bed, chest of drawers, wardrobe and brown linoleum floor) and an equally basic common sitting-room. There was no live-in provision for spouses. At the end of the first month, after all the deductions had been made we were the proud possessors of our first professional pay cheque of £16! Our minimum working week was about seventy-six hours, but one week in four it could be 131 hours. Sleep was a scarce commodity. All the medical staff senior to us were men. They were very helpful and encouraging. Once more we had problems with two of the senior ward sisters. In many ways I could understand their attitudes. Nursing staff tended to be very junior and very sparse. To be landed with novice doctors every year in August did not make their lives any easier. Relationships improved as the months went by and at the end of our time we were almost friends!

After registration what?

The second half of my pre-registration year was spent in the Dermatology department of Glasgow Victoria Infirmary where the chief was a woman. She had some very old-fashioned ideas about treatment, but her results were good. I became more of a counsellor than a clinician in these months. At the time I didn't realize how valuable this would be in later years, but God knew. The dynamics of the department were very interesting. Whenever there was a crisis of any kind, medical or legal, the male second in command was expected to deal with it!

In the middle of the fifth of my six years at university I had become engaged to a young theological student. We had known each other all of our lives, at school and at church, but fell in love in our final year at school. Jim spent six years at Glasgow University while I spent six years in Edinburgh. He had settled in his first full pastorate in Dumbarton when I was in Law Hospital.

We married at the end of my pre-registration year. We decided that I should have some time to settle into marriage and life in the manse before considering re-entry into the medical world. Because of my history of rheumatic fever I knew that I should not delay having children too long. In fact our daughter Leslie Jane, was born eleven months later, on the second anniversary of my graduation!

Compulsory general practice training had not been introduced back in the late 1950s. Our G.P., who was in practice on his own, used to phone me from his surgery and ask if I would go and check on the urgency of house calls near our home. We had no car, so I put my medical gear in the shopping bag attached to the bottom of the pram and pushed the pram round to the patient's house. The baby was left sleeping in the pram – a perfectly safe thing to do in these days – while I saw the patient! On other occasions I helped out in the surgery, but as the baby became a toddler this was no longer possible.

The challenge that the two young men had brought to me at university was continued by one of the deacons in the church in Dumbarton. He and his wife became very close friends. Our friendship had to be discreet because it was not considered proper for a minister and his wife to have close friends in the congregation. We had many stimulating and instructive discussions that always seemed to liven up around midnight. Over these months my feminist leanings were dealt a fatal blow as I pondered the fact 'all scripture is inspired by God'. I began to know that I couldn't split my life into compartments where there was a wife and mother bit, a medical bit, and a church bit. Somehow or other all needed to become one under the lordship of Christ – but how?

The Swinging Sixties

While some young women were screaming with adulation at Beatles' concerts, others were joining the ranks of their bra-burning American sisters. In 1966, London was declared the 'swinging capital of the world'. It was the era when youth culture erupted, declaring that 'morality, the totem of the old, a dirty word' – 'the pill, pot, and freedom' were the order of the day. It was also the time when more serious-minded women also saw the introduction of the pill as the gateway to new freedom, bringing equality a step nearer.

For me, the early sixties were a time of tremendous internal confusion and turmoil. Two months after our second child, David, a model textbook baby, was born, we moved to Dunfermline. Leslie, aged two, had still to learn that the night was for sleeping. She was a very charming and highly intelligent little girl. Like her mother she had a very strong will. Unfortunately it was twenty years too early for any help from Dr James Dobson's books and tapes! I was very happily married. I had two lovely healthy children. But I was not coping with sleepless nights, cleaning a large cold manse, washing endless piles of nappies, answering a constantly ringing telephone, greeting an endless stream of people who arrived without previous arrangement to consult my husband, keeping the children quiet while he was with these visitors in our lounge or while he was working in his study. I did not find fulfilment in presiding over women's meetings. I did it out of duty and not out of any sense of call. I kept thinking of what I might have been doing.

For the year before we were married, I had been involved daily in issues of life and death. Now it seemed that so much of my life was filled with trivialities. That was only partially true, but it was how it seemed to me then. I wouldn't have considered going back to medicine until the children were at school because I believed, and still do, that there are no child-care arrangements that can ever substitute for the one ordained by God to care – the mother. Other people, however, felt differently. I was aware of their unspoken criticism – that money had been wasted on training me. We were both very aware of the financial sacrifices that my parents had made during my student years. No-one except my dear, long-suffering husband knew the inner turmoil that other people's expectations were creating in me. Outwardly everything was sweetness and light, but inside I was like a volcano waiting to blow. I did what was expected of me. More and more of my life, including my care of home and children, was done as a duty rather than a labour of love. There was no doubt that from a financial point of view it would be very beneficial for me to return to medicine. We could never make ends meet financially. Before we were married we had agreed that finance would not be the reason for my return to work in my profession. I would have been earning about three times my husband's salary. We were, and are, old-fashioned enough to believe that that would not contribute positively to the stability of our marriage. Like my father before him, my husband believed that it was his God-given responsibility to be the main provider for the family.

But God........
We were both very weary, physically, emotionally, and spiritually. The little word 'but' is often used in scripture as a bridge which brings God into a human situation where He has been ignored. We were both so busy serving God that we were no longer hearing what He wanted to say to us personally. God engineered our circumstances so that He could get our attention. First He took us to Switzerland minus the children – but plus fifty young people. I didn't mind this at all. I found being with young people much easier than being with other women. Also I was medically responsible for them, so I went equipped to deal with emergencies. But there in a quiet, indescribably beautiful situation I began to hear God speak through my own husband's preaching, and the humility and selfless giving of himself to others by the other leader. I heard God say to me, 'Do you want to get well?' Unlike the man at the pool of Bethesda I wasn't even aware that I was sick!

When we returned home, God had also been working in the lives of two close friends, a Presbyterian minister and his wife, while they were on holiday, and He used them to bring me God's diagnosis of my sickness. I began to realize that I was full of self-pity and resentment, because one part of me knew that what I was doing as wife and mother was important but the other part of me envied my friends who were still in medical practice. Pride made me feel that I was above all that I was doing in the church at that time. I was angry with God because I had done what I felt He wanted me to do. I read Roy Hession's book *The Calvary Road* for the first of many times. I realized that my problems were not in my circumstances or in other people but in me. I learned that repentance was much more than saying, 'I'm sorry'. I experienced the reality of forgiveness and I learned that the blood of Jesus goes on cleansing from each and every sin that is acknowledged and confessed.

My circumstances did not change, but God changed me in my circumstances. People whom I had found really difficult suddenly became much nicer! More importantly, I handed over to God my career/home dilemma. I asked Him to work out for me what seemed impossible. It was as though an enormous burden had been lifted from my shoulders and I knew peace in my heart as I had never known it before. A frustrated housewife began to become a contented home-maker – there is a big difference.

Two years later the way opened up for me to do ante-natal clinics on three afternoons a week when David started school. Three months before I was due to start I discovered that I was pregnant! I went to the clinic as a patient and not as a doctor. If this had happened two years before I would have reacted very differently. Because of the change God had brought about in me, I was able to accept that it was not, as I had thought, God's time for me to return to medicine. I was able to rejoice without any regrets or disappointment over future career prospects when our second son John was born.

The Wind of the Spirit

At the same time as all the laws affecting the morality of the nation were being passed in Westminster, and a great upsurge of occult practice was arising, a fresh wind of the Holy Spirit was blowing through the church throughout the world. Britain was not left untouched. Sadly this caused much controversy throughout the evangelical world. For us, personally, it was a time of reading and searching the scriptures. We saw some of our friends completely transformed as God touched their lives and ministries. Our dry hearts had become thirsty hearts as a result of our new understanding of the relevance of Calvary in our everyday lives.

For some months I had found that people with emotional problems had started to come to me to ask for help. They came because I was a doctor, and there is no doubt that my medical training was of great value in asking relevant questions. The help I was able to give them, however, came from a changed heart rather than medical knowledge. God began to give me a new understanding of healing from His point of view. I no longer saw people as sick bodies that needed medicine. I began to see them as people made up of body, soul and spirit, each part in need of healing. This was long before books on wholeness and healing or even counselling were on the market. When the wind of the Holy Spirit blew into my own life it was as though I had moved into a new dimension of understanding. I found myself asking questions that opened up the real source of the problem. As I prayed God gave me insights that I could never have had by medical knowledge. In a very natural way I discovered that the supernatural gifts of the Spirit are still in operation today. From then until now I have never been sure when I am using medical knowledge and training and when I am using spiritual gifts.

For me this was a very exciting time. My own spiritual life was finding new dimensions in prayer and worship. It was as though God was drawing aside a curtain to show me how my medical training could be of great value in a deepening pastoral concern to see people made whole, body, soul and spirit. I knew that, at last, all the aspects of my life were beginning to come together. Until this point I had always equated practising medicine with earning money – not that there's anything wrong with earning money. But it wasn't God's purpose for me at that time. Another by-product of God's dealings in our lives was that we had learned to look directly to Him as our provider for all our financial needs. The only times that we have had real financial worries since that time have been when we have been foolish, or when God specifically wants to get our attention in some other area and we have closed our ears.

God moves in mysterious ways

Eight months after our youngest son Andrew was born, Jim received a call to become pastor/teacher in a church called Gold Hill in the Buckinghamshire village of Chalfont St Peter. I had never heard of either the church or the place when first contacts were made and it took me some time to be open to the idea. Gradually, as the weeks passed, God began to show me that this was indeed his plan and not a human idea. If anyone had told me as a teenager that the happiest and most fruitful years of my life would be spent in England, I would have thought that they were mad. God knew what was ahead for us when he began to modify my fierce nationalism while at university.

The thing that I appreciated most in those early years at Gold Hill church was that no-one had expectations of me as the 'pastor's wife'. I was allowed to use my gifting in ways in which I felt comfortable. These were years of learning and challenge spiritually.

As the children grew older and eventually began to leave home, I was able to accompany Jim and sometimes to work alongside him in conferences and house parties. Again these were opportunities to receive and be fed as well as opportunities to share. During these years the thinking and studying which has issued in this book developed – not without crisis points, as will emerge in later chapters.

A Grand-daughter's Story – so far

This is the most difficult part of the family story to write because it is about another person who is very much alive and who has her own perspective on the subject of this book. Leslie's whole life has been lived against the background of the development of twentieth century feminism. It is natural that her view of womanhood is in keeping with that of many, but certainly not all, her peers. She is a woman of high integrity who is well thought of, and who has inherited some of her father's natural wisdom to which God has added spiritual gifts of insight. The strong will of the toddler has become an ability to stand firm and keep going when faced with the realities of life.

The oldest child in a family always has the hardest path to follow from childhood to adulthood. Added to that responsibility, Leslie had to cope with three young brothers who were at times a source of healthy sibling rivalry, but who have all grown up to respect their sister's opinions and advice, even although they don't always agree with her.

When we moved to Buckinghamshire it was a real educational upheaval for her and yet she took it in her stride. In Scotland she would not have started secondary education until she was twelve years old. Within weeks of settling into her new school (aged 10½) she was confronted with a series of 11+ tests. (Buckinghamshire has always refused to adopt Comprehensive Education). She gained a place in a new girls' Grammar School in a town five miles away. She enjoyed her school years. Her view of her school was and is probably quite different from that of her parents. It was a complete contrast to the more relaxed co-educational school that we had attended. We certainly became aware that there was a pronounced feminist ethos, which often emerged during our family meal-time discussions. But she was no different at that stage than I had been. It was, however, at this time that I began to think and read about my own conclusions. Almost daily there were pronouncements on women's rights. By the time Leslie was preparing to leave school the Equal Opportunities Commission had already been formed.

Her three good A-levels earned Leslie a place at Edinburgh University to read English Language and Literature. She found that her English Grammar School education had prepared her well for her early years at university. She studied hard (most of the time), had a very busy social life, was involved in, and eventually became Vice-President of, the Christian Union. She made many friends of both sexes. She managed her money well and made few extra financial demands on us. It wasn't until late in her final year that she decided to apply to Goldsmith's College in London to do a P.G.C.E. Soon after she graduated M.A. in the same MacEwan Hall, where her mother had done twenty-four years before, she became engaged to Nicholas, a fellow Scot and fellow student of English. Also like her mother she married one year after her graduation. She taught in a school in Streatham for three years until our oldest grandchild, Kirsten, was born.

I don't think that Leslie found it any easier than I did in those early years of motherhood, but she coped better than I had done. Kirsten was a very colicky baby. Every evening after work Nick paced the floor with his beloved daughter. When Katherine was born three years later after a very difficult pregnancy – three months of which was spent in complete bed rest – the same pattern was repeated only much worse! Katherine had alarming and life threatening symptoms which went undiagnosed for months. Eventually the cause was found to be a profound dietary intolerance to wheat and dairy produce, which lasted until she was five years old.

At this point the family moved out to Oxfordshire. The contrast between city and country life was quite difficult to handle. All the things that Les had been involved in in a busy city situation were no longer there. The local market was the big event of the week! Five years ago she was offered a position in a Montessori Nursery School in a local priory – a job which fits in well with family life and the many other activities in which she is now involved. Who knows what the future holds. Perhaps God has other plans for her in the years after the girls have left home.

The whole family is totally involved in the life of the local Baptist Church. Their home in the main street of the town is open and welcoming to all who knock on the door.

A Century of Change

What does the future hold for the next generation of women in my family in the twenty-first century. Already nine year-old Annie's life is very different from that of her great-grandmother born a hundred years before her. Educationally and socially her life is already so much fuller and more challenging. The prospects as she grows into mature womanhood are wide open. All of our six grand-daughters are being reared by loving Christian parents. They have mothers who are always there for them. They have dads who value and constantly affirm them. Their world of computers and e-mail and the internet would have seemed like science fiction to that little girl of 100 years ago. They will doubtless have homes full of mod. cons. as yet unthought of, which will release them even more than the present generation from time consuming tasks. But will their lives be less stressful? Will they be allowed to choose to stay at home and experience the wonder of a little child's development day by day, or will they be compulsory career women, forced to hand their babies over to others who will not be all that interested in the first smile, the first tooth, the first word, or the first step?

There are still many places in the world where the birth of a daughter is regarded as second best. There are still many little girls who will grow up undervalued and repressed in countries where injustices have not been dealt with. Paradoxically, family life is more generally valued in some of these countries, many of which have been Christianized. Injustice and undervaluing of womanhood have never been in God's heart. His purpose for us has never altered from the beginning of time.

Part Two -
God's Ways in Scripture

3

The Beginning of Time

The beginning of time

'Let's start at the very beginning.' This song from the *Sound of Music* kept running through my head. Earlier that day in September 1984, God had brought me once more to a place of inner peace, away from the turmoil that had been going on for many months. We were in sunny Portugal – a contrast to the majesty of Switzerland, but a country we had come to regard as our place of rest and refreshing away from the pressures of pastoral life.

I had been reading books and magazine articles by Christian feminists. Much of what was being said seemed so right and just. They were all highly intelligent women. Some of them had been to theological college. My theological knowledge had come through listening to my husband and others expounding scripture, through reading books, and listening to tapes. I was not an unquestioning listener or reader, however, and constantly bombarded my husband and his colleagues with awkward questions! If what these books were saying was really true, it would mean that I hadn't been hearing God speak to me in the past, that I had been teaching young women around me what amounted to error and that my life thus far had not been fulfilling God's purposes but my own. These authors were highly regarded in the evangelical world, so I needed to pay attention to what they were saying.

As I sat in the early morning sunshine on a verandah framed with red bougainvillea and looking out over a panorama of gleaming white buildings to the horizon where the clear blue sky and sea met, I called out to God to help me. I confessed that there was criticism in my heart and that I was harbouring wrong attitudes to those with whom I disagreed – and received His forgiveness. I asked God to show me where I was prejudiced and where I was making principles out of tradition and my own ideas (I am well aware that, in some areas, I am my mother's daughter). I asked God to show me from scripture His unchanging principles for womanhood and manhood.

It was at this point that I began to experience and know once more the peace that rules in our hearts where we are completely open to hear and obey God. All day I expected an immediate dramatic revelation of truth, but it never happened! But all that day this song, which I wasn't in the habit of singing, kept going through my head. Next morning I sat down again at the same table on the same verandah with my Bible in front of me. Into my head quite clearly came the words 'In the beginning God'. At that time I thought that God was saying that I was to go through the Bible from beginning to end studying relevant passages in order to fulfil my commitment of the day before. When I began to read these early Genesis chapters it was as though I had never really read them before! Every time I tried to go beyond Genesis 1-3 it seemed that God drew me back again.

Some months before an older friend, a woman whose life was and is a constant challenge to me, pointed out a verse in Ecclesiastes (7:29) which is translated in the Good News Bible, 'God made us plain and simple but we have made ourselves very complicated.' No other version translates this verse in this way, but I have had the authenticity of this translation verified by a very experienced and highly scholarly Bible translator.

I also found that there were several portions of scripture that kept coming up either in devotional reading or at events which I attended with my husband, Jim, in various parts of the country and abroad. It was as though God was constantly reminding me of the commitment I had made and at the same time challenging and encouraging me to keep going.

James 3: 13-18
God has constantly used these verses to make me examine again my attitudes towards others and to expose areas of prejudice and wrong thinking.

The book of Nehemiah
This book tells of the broken walls of Jerusalem and how they were repaired. This book spoke to me of the increasing breaking down of family life, the building blocks of society. It spoke to me of the importance of not just standing by but of being willing to be involved in rebuilding. This was amazingly confirmed when I discovered a book on Nehemiah written by Jill Briscoe called *Fighting for the Family*.

Proverbs 31: 10-31
God had to thrust this passage before me. I was asked to speak on it. I said 'yes', but inwardly groaned. I didn't like this woman because she was so organized and clever. To read of her activities made me feel tired! Frankly it was one of the passages that I found it hard to believe (as 2 Timothy 3:16 teaches us) 'God breathed and useful for teaching, rebuking, correcting, and training in righteousness'. In the course of preparing to speak to others, God spoke into my own life and taught me many lessons that we shall explore later. I now regard this lady as a friend.

Genesis, Genesis, Genesis
For three years I meditated on the first three chapters of Genesis. Increasingly I became convinced that herein lay the key to what has always been in the heart of God for womanhood. Sometimes I would be going about the routine, boring tasks involved in housekeeping when a thought would suddenly come into my head. I would write it down and then research the validity of it when the opportunity arose.

The only people, apart from Jim, that I shared these thoughts with were the members of a Bible Study Group for young mums that I was leading at the time. One of the group, a Wycliffe missionary, gave me a tape of a talk by Elisabeth Elliott on the subject of 'Femininity'. Until this time I was constantly dogged by doubts as to whether what I was discovering was really from God. I seemed to be swimming against an ever-swelling tide. And yet I constantly found a deep sense of God's presence as I studied and meditated. This tape summed up everything that I had felt that God had taught me. Since then I have had the privilege of meeting this Christian stateswoman, whose physical stature is more than matched by her spiritual stature, a woman of strength and gentleness, a woman of intellectual ability, who speaks and writes deep truths with wisdom and humility. We had the privilege of welcoming her, along with her husband Lars Gren, into our home. She assured me that the beliefs that I had would not make me popular, especially among young women – a fact which she had found many times over as she had spoken in colleges and universities in the USA. At the time I was not unduly concerned, because what I had embarked on was, I thought, a private study to be shared with a limited few.

But God.......

On several occasions during 1987 Jeremiah 1 seemed to crop up. It was a challenging scripture, but it didn't seem to have any particular application to me. One autumn Saturday afternoon when Jim was preaching at the induction of one of our young men from Gold Hill to his first pastorate, it was as though the words of Jeremiah 1:4-8 jumped out at me. I had had a growing feeling that God was asking me to share with others, but I had again been struggling with self-doubt – not about the truth of what was in my heart, but my ability to communicate up front. I have always been more comfortable on a one-to-one or small group basis of communication. I felt that God said, 'What is your excuse – too old, too shy, fear of people?' At this point (right in the middle of the sermon) I wrote down words that I felt that God was speaking into my heart. These were words of caution, encouragement, warning and instruction, and a challenge to be willing to speak out. In the years since they were given, they have been confirmed in all that has happened.

Within weeks of this encounter with God, I was invited to speak at a conference for women in the north of Scotland. Until this time most of my up-front speaking had been at our weekly meeting held for young mums – some Christian, but mostly those looking for answers to life's big questions. Since 1987 I have spoken in many places, locally, in this country, and abroad. Over these years there has grown in me such a burden for womanhood that there are times when it has almost become a physical ache.

In His dealings with me, God has shown me that I had moved from one extreme position held in my student years to another, which was not completely scriptural either. In upholding my strong convictions about home and family life I had become very legalistic. Another area that God has dealt with was a shyness that had its roots in pride and a fear of being vulnerable– a fear of people and what they might think of me. This was behind my unwillingness to speak out. He has replaced my reticence about speaking in public with a healthy dose of butterflies in my stomach before each occasion – a reminder of the responsibility He has given me and my dependence on Him. Every time, as I have prepared to speak, God has added new insights. He has also put before me certain guidelines to be observed at all times in preparation and in communicating:

1. In all matters of faith and practice the Bible alone is our clear instruction manual.
2. The church that is the living Body of Christ on earth has a clear call to influence and shape society – not the other way round.
3. God never calls anyone, man or woman, to do anything which is not in accordance with scriptural truth.
4. Scripture needs to be set against scripture and not against what we want it to say. Someone has said, 'Be aware of

your own bias and assumptions and you will be less prone
to baptize them with scripture'.
5.   'Never make a principle out of your own experience. Let
God be as original with other people as He is with you'.
Oswald Chambers, *My Utmost for His Highest.*
6.   'God made us plain and simple but we have made ourselves
very complicated' (Ecclesiastes 7:29 GNB)

A wide-lens view of creation (Genesis 1 – 2:4)

Genesis 1 gives the wide-lens view of creation. It deals with the
immensity of the universe which our finite minds find hard to
take in. The key words in the chapter are GOD and GOOD. 'In the
beginning God.......' 'and God saw that it was good'. *Elohim* is
the word that Moses used for God in this chapter – the maker of
the heavens and the earth, the creator God who planned
everything and brought everything into being, the One who made
the Swiss mountains and the multitude of tiny flowers that grow
there, the God who is one God and yet three persons, who said,
'Let us make man in our image, male and female.' This whole
chapter reaches a climax with these words. None of the planets,
stars, mountain ranges, seas and rivers, or the amazing trees and
plants and flowers, or the variety of living things compared with
the man and the woman He created to bear His image and to
take responsibility for the care of everything else that He created.

A close-up view of creation (Genesis 2)

This chapter moves from the general to the particular, from the
broad sweep to a close up. Moses gives God another name in
this chapter – *Yahweh Elohim* – the God who made himself
known, who spoke to and desired a relationship with the crown
of his creation; the Lord God, the great I AM with whom Moses
had such a dramatic encounter when He called him to lead the
Hebrew people out of bondage in Egypt to the land promised to
Abraham. In this chapter we have an enlargement of the
statement, 'Let us make man in our image, male and female.'

Verse 7 – 'The Lord God formed the man from the soil and breathed life into him so that he became a living being.' It is hard for us to understand how this happened, and yet we see the reverse process when breath departs from the body and it eventually returns to the elements from which it is formed. The human body contains no chemicals that cannot be extracted from the earth.

Verses 8-17 – The Lord God placed the man in very beautiful and lush surroundings and gave him some instructions about the cultivation and care of all that was around him. He also gave him simple rules for living. He spoke about his freedom giving only one restriction to that freedom. There was only one tree in the garden from which he must not eat. To do so would mean an end to his life.

Verses 18-20 – This is the only time that the words 'not good' appear in these first two chapters. God was aware of the man's aloneness but the man, as yet, was not. The Lord God brought the birds and animals to the man to name. He was brought into contact with all the other living creatures for which he had been given responsibility; part of that responsibility was naming them. The man realized that there was no other living creature like him.

Verses 21-23 – The Lord God then completed His work of creation. He created 'a helper fit for him' (NIV) or 'a suitable companion to help him' (GNB). This helper was created –

- For the man
- From the man
- To be given to the man
- To be named by the man

She was not created from the soil as he had been, but from the man's own flesh. Perhaps this is not so hard for us to comprehend in these days when cloning is so much in the news. This is radically different, however, because this being was very different in the intricacies of her cellular structure that made

65

her wonderfully different, as the man noticed immediately. She was no male clone.

Now the perfection of creation was completed and God rested, pleased with all that He had made. He made the perfect man and the perfect woman in His perfect paradise to enjoy the beauty of all that He had made. He made them to enjoy one another, to have children, so that the whole earth would eventually be filled with their descendants. There was food in plenty for all. There was perfect harmony throughout creation. This was *shalom*.

Could God have done things differently?

This thought came to my mind one day as I was pondering these verses in Genesis 2. God could have made one hermaphrodite (androgynous) human being capable of reproducing itself. If all there is to gender difference is to do with reproduction then this would have been a definite possibility. Indeed there have been those who have postulated that this is in fact what Genesis 1:27 is saying, but they have never been taken seriously because the Hebrew text would not support this suggestion. The idea came from Greek philosophy superimposed on scripture. God could have done it this way – but He did not.

• God could have taken a second handful of soil and made the woman. There are many who would feel much more comfortable with this because it fits in much more easily with the idea of undifferentiated equality. God could have done it this way – but He did not.

• God could have taken many handfuls of soil and made many men and women, thus creating a society rather than a family. This would fit in with the view of man and woman held by the evolutionists – with or without God as the creating power. God could have done it this way – but He did not.

• God could have made a woman from the soil, given her instructions, given her the responsibility of naming the animals, and caused her to fall into a deep sleep. Woman could have been called man and man could have been called woman, taken from the flesh of the one created first. God could have done it this way – but He did not.

• God could have made the woman from the soil and caused her to conceive by the Holy Spirit and bring forth a man-child as happened much later in history. God could have done it this way – but He did not.

God created a blueprint for society

God chose to create the man and the woman in the way that He did. He did what He did to complete them in perfection to live in His perfect world, to live in obedience to Him and in fellowship with Him.

He created the man for leadership and direction – signified by the responsibility of naming. He created the woman for support and companionship and the acceptance of the man's loving leadership. He created them equal in value and worth, both fully reflecting His image. He created them wonderfully different not just in anatomy and physiology, but also emotionally and psychologically as well – because His purpose for each was different. He created them first to establish a family, the building block of society, and then society to live in relationship with one another and in fellowship with Him.

We find it impossible even to begin to imagine a sinless relationship in a sinless world. All our thinking and understanding is filtered through the events of Genesis 3 and the effects of that event on our own humanity. The words 'headship' and 'submission' arouse strong emotions in women (and men) today because of the perversion that has taken place in the meanings of these words by the actions, particularly, of men who believe that they are portraying headship when they suppress and intimidate the women to whom they relate, not only in the home but also in society and in the church. Since submission on the part of woman was intended by God to be the reasoned (not blind) response to loving leadership, this word has also become totally perverted in its meaning and is seen in terms of subservience and servility. The only way we can understand the true meaning of headship is to look at the only perfect man who ever lived – Jesus, the second Adam. In Him we see that headship first and foremost demonstrates sacrificial love. Direction, guidance, protection and correction flow from this foundational attribute. There was complete denial of self, and complete submission to the will of His Heavenly Father.

Unfortunately there has never been a perfect woman, but perhaps Mary's response to the news that she was to be the one chosen to bear the long awaited Messiah is the nearest we can come to the portrayal of pure submission. We don't know anything about Mary before the angel appeared to her, but I don't think that it is unreasonable to suppose that God, in some way, had been preparing her throughout her young life. We see from Luke 1 that her submission was not blind obedience. It was a response to coming to an understanding of what was being said.

Genesis 2 ends with the first marriage – the only one to be consummated by sinless people –

Man and woman
Head and helper
Made to be complementary, not supplementary
Made for co-operation, not for competition.

Moses closes the chapter with prophetic words about the meaning of marriage:

For this reason a man will leave his father and mother
and be united to his wife, and they will become one
flesh.

Paradise Lost – Genesis 3
From the beginning God gave human beings the freedom to obey or not to obey – a freedom that He has never removed. For all of us, the choices we make affect our own lives and the lives of

those nearest and dearest to us, and perhaps other people too. Sadly the choice made by the woman and then by the man has affected every other human being ever since.

Verses 2-7 - There is no doubt that the man had conveyed the Lord God's instructions to the woman. Her conversation with the serpent shows that she knew exactly what the Lord God had said. She could not plead lack of knowledge.

Moses reverts to the use of the name Elohim in the conversation between the woman and the serpent. Satan did not have a fellowship relationship with God – he couldn't call God Yahweh Elohim. Why did the serpent not approach the man? Where was the man when the serpent was beguiling the woman with smooth talk? Did the serpent disappear before the man came on the scene? These are questions without answers.

The fact is that the woman listened to the flattery of the serpent. She liked the idea of being like God. She liked the look of the fruit. She ate some of the forbidden fruit. She gave some to the man. What would have happened if the man had refused to be drawn into her disobedience – if he had at that point exerted the responsibility he had been given? The fact is that he had not exercised his God given leadership. Not only did he allow the woman to be in the place of temptation, but also he allowed himself to be persuaded to disobey the Lord God.

The result was immediate. They knew that something dreadful had happened and they hid from God. But perfection had departed. Fellowship with God was broken. Role reversal had begun. Seeds of animosity between man and woman had been sown. Ground had been prepared for sexism and feminism to flourish.

Verses 8-13 – The Lord God, *Yahweh Elohim*, (Moses reverts again to this name) came walking in the garden calling out to the man. The Lord God had given the man responsibility – and so he held the man accountable to Him. The man made an excuse for hiding from God that only served to reveal his guilt. The man said that it was the woman's fault – 'and you gave her to me'– inferring that it was also God's fault. The woman said that it was the serpent's fault because he had tricked her.

Verses 14-15 - The Lord God reversed the order when it came to judgment; he dealt first with the serpent. A curse was put on this creature because it allowed Satan to work through it to bring disharmony into creation. The ultimate fate of Satan is prophesied.

Verse 16 – The Lord God's punishment for the woman was two-fold, both to do with her closest relationships – husband and children. The relationship that was given for co-operation and mutual support would now be open to domination; the relationship that was given for joy would now also be a source of pain. The producing of children, the result of this closest of human relationships, would also be marred with increased pain.

Verses 17-19 – The Lord God's reason for the man's punishment was, 'Because you listened to your wife'. The man's punishment was in relation to the soil from which he had come. (The woman's punishment was in relation to the man from whom she had come.) Enjoyable stewardship and care of God's paradise would be replaced with hard toil away from paradise. His punishment was in relation to making provision for his family.

Verse 20 – Here for the first time the names Adam and Eve are used. Adam named his wife Eve which means 'living' – an acknowledgment that from her their descendants will come.

Verse 21 – The Lord God, in spite of His disappointment with Adam and Eve, shows His continued care for them. Although it was because of their sin that they knew that they were naked, He clothed them and covered their nakedness.

Verse 22 – Because they had eaten of the fruit of the forbidden tree, Adam and Eve were banished from the garden of peace and plenty lest their disobedience take them further in their desire to be equal with God. It was for them truly paradise lost.

How should we regard Genesis?
Genesis and Revelation are the two books of the Bible that have come under most attack down through the ages. They deal not

only with the mysteries of the beginning and the end of time as we know it, but even more significantly with the rise and ultimate fall of Satan.

If the first chapters of Genesis were only an area of dispute between believers and unbelievers there would be no problem. The fact is that these chapters have caused endless disagreement among the people of God down through the centuries. There are those who solve the problem by dismissing the Genesis account of creation as a creational myth amongst many other creational myths that have been found in ancient writings – but even amongst all these myths there isn't one that assigns the high value to womanhood that Genesis 2 does.

However, the acceptance that these chapters are God-breathed through Moses does not end the controversy. There are two other popular interpretations of these verses which differ radically from the one laid out earlier in the chapter. There are also a whole range of views which are usually held by people who feel that the Scriptures need to be tailored to fit the society of a new millennium.

At the one extreme we have the view which ignores the equal worth of man and woman in the sight of God which is stated in Genesis 1:27. Those who hold this position would dwell on Genesis 2:21-24, but would interpret these verses through the words spoken by God to the woman in Genesis 3:16 'and he will rule over you'. The conclusion is that man was made superior to woman in the act of creation, and that God, because of the woman's disobedience, gives man the go-ahead to treat woman in a way which is demeaning and oppressive.

At the other extreme we have the view which would now be quite generally accepted by a large proportion of people in most main line denominations. It is a view which has mirrored the increasingly feminist views of late twentieth century society. This interpretation depends heavily on Genesis 1:27 and on Genesis 5:1 and 2 to support the idea of undifferentiated equality between man and woman. They would dismiss the suggestion that Genesis 2:18-23 speaks of any God-given differentiation in role and purpose between two people of equal worth. Headship and domination are regarded as synonymous – imposed on woman by man after the fall and being the continuing position of women until the coming of Jesus. The death and resurrection of Jesus is regarded as a restoration of the undifferentiated equality of Genesis 1:27, not as a restoration of the perfection of creation as described in Genesis 2:21-24.

It is important, therefore, to continue through the scriptures to find out how women were regarded by God in succeeding centuries.

4

God's Covenant People

What a Mess! When God used the prophet Moses to write the early history of humankind, He made sure that he told the whole story 'warts and all'. The rebellion against God's order, which began in the middle of paradise, proliferated down through the centuries until God decided that enough was enough.

There was one family, descendants of Adam and Eve's son Seth, who had honoured God and obeyed Him for four generations. Noah and his family had demonstrated that it was possible to honour Yahweh in the way that they lived their lives. For this reason they were chosen to repopulate the post-flood world. We have no clear idea of time scale in the Biblical story either pre-flood or post-flood until God breaks in to the life of a descendant of Noah's son Shem around 2000BC. This descendant was called Abram and his wife was called Sarai.

Sarai – who became Sarah, the mother of Israel
How did God's pronouncement to the woman about the possible consequences of her disobedience work out for this remarkable woman Sarai?

When Sarai married Abram, they began their life together in Ur, a highly civilized city in a fertile valley around the rivers Tigris and Euphrates in Mesopotamia. They moved north from Ur to Haran, another highly civilized city, with the household of Abram's father and settled there for some time. When God spoke to Abram, instructing him to uproot himself from Mesopotamia and go to Canaan, this must have been very traumatic for Sarai. She had to leave behind the comforts and considerable mod. cons. to which she was accustomed in her home in Haran and settle for life as a nomad, living in tents. Because they were a wealthy family the tents were probably quite luxurious, but they didn't have the running water and the highly developed sanitary arrangements of Ur and Haran. It is highly unlikely that she had been consulted, but she knew that Abram was responding to the call of Jahweh, the God of their ancestor Shem, so she trusted his judgment.

All went well in Canaan until a famine hit the land. Abram chose to leave the land of God's provision and go to Egypt, where food was plentiful. Because he was afraid that the Egyptians might kill him in order to gain possession of his beautiful wife, Abram persuaded Sarai to say that he was her brother (a half-truth since they had the same father). As he had feared, the king took Sarai into his harem but treated her 'brother' well, giving him gifts of livestock and slaves. Abram's deception was found out when God brought disease on the king's household. Abram, Sarai and their complete entourage were expelled from the land of Egypt.

While in Egypt Sarai had acquired an Egyptian maid-servant. Abram and Sarai's monogamous marriage had produced no children. This was a matter of concern to Sarai, since God had twice told Abram that he would have many descendants. Sarai realized that time was passing and decided to solve the problem by suggesting that her servant girl Hagar should bear children for Abram. Abram listened to his wife Sarai. The situation is very similar to the one that Adam had found himself in. God had spoken to Abram – as He had done to Adam. Sarai persuaded Abram that she had a straightforward solution to the problem – a solution that would require no faith. Humanly speaking Sarai's suggestion was a perfectly acceptable one. God had not specifically said that Sarai would be the mother of Abram's son. According to the custom in the culture in which she had been raised, a barren wife could give her husband a female slave and still raise any resulting children as her own.

But this was not God's way, and Sarai very soon realized it. Unlike Sarai, God did not treat the servant girl Hagar harshly. She had only been obedient to her mistress. God spoke to her and told her that she would have a son called Ishmael who would have many descendants who would trace their lineage back to Abram. Some of the tensions in the Middle East today go back to the fact that Abram listened to his wife rather than to God!

El Shaddai – the Almighty God

God spoke again to Abram, making it plain that He was the Almighty God and would not tolerate disobedience. This time He made it plain that His purposes would be fulfilled through Sarai, his wife. God instituted a covenant relationship with Abram and his household which would be physically confirmed by the circumcision of every male. God changed Abram's name to Abraham – 'ancestor of many nations' – and Sarai's name to Sarah – 'princess'. Abraham's response to this awesome meeting with God was to laugh at the prospect of a child being born to them at their advanced age. He suggested to God that He should settle for Sarah's solution and accept Ishmael as his heir. God responded with the promise that he would bless Ishmael – but Sarah would bear a son within one year.

Sarah's Laughter – Derision or Incredulity?

Three months later Sarah heard God's messengers tell Abraham that the countdown was now nine months. Sarah's response was exactly as Abraham's had been – laughter. Any woman, long past childbearing years, would have responded in the same way. Sarah had weathered all Abraham's adventures and had known God's protection and provision throughout these long years of travelling. She knew God's promise to make Abraham the father of a great nation, but she just could not believe that God could fulfil through her His prophecy that there would be kings among her descendants.

Despite her old age she was still a beautiful woman – a fact that caused Abraham to allow her once more to be taken into a king's harem during the year that preceded Isaac's birth. But God protected Sarah and allowed her to be given back to Abraham untouched by the king, so that there could be no doubt about who Isaac's father was. Isaac was born at the time that God had said he would be.

Sarah's laughter was not directed towards Abraham but was a response of complete incredulity – an inward struggle to believe that with God nothing that He has promised to do is impossible.

Twice before Abraham had yielded to Sarah's requests in relation to Hagar, and Abraham had had to live with the consequences. This time God intervenes and tells Abraham to go along with her request. God knew that Sarah's desire was to get rid of Ishmael and his mother. Sarah knew that Abraham loved his son. She wanted to make sure that Ishmael would not inherit Abraham's wealth. God's desire, on the other hand, was that it would be clear that His purposes were to be fulfilled through Isaac. God said 'Listen to what Sarah tells you'

Did Abraham rule over Sarah?

In looking at this question it is important to note that in Genesis 3 God did not instruct the man to rule over the woman. He said to the woman that this would be a consequence for her of their disobedience, which would cause difficulty in man/woman relationships.

Abraham and Sarah were both sinful human beings loved by God, and chosen by Him to fulfil His purposes. They had no scriptures to guide them in their daily walk with God, but Abraham learned by experience to hear God's voice and to walk by faith. Sometimes he chose to go his own way and had to take the consequences.

There is no doubt that Abraham was not always a model husband, but through the whole story there is a thread running that indicates that Abraham did love Sarah and valued her as a person. They obviously communicated with one another, because she knew that their God had a special purpose for Abraham. One wonders why God never spoke to Sarah directly as He did to Hagar. Did she not expect that God would speak to her? The narrative indicates that she remained a beautiful woman, which according to the apostle Peter was not just a physical beauty (1 Peter 3: 3-6). That Abraham's love for Sarah was not merely a physical attraction is suggested by his faithfulness to her in spite of the fact that she bore no children; he could easily have set her aside because of her barrenness. Abraham certainly had children by Hagar and then by Keturah. It is not clear whether Keturah became his wife after Sarah's death – but Sarah is the wife whom he mourned and beside whom his sons Ishmael and Isaac buried him before going their separate ways.

There are those who would put other interpretations on the story of these two people, portraying Abraham as an overbearing husband and Sarah as an unsubmissive wife who treated her husband with contempt. But does this picture fit in with the importance given to them in Romans and Galatians, where Paul uses them as representing the faith covenant with God that we have in Christ Jesus? With God nothing is impossible – even today.

On a personal note

Sarah's reaction when she overheard God's messengers prophesy the birth of Isaac was exactly my inner reaction when Jim walked into the manse kitchen one morning in the early 1980's and said, 'God has just told me that He will give us a house.' I wasn't as honest as Sarah – instead of laughing I made a pious response to the effect that I had no doubt that, when the time came for us to vacate the manse, God would put a roof over our heads.

Jim had been concerned for some months that, if he died, I would be left homeless with three lads to feed, clothe and educate. Our daughter was already married. His concern arose out of seeing this happen to the family of one of his contemporaries in the ministry. He knew that God would take care of us but he felt that some responsibility for his family rested on his shoulders.

He was quite deflated by my response and never mentioned this again to anyone but God.

Some months later a friend said to me that, while she had been praying for us, she felt that God had told her that he was going to give us a home of our own! I had to listen this time – but how could this possibly happen? We had very few savings. God had regularly supplemented our salary in very unexpected ways when things like school uniforms and sports gear had to be bought. He had always provided us with good holidays, often through the generosity of people in the church. He had always enabled us to change our car when it became obvious that that was necessary. Moreover we had always had a reliable car. However, we had no rich relatives who were about to die and leave us a legacy. Even a modest three bedroom semi in our area cost about £80,000 (now much more than double that amount). It is very easy to believe scripture in our heads, but when it comes to personally appropriating God's promises it can be a different story. I found that I could have faith for promises God had made to others and could rejoice in God's miraculous provision for others – but this was different!

One Monday morning a few months later Jim opened a letter, and I heard him gasp. He handed it to me. It was from two people who had always been very caring towards us in every way. This letter said that they had been concerned for some time that, unlike other members of the pastoral team at that time, we did not have our own home but lived in tied accommodation. They went on to say that they believed that the Lord had prompted them some months before to realize some assets and divide the resulting funds between their own family and us. The sum mentioned would have bought us a very large house almost anywhere else in the country! Because of taxation problems the money was put into a trust fund on our behalf which was then added to by others!

Thirteen years ago we moved into our own very spacious and comfortable home. If we want to uproot and move we are free to do so. We have complete freedom to use the resources to provide us with a home here or anywhere else for the rest of our lives. God did what He said He would do. I have learned to listen when Jim says that God has spoken to him! Like Abraham, he has made mistakes – and has had to live with the consequences, but I know that he is a man of faith who wants to be obedient to God.

Other 'holy women of the past who put their faith in God'
Many centuries had passed since the miracle of Isaac's birth. God had kept His promise and had made a mighty nation out of the descendants of Abraham and Sarah. Famine had once more sent Abraham's grandson and his family into Egypt, away from the land of God's promise. For many years they lived comfortably, but as generations passed and their many descendants remained there, they became slaves to the Egyptians. God chose Moses to lead his people out of slavery and back to the land that He had given Abraham. Because of their rebellion and unbelief, forty years passed between leaving Egypt and entering again into the land that God had prepared for His people. Joshua, not Moses, led the people in. Each tribe, descendants of Joseph and his brothers, were allotted land. It is interesting to note that Joseph's great, great, great grandson Zelophehad (Manasseh's descendant) had no sons but had five daughters (Joshua 17:3). As Moses had promised (Numbers 27:1-8), they were allotted land in the same way that Manasseh's male heirs were allotted land.

Before Joshua died he called together all the leaders of Israel and challenged them to 'fear the Lord and serve Him with all faithfulness' (Josh. 24:14), which they promised to do. Within two generations the people of Israel had forgotten the instructions given them through Moses and the promise they had made to Joshua and had begun to worship other gods. They turned their back on their covenant relationship with God, and 'everyman did what was right in his own eyes' (echoes of twentieth century Britain?). People worshipped Baal and Astarte, male and female fertility gods, instead of Jahweh. Time and time again God allowed the land He had given to the Israelites to be invaded and the people to be oppressed by those who occupied the land. Then they would turn again in desperation to Jahweh and cry for deliverance. Time and time again their faithful God would hear their cries of repentance and bring deliverance. Each time God raised up a leader who led them to victory over their enemies.

Those who were used by God in this way were known as judges. Moses first appointed judges in each of the twelve tribes of Israel when the responsibility of total leadership weighed heavily upon his shoulders. They were to be 'wise and understanding and respected men from each tribe' (Deut 1:13). After the death of Joshua and Eleazar, the judges were the only people left to hear from God and to convey God's desires to His people.

Deborah – a mother in Israel

For twenty years the people of Israel had been oppressed by a Canaanite king called Jabin. God had, once more, allowed this to happen because of the wickedness of His people. There was, however, a woman who was faithful to Jahweh. She was a prophetess in the tribal area of Ephraim. She was acting as a judge for the people at that time and was obviously known throughout the land as a woman who heard God speak and gave wise counsel. Yet again the people of Israel were repenting of their disobedience and looking to God to bring them deliverance. God spoke to Deborah and told her to send to Naphthali in the northern part of the nation of Israel for a man called Barak. God had said that Barak was the one who would lead His people to victory over their oppressor King Jabin.

Barak was none too keen to take on the task that God was giving him. He reluctantly agreed to do what God had said, but only if Deborah went with him – a very unusual request for a warrior to make! Deborah agreed, but made it plain that this was a compromise and not what God wanted. She went with him and once more the Canaanites were driven out of the land but the credit went to Deborah and to another woman, Jael, who killed the leader of Jabin's army.

In her song of victory Deborah describes herself as a mother in Israel – not as a crusading Joan of Arc , but as one who jolted the men of Israel into assuming their God-given responsibilities.

Women like Deborah – mothers in Israel

Although Deborah is unique in the pages of scripture, there have been many women down through history who have held fast to their faith in God when men have turned their backs on Him and have worshipped at other altars. Many of these have been unsung and unknown except to those closest to them. I am sure that this was just as true of women in Israel as it has been among women in Christendom. As far back as the Middle Ages in Europe there were women who were educated in theology as well as in other disciplines who kept the fires of faith burning. They challenged the weakness of men and brought peace where there was division and rancour without taking on themselves any function not scripturally appropriate to their womanhood.

Hilda of Whitby was one of those. She was a woman of wealth and royal connections. She set up a community for the theological training of young men at Whitby Abbey. She was responsible for bringing reconciliation between the two main streams of the church in Britain at that time. Several of the men who were educated in her college became bishops.

In more modern times we have the amazing life of Susannah Wesley, whose prayers for her children resulted in the ministries of her sons Charles and John. Their influence throughout the land was said to have saved England from the bloodbath of revolution as happened in France.

Many women missionaries, some well known, others known to God alone, have gone from our shores to carry the Gospel in word and action to the far corners of the earth. Many have had to assume responsibilities which God intended men to carry, but men did not respond to God's call to go.

This has been true at home too. There are churches that are thriving today because of the prayers and commitment of women of previous generations who have kept going during war and peace where men were absent or unwilling, as Barak was, to take on their responsibilities.

In the later years of his theological studies, my husband was student pastor of a little church in a poor area of Glasgow. This church was financed by a well-to-do church in a wealthy area of the city. There was a woman there who supported the raw, inexperienced young men sent to this church to gain experience. She had been a missionary with Mary Slessor in Calabar. She sought neither position nor glory, but was always there in the background to encourage and advise. She was known and loved in the awful slum tenements around the district where many people feared to go. Like Deborah, she was a true mother in Israel. Without her these young men would have become very discouraged. It would seem that none of the men in the parent church were willing to give the care and commitment that she gave.

Ruth – *a daughter-in-law*

Deborah's influence on the people of Israel was timely but brief. No more is heard of her after the defeat of the army of King Jabin.

There was another woman, however, who lived around the same period as Deborah. Ruth was not from Israel but from the neighbouring country of Moab. The people of Moab originated from an act of incest perpetrated by the daughter of Abraham's nephew Lot's eldest daughter. By making her father drunk she had intercourse with him which led to the birth of a child, called Moab by his mother. His descendants became a nation who worshipped a god called Chemosh, whose worship involved the practice of child sacrifice. It was through the land of Moab that the children of Israel finally entered the land that God had given them. Moses had led them to the border, but was not permitted by God to go any further. It was there in Moab that Moses taught the Israelites God's rules for living given on Mt Sinai many years before. It was from Mt Pesgah in Moab that God showed Moses the land that He had promised. Moses died and was buried in a valley there.

Ruth, the Moabitess, had married an Israelite man, the son of Elimelech and Naomi, who had left their home in Bethlehem in Judea and had gone to live in the pagan land of Moab in a time of famine. Father and sons died, leaving Naomi and her daughters-in-law without means of care and support. Both young women were childless. Naomi decided that she would return home to the city of Bethlehem. She encouraged her daughters-in-law to stay behind in their own land with their people, but Ruth responded with the well-known plea to be allowed to go with Naomi. This was a very brave and unusual decision for this young woman to make. In doing so she was severing her family and religious ties. Her decision was to follow the God of her late husband's family and to become one of His people. This decision was to affect the history of the whole world in future generations. Ruth's later marriage to Boaz – a kinsman of her first husband – led to the birth of a son, Obed, and two generations later to the birth of her great-grandson, who became King David. Twenty-eight generations later another gentle young woman gave birth to a son called Jesus, who was 'of the house and lineage of David'.

The story of Ruth is such a contrast to the faithlessness of the people of Israel at the time of the judges. While they were turning to the pagan gods of countries like Moab, this young woman committed herself to following Jahweh the God of Israel. In faith she went with her mother-in-law to a land unknown to her and in so doing became the mother to a future line of kings!

Naomi – *a mother-in-law in Israel*
There must have been something very special about Naomi's attitudes and actions that triggered off such a response of

devotion from Ruth. Naomi could have insisted on Ruth going back with Orpah to her own pagan people, but she didn't. Not only did she take Ruth to Bethlehem with her, but she also made sure that her future was secure by encouraging her to marry again.

With the death of her husband and two sons, Naomi could have wallowed in self pity and have made life a misery for her daughter-in-law. Instead she took control of her circumstances and made the decision to return to her own home town, where her people were. We know how significant that decision was in the purposes of God. When Ruth's son Obed was born, Naomi rejoiced that she had been given a grandson. It was as though all the grief of the past had been swept away. How much greater the rejoicing would have been if Naomi had known the significance of this child's descendants!

Naomi and Ruth were two gentle, courageous women. Their relationship is a model to be copied.

Mother-in-law – a figure of fun

Many cruel and cynical jokes have been made about mothers-in-law. It is a sad fact that this has come about because of the reality that many marriages are put under strain by the interference of the mother-in-law, particularly in sons' marriages.

When Moses wrote down the account of the beginning of time, God gave him a prophetic word about marriage. 'For this reason a man will leave his father and mother and be united to his wife and they will become one flesh.' This verse comes in scripture at the end of Genesis 2, before the events of Genesis 3. It seems strange that God would put this into His written word at this point, before there were any children born! It makes clear how God views this relationship between man and woman. Jesus quoted it when He was questioned about divorce. The 'leaving' has to come before – as the older versions put it – 'the cleaving'. There must be a significant break in the old parental relationships before the cleaving can be worked out not just in physical relationship but in every-day living. If a mother doesn't begin to learn to let go as a child matures into adulthood, then this further change in relationship will be very painful. It's not that parents (both sets) cease to be parents, but parenthood assumes new boundaries.

Jim had the moving experience of giving our only daughter Leslie away, putting her hand into the hand of the young man standing at her side, and then, changing roles, he married her to that young man. This was a deeply emotional experience for him, even although he had no doubt in his heart that she would be secure in every aspect of her life, spiritually, emotionally, and materially, in Nick's care.

For both of us, as parents, this was a very happy day and yet we realized that this was the first step in new family relationships. When she had gone off to university for the first time some years before we both found that her empty bedroom tugged at our heartstrings – but now it was no longer her bedroom. Her home was elsewhere. On that day I became a mother-in-law!

Since then three sons have married. Jim has had the privilege of performing the ceremony on each occasion. Each wedding day has been different, but each has been an occasion of joy. Each time we have felt that we were not losing but gaining, and have rejoiced at the expansion of the family. There is a very definite change in relationship that has occurred, however, which is as God intended it to be. One household has become five households. Each has a different character which mirrors the personalities, creativities and interests of each couple. All are totally involved in serving God in very different ways. God has been very gracious to us as parents and as parents-in-law.

Everything I have said thus far is true, and yet from time to time I recognize a very definite 'mother hen' tendency within myself – not towards my own children as individuals but towards them as families. I don't want them to make the same mistakes that we have made. I want to smooth out the rough patches for them. But the only real mistakes are the ones that we don't learn from. We all learn by experience – often the hard way. There are times for praying and not interfering. Advice should only be given when asked for, but even when it is asked for we shouldn't expect them necessarily to take it!

Recently, in the Far East, I heard of one mother-in-law who treated her son's wife like a live-in slave. This is a Christian family, but old cultural habits (not just in the East) still often dictate attitudes more than scripture does. This young woman has three young children, one of whom has a serious physical condition, and yet her mother-in-law – who is not by any means elderly – expects this woman to attend to her every whim, giving no help whatsoever with the running of the home or caring for the children. The young woman in question is the well-educated, gifted wife of a pastor!

This is an extreme example but I have observed similar tendencies in the western world. We need to make it easy for our children and their spouses to show us honour and respect. This will never happen by making constant demands on their time and interfering in their personal lives. We mothers find it much harder than fathers do to stand back and allow our married children to live their own lives – but do it we must, or the mother-in-law jokes will cease to be jokes and become experiences of personal pain to our children and sources of tension and frustration in their marriages.

Hannah – *whose prayers were answered*

Hannah was another woman who lived towards the end of the time when Israel was ruled by the judges. Hannah had borne no children. Whereas Sarah didn't seem too upset by the situation, and did not seem to see it as a reason for pleading with God, for Hannah her barrenness was a source of deep pain. That her husband loved her and did not neglect her because of her childlessness was no consolation to her. Hannah came before God and, in silent prayer, she poured out all her pent-up grief and resentment, promising God that she would give her son back to Him to serve as a helper to Eli the priest at Shiloh. When God answered her prayer and her son Samuel was born, her husband, Elkanah, supported her in the promise she had made.

Samuel became the last great spiritual leader of Israel before the period of the kings. It was he who anointed Ruth's great, great grandson David as king of Israel. So Hannah too played a part in God's countdown to the coming of the Messiah. The song that she sang when she left Samuel to serve God in Shiloh is regarded as a kind of forerunner of the song sung many generations later by Mary that is known as the Magnificat. The sacrifice that Hannah made in presenting her first- born son to God bore fruit in his outstanding leadership of God's people. He combined his role of leader with a very real ministry of listening to God's voice.

The people of Israel, however, decided that they wanted to be like the pagan nations around them. They wanted to have a king to rule over them and lead them in battle. They also knew that Samuel's sons were not God-fearing men like their father. Samuel told the people that, although this was not God's best for them, he had been instructed by God to anoint a young man named Saul from the tribe of Benjamin as king.

Polygamy – did God approve?

This is probably a good point at which to look at the subject of polygamy among the people of God. God's intention as laid down in Genesis 2:24 and affirmed by Jesus (in Matthew 19:5) was monogamy.

Abraham's father must have had more than one wife – otherwise Sarah could not have been his half sister. There is nothing to indicate whether this was because of the death of one wife before he married another. As we have already noticed, it is uncertain whether Keturah became Abraham's wife after the death of Sarah or while she was still alive.

In Deuteronomy 21:15 the existence of polygamy is mentioned in regard to rights of inheritance. God recognizes that polygamy exists and wants to see fair treatment. The children of 'an unloved wife are not to be given less than the children of a loved wife'. God recognizes the reality of the situation, but does not express approval. Moreover it does not seem to have been the necessary norm among men. Naomi seemed to be Elimelech's only wife, while Elkanah had a loved wife, Hannah, and an unloved wife, Peninah.

It could be that this was part of the practical outworking of God's pronouncement to the woman in Genesis 3. On the other hand it may have been that, when there was so much fighting and warring, the balance of the male/female ratio was so upset that it was a way of giving protection to women, who otherwise would have been at the mercy of unscrupulous men.

Nothing has been hidden about the polygamous relationships of David and Solomon, his son. David's marriage to Abigail could well substantiate the second suggestion (Abigail's story is told in 1 Samuel 25). Abigail had done a very courageous thing when she went against Nabal's instructions to his servants. Her actions demonstrate that submission is not blind obedience. She knew that her husband's decision not to help David was a very wrong and dangerous one. She listened to what the servants said and took action which caused David to change his mind about slaughtering Nabal and his household. Her husband's reaction when she confessed what she had done caused him to have a heart attack, which led to his death within days. David's response was to send a proposal of marriage to her! Admittedly Abigail is described as beautiful as well as intelligent. That David had an eye for pretty women is shown clearly in his attraction to Bathsheba (2 Samuel 11) which was a very different situation, however. 'The thing that David had done displeased the Lord.' David repented of his sin but still had to face the consequences of God's anger about his adulterous relationship with Bathsheba. David's eight wives were all from Israel, but Solomon married foreign women. This was not pleasing to God, because these women introduced the worship of pagan gods. Eventually Solomon began worshipping these gods himself and turned his back on Jahweh. God's punishment of Solomon was to take away most of his kingdom, leaving his successors to rule over the tribes of Judah and Benjamin.

Faithfulness to Jahweh in worship and obedience to His instructions seemed to be God's priority at that time – not the number of wives, but their origins and beliefs and the influence they had on the nation.

Queens in Israel

Unlike some surrounding nations, God's people did not have queens who were anointed by God to rule, but had queen consorts. Few of them were even given the title of queen. Those who were known as queen were amongst those who introduced the worship of foreign gods.

Maacah was the first of these women. She was an Israelite, the daughter of Absalom and the wife of Rehoboam. Her influence went on through the reign of her son, Abijah. It was her grandson Asa who deposed her from her role as queen mother and had her idols destroyed (2 Chronicles15:16).

Jezebel was the daughter of a Phoenician king. When she married Ahab of Israel, she brought the worship of Baal and Asherah. Elijah's well-known confrontation with the prophets of Baal on Mount Carmel did not endear him to Jezebel. She was a powerful and evil woman whose influence continued after her husband's death. She eventually met a violent death, as Elijah had prophesied. (1 Kings 16:31, 1 Kings 19:1 and 2, 1 Kings 21:1-25 and 2 Kings 9:7)

Ahab's daughter Athaliah married King Jehoram of Judah. She may well have been Jezebel's daughter – her behaviour would certainly suggest strong genetic links with Jezebel! She plotted the extermination of the royal family of Judah following the death of her son Ahaziah. Having thought that she had succeeded, she appointed herself queen of Judah. But God preserved the line of David as He had said that He would do. Her grandson Joash had been hidden away by his half-sister, and he was anointed rightful king of Judah. Athaliah was put to death in disgrace (2 Kings 11:1-16).

A Persian king with a Hebrew queen

Esther was a young woman from the tribe of Benjamin. King Nebuchadnezzar had taken her family into exile. Her parents had died and her cousin Mordecai adopted her into his family. She had been brought into the king's palace when the king set aside his queen for disobeying him. It might have been better for God's people if their king, Ahab, had dealt similarly with Jezebel! But marriage was not to be held lightly amongst God's people, as David had discovered.

Esther was chosen to be part of the king's harem. Mordecai told her not to reveal her nationality, and in obedience to him she did not do so. Soon after becoming his queen she saved the king from being assassinated. She won the king's favour and respect. The Hebrew people were in great danger. Under Mordecai's guidance, and displaying great courage and boldness, she saved the lives of her people in exile in Persia.

Jezebel and Athaliah brought harm and destruction to the people of Israel and Judah. Esther's marriage to a foreign king brought him nothing but good. Her trust in the God of her ancestors brought justice into a corrupt society and saved her own people from annihilation.

Sarah, Deborah, Ruth, Naomi, Hannah, Esther

The lives of these women span 1,500 years of history. Unlike us they lived in a world that changed slowly. Generation upon generation lived in much the same way. Sarah was the only one who lived before God gave Moses His rules for living. The Law given to Moses was the framework within which the people of Israel lived. Before he died, Moses reminded the people of Israel – men, women and children, of the covenant that Jahweh had made with them, His chosen people. Obedience to the law would bring blessing and disobedience would bring curses on every aspect of their lives, their land, their livestock, their health, and the health of future generations.

So what specifically did the law say that affected women?

1. Family

The law commanded that honour and respect should be shown not only to the father but also to the mother. Abuse shown to a father or mother, whether in word or in physical action, was punishable by death. This was in contrast to the practice in surrounding nations where only the father was regarded in this way.

2. In marriage contracts

The giving of the Law changed some rules of marriage. Under the new conditions set out, Abraham could not have married Sarah, his half sister. Betrothals among ordinary people were normally arranged between families. The young man's parents usually chose a suitable wife for their son and began negotiations with the girl's parents. Sometimes a young man would see someone he wanted to marry and ask his parents to negotiate a betrothal for him. The betrothal was sealed by the man agreeing an appropriate sum of money with the girl's father, otherwise he would be required to work for the father for an agreed time before the marriage. Sometimes a young woman would be asked if she was in agreement, but more usually she just had to go along with the wishes of the bridegroom and her parents. On her marriage, her father would give her a gift – usually servants or land. The bridegroom also gave his bride a gift – usually clothing or jewellery.

This is an area where one can read into such negotiations what one wants! It is true that the Hebrew word for betrothal has the sense that the bridegroom was making the bride legally his own. This could be regarded as the man being willing to take complete responsibility for the future well-being of his bride in place of her parents. On the other hand it could be interpreted that the wife was becoming the equivalent of a more sophisticated slave. Much is made of the fact that a husband, for instance, Abraham, was sometimes addressed as 'adon' (lord) – a word certainly used in the slave/master context, but also used to denote respect towards someone highly regarded. In any of the relationships we have looked at there does not seem to be any indication of a master/slave relationship. In practical terms, as is true today, there would certainly be men who demeaned and undervalued their wives but that does not mean that it was the norm. It was certainly not an attitude approved of by God then or now. It is true, however, that when it came to marriage breakdown and divorce (which God hated) women were on the losing side.

3. Slaves

When the word slavery is mentioned, we immediately think of the horrors of the slave trade which caused thousands of Africans to be herded like cattle on to sailing ships and transported to the Southern States of America, where their lives were lived in misery and degradation. The Hebrew people had lived in this kind of slavery in Egypt and had known oppression and cruelty.

When the Law talks about slaves it is not in these terms, but rather in terms of servants who could not walk away from their employment at will (Exodus 21:2-11and Leviticus 25:35-54).

A Hebrew man who was in financial difficulties could, with his family, become a slave for seven years, during which time he could earn money and resolve his difficulties. Then, after seven years had passed, he became a freed man. At this point he and his wife and family were released from any further obligation. If, however, the man was single when he became a slave and was provided with a wife by his master, only the man was free to go after seven years. Presumably this was because the wife had been a slave before her marriage – perhaps because her father had sold her as a slave because of his financial difficulties! She could, however, be bought back by her family if she had not married. If a woman slave was given to the master's son as a wife she became a daughter of that family.

Ill-treatment of slaves was a punishable offence – male or female. Both male and female slaves were regarded as persons, not possessions, and were afforded the same freedom to worship God and observe the Sabbath and festivals as their masters. Foreign people, however, men and women who had been taken as slaves, had fewer rights and were regarded as possessions which could be handed down as an inheritance to the owners' children (Leviticus 25:46).

4. A woman's relationship to God
The law was read to all men, women and children (Deuteronomy 31:12 and Nehemiah 8:2). A very important part of the law related to the worship of God. It was considered very important that men, women, and children knew what God expected of them. The worship of God was at the centre of every part of their lives. Mothers were responsible for the religious instruction of young children. Parents were expected to model what was being taught by the way they lived their lives and their attitudes to those around them.

There are many instances of God speaking to women and dealing directly with women. Deborah was only one prophetess among others. God gave women songs of worship and they took a part in times of rejoicing among God's people. Women and children were alongside their men folk as they offered sacrifices. Families were involved together at the celebration of the Passover and the Feast of Tabernacles.

The conduct of worship, however, was a different matter. The priestly office was given only to a few chosen men who were descendants of Aaron. The priests represented the people before God. They were responsible for seeing that the rituals of the sacrifice were properly carried out. They led the people in worship and were responsible for seeing that the law was taught. In every other nation where pagan gods were worshipped priestesses abounded. But not among God's people.

Lastly.....Mrs Proverbs
The last verses of the book of Proverbs pose quite a problem for those who believe that women have always had a raw deal in life. There is disagreement among scholars about the authorship. Some think that Lemuel was another name for Solomon, while others believe that he was a descendant of Ishmael. Wherever

the truth lies, these verses have been included in our scriptures and so merit our attention. I believe that this alphabetical poem is there to show how highly God values woman, her gifting and ability and her importance in upholding godly standards in the home and in the wider society in which she lives. Everyone respected her – her husband, her children, and her neighbours. There is much that can be learned from this woman — but that must wait until later chapters!

Israel – a Patriarchal People
Patriarchs

A patriarch is the male head of a family or clan. The people through whom God chose to reveal himself were a patriarchal people – inheritance passed from father to son. Patriarchy is not the result of the disobedience of Genesis 3, but was established in the perfection of creation in Genesis 2. Patriarchy was and is God's intention, not fallen manhood's invention. It has to do with leadership and direction, not domination and suppression. It has nothing to do with superiority and inferiority, but has everything to do with the orderly functioning of a family, tribe, or nation. Although our attention has been focused on one nation in 1,500 years of their history, patriarchy is a universal fact. All attempts to find a truly matriarchal society have failed. After a lifetime working amongst tribes in Samoa and New Guinea, Margaret Mead the anthropologist concluded 'men have always been leaders in public affairs and the final authorities in the home.' There is no doubt that there have been many men – God-honouring men included – who have used their patriarchal position to oppress and suppress those under their leadership, particularly but not exclusively women – but this is the distortion by fallen man of the purposes of God.'

The early patriarchs of God's people were Abraham, Isaac, and Jacob, who became Israel and whose twelve sons became the patriarchs of the twelve tribes who made up the nation of Israel.

Priests

God, through Moses, the patriarch and prophet, instituted priesthood in Israel. Until this time there was no official priesthood. Sacrifices were offered to God by the head of the family at various sites with some special religious significance.

By God's command Moses set apart his brother Aaron and his sons to serve God as priests. Moses and Aaron were from the tribe of Levi. Other men from the same tribe were to assist them in the ritual duties of worship and sacrifice ordained by God. The high priestly office was to be handed down from generation to generation of the descendants of Aaron. The priest was seen as an intermediary between man and God. There is no feminine form of the Hebrew word for a priest.

In the 300 years from the institution of the priesthood to the building of the first temple there were various places of worship where the priests performed the rites of sacrifice. In times of rebellion against God, the strict rules that He had given were not obeyed and it seems that, at these times, any Levite performed the priestly duties.

During the period of the monarchy, the priestly office lost some of its spiritual authority. For example, David became the leader of the religious life as well as the civil life of the nation. The priests still performed all the ritual part of the office, but the king gave spiritual direction. There were good and godly priests, but there were also evil priests (e.g. the sons of Eli). There were men who upheld God's rules and led the people into righteous living, and there were those who lived in disobedience and who bent God's rules to suit themselves – but the priestly line continued in spite of this, right through the spiritually compromised and politically turbulent times of the inter-testamental period until the beginning of the New Testament. Then we read of an upright priest called Zechariah and his wife Elizabeth, both of the line of Aaron whose son was John the Baptist.

Kings

Although it was not God's best for His people, He had recognized from the time of Moses that, one day, Israel would want a king (Deut 17:14-20) and specified that this would be a man of His choice – someone who would live by His rules given in the Law. The monarchy lasted about four hundred years. God first chose Saul, from the tribe of Benjamin, but his disobedience caused God to reject him as king. With the anointing of David as king the monarchy moved to the tribe of Judah. As we have already noted, the disobedience of David's son Solomon caused the splitting of God's people into a Northern Kingdom, Israel, and a Southern Kingdom, Judah. But God had promised David that his dynasty would never end. The monarchy ceased during the period when the people of Judah were exiled in Babylon. David's line, however, continued and re-emerged with the appearance of an angel to a man called Joseph in the city of Nazareth several hundred years later.

Prophets

The role of the prophet was quite different from that of the priests and kings. The latter were offices of leadership and authority for the ordering of the religious and secular life of the nation. Both operated under God's appointing and anointing, and carried God's delegated authority. The prophet's role was quite different. The prophet was someone who heard God speak, who knew God's mind, who felt God's emotions and was willing to speak out at any cost. The prophet was not always a popular person with kings, priests, or people. It was through the prophet that God rebuked His people when they turned away from Him. It was through the prophet that God entreated kings, priests and people alike to repent of disobedience and rebellion so that they would again know His blessing on their lives. The message of the true prophet was always in accordance with God's law. False prophets bent or contradicted God's law and often presented a compromise solution. Prophecies were, and are, delivered under the anointing of God on a specific person, at a specific time, for a specific reason. There was no inherited line of prophets as there was for priests and kings.

We have already noticed that there were women with prophetic gifts. There is a feminine form in Hebrew for the word prophet. Abraham was the first person to be called a prophet by God. Moses and his sister Miriam were both regarded as prophets. Deborah's prophetic role was crucial in rescuing God's people from tyranny and restoring them spiritually. During the monarchy, in the reign of Josiah, Huldah prophesied the destruction of Jerusalem, and her prophecy helped to bring about religious renewal. On the other hand, a prophetess Noadiah (described in the Good News translation of the Old Testament as 'that woman') was among the prophets who tried to deceive Nehemiah and discredit him when the rebuilding of the walls of Jerusalem was near completion.

A Potted history of God's chosen people

- God kept His promise to Abraham and made a great nation of the descendants of the son born to Sarah.
- Their grandson Jacob became the father of twelve sons who became the leaders of twelve tribes enslaved in Egypt for 450 years.
- Moses of the tribe of Levi was chosen by God to lead them out of slavery in Egypt, but Joshua was chosen to lead them into Canaan, the land of God's promise.
- Eleven of the twelve tribes were given land to inhabit, the tribe of Levi, to which Moses and his brother Aaron belonged, supplied the priests to all the other tribes.
- After the tumultuous years of the judges, the people demanded of Samuel – the last and greatest of the judges – that they should have a king.
- God allowed them to have what they wanted and Israel became a kingdom with Saul, then David.
- Solomon built the temple at Jerusalem.
- Because of Solomon's marriage to an Phoenician princess leading to the worship of pagan gods the largest part of

the kingdom was taken away from David's descendants – only Judah and Benjamin remained.

- Kings of the Northern Kingdom (Israel) continued in disobedience, despite the pleas of the prophets.
- God allowed Assyria to swallow up the Northern Kingdom and its people were taken into exile while Assyrians settled in Israel.
- God allowed the Assyrians to occupy Judah, but Jerusalem, although besieged, did not fall to the Assyrians because King Hezekiah returned to the worship of Yahweh and restored the temple.
- Judah's obedience to God depended on who was king.
- In spite of the warnings of the prophets that God would not tolerate disobedience, the people of Judah went on sinning.
- As Jeremiah prophesied, Jerusalem was overrun by the Babylonian King Nebuchadnezzar (who had conquered Assyria), the temple was destroyed and most of the people of Judah were taken into exile in Babylonia for seventy years.
- The OT scriptures draw to a close with the return from exile of some of the people of Judah (now called the Jews).
- The temple was rebuilt and the walls of Jerusalem were restored under Nehemiah's leadership.
- Ezra, a descendant of Aaron, called the people together in Jerusalem – men, women, and children who were old enough to understand – so that he could read, once again, God's rules for living given to Moses a millennium earlier. Later all the people were called to confess their sins of disobedience and to commit themselves to Jahweh. Scenes of great rejoicing followed.

Malachi – My Messenger

Among the last prophetic words of the OT were those recorded in the book of Malachi, in which God:

- Declared His unchanging nature.

- Reaffirmed His steadfast love for His people.
- Reprimanded the spiritual leaders (the priests) for living ungodly lives, giving no example to the people.
- Condemned the priests for the fact that they were not teaching the people truth, thus breaking the covenant that God had made with the tribe of Levi.
- Reaffirmed monogamy as His creational intention and condemned the cruelty that easy divorce inflicted on a wife.
- Condemned the oppression of widows and orphans.
- Stressed the importance of the giving of tithes as part of their worship.
- Spoke of a messenger who would come to prepare the way of the Lord.

And then for 400 years not another clear prophetic voice was heard. God was silent. The care of His people was left to the priests – which did not prove beneficial to Jewish women.

5

When God was silent

In most copies of the Bible only two or three pages separate the end of the Old Testament from the beginning of the New Testament. On one of these pages in my own Bible I have written two things. Firstly, 'Twelve generations passed before God spoke to His people again.' Secondly, there is a reference to Luke 1:5 and 6, which says, 'In the time of Herod the king of Judea there was a priest named Zechariah who belonged to the priestly division of Abijah: his wife Elizabeth was also a descendant of Aaron. Both of them were upright in the sight of God observing all the Lord's commandments and regulations blamelessly.' It would be easy to conclude that the words of Ezra and Malachi were listened to and, at last, the Judean remnant of God's people had lived in obedient expectancy of the coming of the Messiah, which had been prophesied. But nothing could be farther from the truth!

The challenge to do some digging into what had happened in these years came from the fact that at the end of the Old Testament women were present with their menfolk when the Law was being read and taught, and yet when we come to the unfolding of the gospel narrative, women were separated in worship in the temple and in the synagogues, and they were not thought worthy of being taught. Generally they were not treated with the dignity or respect which God had intended from the time of creation. Women like Elizabeth seemed to be the exception rather than the rule. How and when this happened is not easy to discern, but there are historical happenings that would certainly have influenced attitudes to women.

Four centuries is a long time!

Perhaps it would help us to understand the span of time between the two testaments if we look at our own history here in Britain. Four hundred years ago was the time when the crowns of England and Scotland were joined under James the Sixth of Scotland, who became James I of England. Spiritually it was just after the spiritual awakening of the Reformation. This was the time of the Gunpowder plot. It was the time when the first settlement of English and Scots took place in Ulster across the Irish Sea and in Virginia across the Atlantic Ocean. Shakespeare had just written Hamlet, Galileo had just invented the telescope. Those of us who studied history at school learned just how much happened politically, socially, scientifically and spiritually in the years since then. Our nation has known war, civil and international, and peace. Many external influences have come to us from other lands. We have prospered and we have declined. The lives of men, women and children have been deeply affected by change – especially in this last century. We have known God's blessing on our nation when we have honoured Him and stood for His timeless values. We are learning what happens when we turn our backs on Him and allow other gods to infiltrate the spiritual fabric of our people. Four hundred years is a long time!

The same was true for the remnant of God's chosen people (who were now known as the Jews) during the 400 years before the millennium that changed BC to AD. Unlike Britain, however, this tiny Middle Eastern land, which is still so much a focus of international attention, was constantly invaded and overrun by foreign powers bringing with them many different pagan influences. In a sense this was not new because, as we have already seen, the children of Israel constantly struggled to keep possession of the land that God had given them. Until this point the pattern had been of spiritual decline leading to invasion by surrounding tribes and nations, and spiritual repentance leading to the restoration of their borders. Each time such an invasion had taken place, God had spoken through his prophets against his people adopting the religions that the invaders had brought with them – sometimes to no avail.

This pattern had changed, however, when God allowed the Assyrians to invade the northern kingdom of Israel, dispersing many of its people to other lands, and repopulating the area with foreign settlers with their false gods (c 720BC). Just over a century later, as has been already noted, God allowed the same to happen in the southern kingdom of Judah when the Babylonians took many of the people of Judah into exile. When the Persians took over from the Babylonians (c 539BC) some of the Jews were allowed to return from exile and the temple and the city of Jerusalem were rebuilt. The area around Jerusalem now called the province of Judea under the rule of a Persian governor was all that remained of the southern kingdom. Persian rule continued into the fourth century BC. Although God continued to speak to the remnant of his people through the later prophets the invaders were not turned out as before but remained in control until other invaders replaced them.

Beyond the Eastern Mediterranean

To the people of Judea the world consisted of the nations which immediately surrounded them and those along the Eastern Mediterranean. But great civilizations had grown up all over the world completely unknown to the people of the Middle East. The whole planet earth was populated with peoples, some of whom were much further advanced in art and architecture and early scientific discovery than were the people chosen by God. The search for knowledge and understanding and a desire to explore and conquer other tribes and nations was deeply rooted in men everywhere. Human beings also knew that there were powers outside themselves that had influence on their lives. They invented gods whom they constantly tried to appease. In every part of the world men ruled over women as God had said they would. Women were not always treated badly, but they were definitely regarded as inferior in every way – a situation which is still true in many lands today. It is the inevitable result of fallen human nature without the knowledge of the One who created the world and everything in it.

Near East and Far East in the sixth century BC
Around the same time as the Jews were returning from exile and the temple in Jerusalem was being rebuilt, there were some interesting men influencing the thoughts of people in Nepal and in China.

Nepal
In Nepal a young, wealthy and highly educated prince who had a wife and a harem of dancing girls for his amusement, became dissatisfied with his way of life and the religious practices of his people. He left everything, including his wife and his harem, and became a homeless wanderer searching for the meaning of life. His inborn sense of right and wrong, planted in him by God (Romans 1:20: 'For since the creation of the world God's invisible qualities – his eternal power and his divine nature – have been clearly seen, being understood from what has been made, so that men are without any excuse') led him into developing a philosophy based on acquiring knowledge and wisdom, on ethical conduct and on inner meditation. It was a philosophy which had no dependence on any power outside himself. His name was Siddartha Gautama, better known as the Buddha, who lived from 563 – 480BC Gradually he gathered disciples around himself and taught them how to live according to his highly disciplined code of life. At first he excluded women because he felt that they were dangerous and greedy, but in his lifetime relented on this stance. In the century after he died his teachings spread to China in the east and to India in the south and to the west. Buddhism became a religion without a god, but where statues representing the Buddha became and have continued to be a focus of veneration.

China

In China there were two philosophers who, like Gautama, became disillusioned with the religious practices of their people. They were also rich young men who opted for a simpler way of life. Confucius lived at more or less the same time as Gautama (571 – 479BC). His philosophy emphasized the importance of devotion to the family, living and dead. He advocated peace, justice and compassion for others. Self-discipline and inner contemplation were seen as the ways to achieve these virtues. The aim was to become a person of superior merit. Confucianist thought spread quickly throughout the Far East and is deeply embedded in the thinking of many of the people in that region today. Sadly, even many of those who have become committed Christians would put obedience to the family heads above their loyalty to Jesus' teaching on the subject.

Lao-Tzu, the founder of Taoism, also lived in the sixth century BC. He was more of a mystic than Confucius. His concern was more to find personal peace by union with nature than to affect the surrounding society.

Both of these men were philosophers looking for the meaning of life, but both philosophies have become religions without a god. All of these 'isms' like the 'isms' of today (as was noted in an earlier chapter) have a deep effect on the way people think and act. As trade routes developed from East to West and West to East, these philosophies and some aspects of Hinduism (India's main religion) became intermingled in the minds of travellers and soldiers in the centuries ahead.

Although these religions have many positive aspects, they afforded no more dignity or respect to women than the old ways of thinking in these lands. The family patterns which have continued in these vast areas of the world have given women little importance or status.

Eastern Mediterranean in the fifth and fourth centuries BC

During the fifth century BC when God's prophetic voice to his people had ceased, another powerful civilization, which was at this time also under Persian control, was emerging. Across the Mediterranean Sea and to the west were the city-states which eventually became the nation of Greece. This region excelled in architecture and sculpture and produced some of the best known philosophers of ancient times. The fifth century produced Herodotus, a much-travelled historian, and Hippocrates, who is still regarded as the father of modern medicine. It was the era of Sophocles, the playwright, and Socrates, the soldier, sculptor and philosopher – who had a disciple called Plato who lived into the fourth century BC. In turn he had a pupil called Aristotle.

It was said that there were no atheists in Greece. They believed in a multiplicity of gods who controlled different aspects of life. Greek religion had a negative effect on personal morality. Many of their gods and goddesses were concerned with fertility, and prostitution, e.g. Artemis, daughter of the chief god Zeus, often depicted as a huntress, was goddess of birth and fertility. Her temple at Ephesus became one of the Seven Wonders of the World. The temples abounded with priestesses whose functions were often more to do with prostitution than with religious ceremony. As in the Far East, it was the philosophers who were concerned about morality and ethics, and who had a desire to know the meaning of life (Romans 1:20 again!).

One of Aristotle's pupils was a young Macedonian (Northern Greece) prince called Alexander. He was only twenty when he succeeded his father King Philip of Macedonia in 336BC. He was a young man with a brilliant mind, an outstanding military leader, who enjoyed life to the full! He raised a huge army and swept through all the regions occupied by the Persians, including the areas once known as Israel and Judah. He was crowned King of Egypt and then led his armies eastwards along the Persian Gulf as far as India. In India he developed a growing interest in Hinduism and Buddhism. His success led him to believe that he was invincible and eventually to believe he was a god to be worshipped and obeyed. His reign was short-lived; he died at the age of thirty-three. His empire was split among his generals, who had been influenced deeply by their king. One of them, Ptolemy, became King of Egypt and another, Seleucius Nicator, ruled over the remainder of Alexander's empire. In turn they ruled over the remnant of Judah around Jerusalem until the middle of the second century BC.

The Jewish people under Greek rule fourth – first century BC
The other invaders mentioned earlier in this chapter who came to replace the Persians were the Greeks – the Ptolemies and the Seleucids. As the Assyrians had done in the northern kingdom in the seventh century BC, the Seleucids placed settlers throughout the whole area that had once been Israel and Judah. They increasingly imposed their pagan culture and customs on the people, while, at the same time, giving freedom to the priests to go on observing the rituals of the temple worship according to the law of Moses.

By the beginning of the second century BC, however, the increasing Hellenization (imposition of Greek culture) was causing ordinary people to compromise their traditional beliefs. In the apocryphal book of 1 Maccabees 1 it is recorded thus:

> It was then that there emerged from Israel a set of renegades who led many people astray. 'Come,' they said, 'let us reach an understanding with the pagans surrounding us, for since we separated ourselves from them many misfortunes have overtaken us.' This proposal proved acceptable and a number of the people eagerly approached the king who authorized them to practice the pagan observances. So they built a gymnasium in Jerusalem, such as the pagans have, disguised their circumcision, and abandoned the holy covenant, submitting to the heathen rule as willing slaves of impiety.

It should be added that the gymnasium was more than a fitness centre – nudity was an essential ingredient of participation.

Until 173BC the high priesthood had been handed down as God had intended that it should be. Onias III protested against the increasing effect that Hellenization was having on God's people. He was deposed from the position in favour of his brother Joshua, who had taken the Greek form of his name, Jason, and who had secured the position by bribery. He, in turn, was deposed for a brief time by a man called Menelaus (Menahem in Hebrew), a brother of the temple administrator, who had no claim to the office. He too obtained the position by paying money. Spiritually things went from bad to worse, with many Jews becoming increasingly compromising. This led to an eventual embargo on the practice of orthodox Judaism, culminating in an attack on Jerusalem by the army of Antiochus IV. He entered the temple on a Sabbath in 165 BC while worship was in progress. The temple was desecrated, with all manner of immoral Greek religious rites being enacted. A pig was sacrificed on the altar and an attempt was made to force the worshippers to eat pig meat. A much-revered scribe called Eleazar chose martyrdom rather than do so; many more of the faithful followed his example. Copies of the scriptures were burnt and many atrocities took place. Sabbath worship and circumcision were punishable by death. A huge statue of Zeus was put in the temple. The full account of all that happened is recorded in 2 Maccabees 5 and 6.

But God...

But God still had faithful followers. Some of these were the supporters of the murdered Onias III. They became known as the Hasidim – 'the loyal ones'. Many of them were martyred when they refused to bow down to worship the statue of Zeus set up in the temple.

The other main group were followers of an elderly priest called Mattathias, who had refused to offer incense to Zeus. With his four brothers, Mattathias' son Judas Maccabeaus raised an army of loyal Jews, who within three years had retaken Jerusalem and cleansed and rededicated the temple. The consecration of the altar took place on the third anniversary of its desecration. The anniversary of this event is still celebrated every year by Jews everywhere at Hanukkah, or the Festival of Lights.

The Hasidim had supported the Maccabees and had hoped to see the high priesthood restored, but this did not happen and a puppet high priest, Alcimus, was appointed by Antiochus, the Seleucid ruler. Things began to go against Judas Maccabaeus in his struggle to rout the Seleucids. He was killed in a battle in 161 BC and the Seleucids gained the upper hand again. His brothers Simon and Jonathan went into hiding for a time when the authorities tried to get rid of the Maccabaean sympathizers. Eventually, in 160 BC Jonathan, a much weaker person than his brother, managed to steer a middle course between rival Seleucid kings. One of them appointed Jonathan high priest (152 BC) in Jerusalem, which made him leader of Judea. He was killed by another Seleucid in 143 BC.

The Hasmonean Dynasty

From 167BC–40 BC the descendants of Mattathias were the leaders of the Jewish people. When Jonathan Maccabaeus was murdered in 143 BC, his brother Simon negotiated a peace in which nearly all the demands of the revolt begun by his brother Judas in 167 BC were met. This era of Jewish history was known as the Hasmonean Dynasty. Simon became high priest and ruler of Judea. This was the most peaceful period for the Jewish people in the whole of the intertestamental period. It ended in 135 BC when Simon and two of his sons were murdered by his son-in-law Ptolemy.

Under Simon's son, John Hyrcanus, Judea was led towards secular rule. His armies extended the area under Hasmonean control. He secularized the role of the high priesthood. His son Aristobulus was a very unpopular and ruthless leader, who styled himself as a king. His brother Alexander succeeded him, and when he died, his wife (Alexandra Salome) took the Hasmonean 'throne' (as Athaliah had done) for nine years while her son Hyrcanus II acted as high priest. In these later years of the Hasmonean dynasty its leaders had lost sight of the spiritual origins of their family's revolt. The high priesthood became more an office of political power than of spiritual leadership.

And then the Romans came
In 63 BC 12,000 Jews were killed when the Romans came. Pompey marched right into the temple and entered the Holy of Holies – an action which caused outrage among the Jews and evoked the memories of a hundred years before. The Romans did promise that the Jews could continue to practice their faith unhindered. Hyrcanus II (son of Salome) was appointed High Priest. The Romans also appointed puppet kings, one of whom was Herod, whose second wife Mariamne was the granddaughter of Hyrcanus II.

Herod decided to rebuild the temple on a much grander scale than ever before. This was a political rather than a spiritual rebuilding – an attempt to curry favour with the Jews. This temple had several additions – market stalls and room for money changers, a place for theological debate – and a Court for Women! It was completed in 9 BC, just before the birth of Jesus. But Herod also built a temple to Augustus, the Roman emperor at the time, to curry favour with the Romans, who were obliged to treat their emperors as Gods.

Assyria, Babylon, Persia, Greece, Rome ...
All of these nations had overrun God's promised land in the 500 years before Jesus was born. Israel had long since gone. All that was left of Judah was the province of Judea. Many of God's chosen people had been scattered around the Mediterranean area as they were displaced from their homeland. Because of these dispersions, there were those in these lands who had come to believe in Jahweh, the God of the Jewish people. The reverse was also true. The pagan attitudes and beliefs of the conquerors had become intermingled with the true faith of Abraham's descendants throughout Judea.

The laws of conduct of some of these neighbouring nations were similar in some respects to the Law of Moses, but none of them gave value and dignity to women as the Law of Moses did. The general attitude to women, not only in the Middle East but throughout the world, was sexist and even misogynist in some cases – which is still true in some parts of the world. The attitude that most men had towards women was summed up by a Roman who said that 'wives are for child-bearing, mistresses are for cohabitation and casual relationships are for sheer pleasure'. The two happiest days of a man's life were said to be the day he married and the day he buried his wife! For the most part women were regarded as creatures who bore children and who made themselves outwardly beautiful for the benefit of men.

Did some of these attitudes rub off on young Jewish men who compromised their beliefs as the Hellenization of Judea progressed? Domination by men, as opposed to Godly leadership, will always produce a reaction of defiance in women, instead of submission. The difference in attitude between a Jezebel (a daughter of a sexist, polytheistic nation) and an Esther (a daughter of a nation whose God honours womanhood) has already been noted. The reaction of defiance may go on smouldering underneath for a long time before it erupts in anger and frustration or manifests itself as a scheming manipulation. Was something of this kind beginning to happen amongst Jewish women living in an atmosphere of spiritual compromise? Was this the reason for a hardening of attitude towards women among the religious leaders of the time? Or had even those in spiritual leadership been affected by the sexist attitudes of invading armies?

The Spiritual Leaders of the Jewish People

At the end of the Old Testament the temple in Jerusalem was the hub of the spiritual life of the Jewish people. The high priest (always a descendant of Aaron) and the other priests (also from the tribe of Levi) were responsible for the spiritual care of the people.

At the beginning of the New Testament several other names appear. Who were the Sanhedrin, the Pharisees, the Sadducees, the scribes, the rabbis; and when did the synagogues appear?

The Sanhedrin

The Sanhedrin is thought to have its origins in the seventy elders appointed to assist Moses – a concept that was reintroduced by Ezra after the Babylonian exile. It was the highest court of the Jews, and dealt not only with religious affairs but with civil law and social aspects of life as well. Originally it was made up of Sadducees, but after the time of Queen Alexandra, Pharisees and scribes were included as well. The Great Sanhedrin at Jerusalem in New Testament times was made up of the high priest, members of privileged families, the tribal heads of the people and the scribes. Some of the above mentioned were Sadducees and some were Pharisees.

Sadducees

The Sadducees came mainly from a line of priestly aristocratic families. They adhered rigidly to the five books of Moses (the Pentateuch). They did not believe in life after death.

Pharisees

The Pharisees on the other hand were drawn from the people rather than the priesthood. They came into being during the Maccabean dynasty. They were originally part of the Hasidim, who refused to be part of the perversions that the Greeks imposed on temple worship. They broke away from the Hasidim at the time when Simon Maccabaeus brokered peace for his people. They regarded themselves as expert interpreters of the law. They made the law of the Pentateuch (to which the Sadducees adhered rigidly) much more complicated, e.g. 'Remember the Sabbath day' as interpreted by the Pharisees had thirty-nine unbreakable Sabbath observance rules'. It is interesting that Queen Alexandra favoured the Pharisees because they certainly were not pro-women!

Scribes

The profession of scribe had a long history in Israel and Judah. They were employed in public administration by the royal household, by the military and in the temple courts. Ezra was both a priest and a scribe. From that time on the scribes assumed an important role in the study of the law. They became defenders of the law during the Greek occupation when there was so much pressure to conform to Greek culture. During the inter-testamental period they wrote down much of what we know as the Old Testament. They elaborated on the law given to Moses in order to apply the law to contemporary situations. Most of the scribes belonged to the party of the Pharisees. They were the originators of the synagogue service.

Synagogues and Rabbis

The word synagogue only appears once in the Old Testament and that only in the Authorized Version (Psalm 74:8). This is not surprising since it is a Greek word, which means a meeting place. During the time of the Babylonian exile, when the temple had been destroyed and people were far from Jerusalem, these 'meeting places' became centres for education, civil government and also a place of worship on the Sabbath. There was no altar, so no sacrifices were offered. It seems that at some point during the development of the synagogue as a place of worship, it became the rule that the women were separated from the men - a custom still practised by Jews today.

We tend to associate the word 'synagogue' with the word 'rabbi' because today the rabbi is the authorized teacher of the law ordained to do this work. In liberal and reformed branches of Judaism today there are women rabbis as well as men. But biblically, the word 'rabbi' was a term of respect used towards someone in high position. It came to be synonymous with a teacher of the law.

Why are all these people important to our subject?

Somewhere amongst all of these people there grew a degrading and a hostility towards women which Jesus constantly opposed in his ministry. This antagonism increased rather than decreased in the early Christian era. The popular belief among the rabbis was that the fall in Genesis 3 was totally the fault of the woman; it was she and not the man who had brought corruption on mankind. It was in AD150 that a man called Rabbi Judah said, 'A man must pronounce three blessings every day, "Blessed be the Lord who did not make me a heathen, blessed be He who did not make me a woman, blessed be He who did not make me an uneducated person"'.

It seems highly likely that the general moral decline that existed among the people of God in the late intertestamental years played some part in the antipathy towards women, and particularly towards single women. It may well be that part of the blame could be attributed to the attitude and behaviour of some women who were attracted to Greek culture. The fact remains that immoral behaviour was always seen as the sin of a woman and not of a man. One famous Rabbinic School (Hillel) declared that a man could divorce his wife for burning his food or if he met a prettier woman. Compare this attitue with the words of Malachi 2:14-16:

> You ask 'why'? It is because the Lord is acting as the witness between you and the wife of your youth, because you have broken faith with her, though she is your partner, the wife of your marriage covenant. Has not the Lord made them one? In flesh and spirit they are his. And why one? Because he was seeking godly offspring. So guard yourself in your spirit, and do not break faith with the wife of your youth. 'I hate divorce', says the Lord God of Israel.

When God's original intention, or even the situation at the end of the Old Testament is compared with the attitude to womanhood and marriage at the end of the inter-testamental period, there are evidences of serious decline.

In conclusion

Because of the large silent gap between the two parts of our Bibles, it is easy to imagine that the land into which Jesus was born was full of people who had been faithful to their religious heritage. But it was like our own nation today, a multi-racial, multi-faith and morally compromised nation, where the religious leaders were at loggerheads with one another because some held rigid views while others were totally compromised. Both had lost sight of the living God. It would be wrong to give the impression that God had no concern for those who were not part of his chosen people, but throughout their history God was concerned to preserve his people's knowledge of Him as the one true God, the Creator of all. In allowing his people to be dispersed, he was also scattering seeds of faith. Colonies of believing Jews had sprung up around the Eastern Mediterranean. The presence of so many foreigners in the territories he had once given to his people meant that there were people of many nations there when he broke in once more in Jerusalem at Pentecost, and all over the Mediterranean as the Church spread.

In spite of all that had happened, there was still a remnant of believing people who eagerly and longingly awaited the intervention that God had promised – the coming of the Messiah. There were ordinary people like Simeon, Anna, and a young girl called Mary. There was an elderly priest called Zechariah and his barren, elderly wife Elizabeth.

6

Immanuel – God With Us

The Silence is Broken

'In the time of Herod King of Judea there was a priest named
Zechariah, who belonged to the priestly division of Abijah; his
wife Elizabeth was also a descendant of Aaron. Both of them
were upright in the sight of God, observing all the Lord's
commandments and regulations blamelessly. But they had no
children because Elizabeth was barren; and they were both well
on in years'(Luke 1:5-7). Zechariah's response to the angel
Gabriel was almost identical to that of Abraham when he was
told of the impending birth of a son. The story of the new
covenant begins, as the old covenant did, with the birth of a
child to the elderly barren wife of an elderly man.

Zechariah was performing his priestly duty of burning incense
– the symbol of prayer – at the altar in the temple. He did this
every day at the hour of prayer while people in the outer courts
gathered to pray. I wonder if Simeon and Anna were among the
people – Simeon in the inner court and Anna in the women's
court. I wonder how many people realized when they saw
Zechariah emerge unable to speak that God's silence had been
broken and that God's promised deliverance was drawing near.

Elizabeth

It must have been quite a shock for Elizabeth when Zechariah
returned home after his period of temple duty unable to tell her
what had happened. Presumably he communicated by writing

(which meant that Elizabeth must have been able to read). Was she as incredulous as Sarah had been, or did she know, because she was well acquainted with the scriptures, that with God nothing is impossible? Her only recorded comment is, 'The Lord has done this for me, in these days he has shown his favour and taken away my disgrace among the people' (Luke 1:25). This is an indication of how little value was placed by society on a childless woman. In the succeeding months Elizabeth knew that something very special was happening within her body. When her young relative Mary came to visit, she was given prophetic insight by the Holy Spirit as the child within her leapt for joy and she spoke out the first word of knowledge given to anyone in the New Testament record (Luke 1: 42 and 43).

When Zechariah's speech returned as he named his son John, he prophesied over the infant using words confirming the prophecy given by Malachi so many centuries before about the one who would prepare the way for the Lord (Malachi 3:1 and Luke 1: 68-79).

What a privilege to be chosen by God to be the mother of such a child! I wonder if she knew in her heart just what these words of prophecy would mean for her son in the years that lay ahead.

Mary

We have read and heard the story of the birth of Jesus from Luke's gospel so often that we don't even stop to think about this teenage Jewish girl who was suddenly confronted by the angel Gabriel. Angelic visitations were not every-day occurrences. In fact Gabriel's only other appearance recorded in scripture before his meeting with Zechariah was to the prophet Daniel, hundreds of years before.

The record says that, 'Zechariah was gripped with fear'. If this was true for a priest in the temple, then perhaps the scriptures are somewhat euphemistic in saying that Mary 'was greatly troubled'. Perhaps phrases like shaking in her sandals, or terrified out of her wits, might be appropriate! After 400 years of silence this stranger was saying that she, a Jewish teenage girl was highly favoured by Jahweh, that she was going to become pregnant and give birth to a son – a son who would be called the Son of the Most High – wow! Did her thoughts immediately turn to Joseph, her betrothed husband, and what he and his family would say and do? The scriptures had very stern things to say about a young woman who became pregnant before marriage – that she could be stoned to death (Deut. 22:20). Or did her thoughts turn to another scripture which said that a virgin would conceive and bring forth a son (Isaiah 7:14)? But with the angel's 'Fear not', Mary's fear turned to questioning – a very understandable reaction. This was followed by a growing realization that God was speaking to her through this stranger, and her questioning turned to an unconditional submission to the purposes of God. Although the situation is unique, this is a very clear picture of what is meant by submission. This was not, as already noticed in an earlier chapter, teeth-grinding obedience, but a conscious decision to co-operate unconditionally whatever the outcome might be. Mary did not know that an angel would visit Joseph too. When she said, 'May it be to me as you have said,' she had no idea what the consequences would be for her, for Joseph, for women or for the entire human race from then on!

Mary's visit to Elizabeth must have been a confirmation for both of them that these angelic visitations had been real – the one an elderly, until now barren, married woman who had for years borne the deep personal pain and the scorn of others because she was childless, and the other a teenage virgin, betrothed but not yet married. Surely only God could bring about such circumstances! Did they talk together about the seemingly impossible births of Isaac, Samson and Samuel? Mary's song of worship would suggest that they were mindful of these women way back in the history of their people, since it is so much like Hannah's song of worship(1 Sam 2: 1-10). Mary's song of praise is all the more amazing when it is considered against the background of all that had been happening to the people of God in those last centuries BC. No matter what the circumstances, God is faithful and keeps his promises. Mary could face the coming months with that assurance deeply rooted in her heart.

Joseph

Joseph could have divorced Mary (betrothal was as binding as marriage). He could have had her humiliated publicly by doubting her virginity. He could even have had her stoned to death. It says much for the character of this young man that he had already decided that he would not cause Mary any public disgrace, but that he would divorce her quietly. Before he was able to take any action, an angel appeared to him in a dream. Without any questioning he took Mary home as his wife when she was already several months pregnant – which would certainly have set a few tongues wagging about his moral purity.

Joseph accepted his responsibilities immediately as a young father. No-one will ever know how he felt when the child was born in such humble circumstances but surrounded by such dramatic events. In obedience to God's laws the child was circumcised on the eighth day and later was presented in the temple 'to be consecrated to the Lord'.

It was then that Simeon and Anna made their appearance. Simeon is described as a devout man on whom the Holy Spirit rested. God had told him that he would not die before he had seen the Messiah. When Mary and Joseph came to the temple to present the infant Jesus, Simeon took him in his arms, recognizing who he was, and praised God. He then blessed Mary and Joseph and spoke a special word to Mary. Anna, an elderly widow, whose life was devoted to prayer and the worship of her God, also prophesied over the baby. She too recognized who he was.

According to Matthew's gospel an angel appeared to Joseph (not to Mary) on two further occasions. The first was to tell him to take his wife and child to Egypt to escape Herod's slaughter, and later to direct him back to Galilee to live – an area where they were out of the new king's jurisdiction. After a boy's fifth birthday, a Jewish father took responsibility for his instruction, guidance, and teaching a trade. At twelve a Jewish boy officially became a man. In Luke's gospel the story of Jesus in the temple demonstrates his desire to be obedient to his earthly parents and yet, for the first time, it is clear that he knew that obedience to his heavenly Father came first as 'he grew in stature with God and man'.

'Mary stored away all these things in her heart'

Mary was the only mother who had ever given birth to a normal (by God's standards) child. It is impossible for someone who has given birth to four normal (by human standards) children to imagine what that must have been like! We have all known children whose mothers have thought that they were as near to perfection as is possible while those observing these paragons of virtue have seen over-indulged, priggish, undisciplined little monsters! But Mary's first-born child was normal with the normality of God's first creation – the normality that God said was good. This normality allowed Jesus to grow from babyhood to boyhood and boyhood to manhood without being regarded as a freak by his siblings and friends.

The Protestant tradition has tended to give Mary less significance than she deserves, while the Catholic tradition has endued her with significance which the scriptures do not authenticate. It cannot be denied that Mary was a remarkable woman – remarkable because throughout the years of her son's earthly ministry she was there in the background with the others who travelled with Jesus and his disciples. She never claimed any special attention because of who she was.

Only John's gospel records the story of the wedding at Cana in Galilee. I wonder what Mary's expectations were when she told her oldest son that the wine had run out. I think we read much more into her words than she meant. Jesus was right at the beginning of his public ministry. He was a guest at this wedding with his mother because they had been invited. It would seem a natural thing for a mother to turn to her son to help their friends in an embarrassing situation. His reply must have been puzzling to her – perhaps her mind went back to the time at the temple in Jerusalem. It would seem that this simple story contains the final leaving behind of family relationships, as Jesus, Mary's son, enters fully into the years of public ministry as Jesus the Messiah. The human Jesus had honoured his earthly parents by obedience in the home, but from now on Jesus, the Anointed One, would do only what his Father told him to do. Mary's simple statement triggered a response that must have led to the Father's go-ahead to his Son. His quiet and unobtrusive response brought pleasure to the wedding guests who gave all the credit to their host – but to his disciples it brought belief and faith.

It was as Mary watched the horrors of the crucifixion that Jesus gave the care of his mother to John, the beloved disciple. As a mother I can't imagine how she coped as she watched him suffer such agonies as he neared death. I wonder if John and Mary talked about the time at Cana in the succeeding years before John, under the inspiration of the Holy Spirit, wrote his account of Jesus' earthly life. Could this be why the story only appears in John's gospel?

There is only one more mention of Mary. She was a woman amongst other women who met in Jerusalem with the eleven disciples to pray as they waited for the empowering of the Holy Spirit – the comforter whom Jesus had promised he would send.

Jesus – the friend of publicans, sinners – and women

Jesus' earthly ministry lasted for only three short years, but he had lived for thirty years before then. Unlike John the Baptist, his preparation for ministry was a life lived out amongst family and neighbours. Joseph was a carpenter and had passed his skills on to Jesus, who worked at that trade. He lived in Nazareth and attended the local synagogue Sabbath by Sabbath. He knew all about people. He saw the way in which the teachers of the Law treated ordinary men and women. He knew the publicans, who were the men who gathered the taxes for the Roman army of occupation. He knew that they were hated – not just because they were collaborators with the enemy, but also because they charged more than they should have in order to make personal profit. Jesus saw blind beggars and despised lepers. He saw women who had become prostitutes, perhaps because their husbands had divorced them for some trivial reason and it was the way to avoid becoming destitute. He knew that these people were the outcasts of society (sinners). He knew that widows and orphans were not being cared for. He knew that there were men who valued their wives less than they valued the tools of their trade. He knew that there were men who regarded women as only being a little higher than their animals. Jesus didn't spend the first thirty years of his life with a closed mind and blinkered eyes. He lived and worked in the real world. The Bible tells us that Jesus 'was tempted in every way just as we are, yet was without sin' (Hebrews 4:15).

During all these years when Jesus had matured into manhood, there were no sermons, no ministry, no miracles, until that amazing day when he met John the Baptist by the river Jordan and was baptized in water and then anointed for ministry by the Holy Spirit. This was followed by forty days of fasting and testing by Satan to the point of exhaustion. Only then, as he emerged from the wilderness full of the Holy Spirit, did he open his mouth in protest at all the injustice and social and religious oppression that he had observed throughout these years. He stood up and spoke in the synagogue he had attended since childhood, quoting from a 700 year old prophecy (Isaiah 61). He identified himself as the fulfilment of these scriptures. Jesus did not come to establish a great new order but to redeem and restore the perfection of creation, so that fallen manhood and womanhood would be able, once more, to be in a right relationship with God and with one another. Jesus lived by God's standards as contained in the Law of Moses – not by the hundreds of rules and regulations added by those who regarded themselves as experts in interpreting the law. He lived in the freedom that came with obedience to the teaching of the Law and the Prophets, not the bondage of hundreds of rules that obstructed people's relationship with God.

Jesus did not conform to the pressures and restrictions of the culture in which he lived – a fact that caused him to be constantly in trouble with the religious and civil leaders as he spoke out against injustice and oppression, without ever encouraging people to react with civil disobedience as some would have wanted him to do. Jesus treated people as God had always intended that they should be treated – justly and fairly, but never making light of sin. Many of the women of Jesus' day were among the oppressed and the outcasts of society.

1. Jesus affirmed the creational equality of man and woman in value and worth

a. By re-establishing the fact that even although woman was created in a different way from man, both were created in the image of God.
The Pharisees tried to trap Jesus on the subject of divorce (Matthew 19:4-6). In answering them he quoted two texts from Genesis (1:27 and 2:24) affirming God's purpose in creating male and female, and his intention that marriage was a lifelong commitment between one man and one woman.

As part of the Sermon on the Mount – spoken of as the Manifesto of the Kingdom – Jesus condemned the lustful attitude of some men towards women that was (and is) prevalent in a sexist society. He did an unheard of thing in focusing on men and not on women where sexual immorality was concerned. (Matthew 5:28). He pointed out the seriousness of even looking at a woman in a lustful manner (Matthew 5:29). On the other hand Jesus never made light of a woman's moral failure.

In tackling these attitudes in men, Jesus was addressing the wrong understanding of Genesis 3 – which suggested that evil came into the world because of the woman alone. This was the root cause of the wrong attitude to women which had developed over the previous centuries and was, more than likely, the reason why men and women became separated in worship in synagogue and temple. The teachers of the law did not like the way in which Jesus gave women dignity and respect. They tried hard to insinuate that Jesus' association with women must have some unhealthy motive – but in the story of the woman taken in adultery Jesus turned the tables on the Pharisees by suggesting that they look at their own attitudes and actions. Only then did he deal with the woman's wrongdoing (John 8: 1-11)

b. By teaching women spiritual truths alongside men

Men and women gathered together around Jesus in the countryside where so much of his teaching about the King of God was given. He taught through parables, some of which were based on everyday occurrences in the running of a home and the feeding of a family. Jesus listened to women and responded to their questions. He acknowledged their spirituality and their ability to understand the truths about which he spoke. It was much-maligned Martha who recognized who Jesus was – 'Yes, Lord, I believe you are the Christ (Messiah) who was to come into the world' (John 11:27). He was not afraid to be seen speaking to a woman – something which was completely foreign to his culture. No respectable man would be seen holding a conversation with a woman – especially when that woman was a Samaritan. Even the disciples struggled with that! But Jesus spoke words of knowledge that confronted the moral laxity in this woman's life and opened her eyes to who he was. She rushed away to tell others – many of whom came to believe in Jesus. Jesus recognized a woman's capacity to gossip good news to others. Was this the reason that Jesus' first appearance and words after the resurrection were to the women and not to the disciples? He knew that they would be quick to acknowledge the reality and would be anxious to share what they had seen and heard.

c. By bringing healing and deliverance to those who were sick and in need of deliverance

Jesus set a woman free from an evil spirit that had crippled her for eighteen years. He did this in the synagogue where women were more or less ignored. Moreover he did it on the Sabbath! When challenged by the synagogue authorities, he accused them of having more consideration for their animals than they had for this poor woman who was a daughter of Abraham (i.e. as much an heir of God's promises as were the sons of Abraham) (Luke 13:10-17).

Jesus had the same attitude to the woman who touched the edge of his cloak. He could have ignored what happened; this woman was ritually unclean because of her haemorrhaging. He should not have looked at her or spoken to her, but he had compassion for her suffering and commended her faith and healed her (Luke 8: 43-48). This healing took place as he was on the way to the house of Jairus, a synagogue official. This man was concerned about his only daughter, a fact which must have commended him to Jesus, because daughters were not usually given much consideration. This was not only a healing, but also a bringing back to life (Luke 8:49-56).

The scriptures do not recount the circumstances but simply state that Jesus carried out a radical deliverance on Mary Magdalene, to whom he appeared first on that resurrection morning. Jesus' earthly ministry was first and foremost to the Jews, but he recognized the faith and discernment of a Canaanite woman who discerned who he was. Because of a mother's faith a young woman was set free from demon-possession Matthew 15:21-28).

d. By his compassion and care of widows and those who were bereaved
Tradition has it that Joseph had died long before Jesus' ministry began. Mary would have been a widow. When Jesus encountered the funeral procession of a widow's only son, we read that 'his heart went out to her'. He knew that there was nothing left to her but a life of poverty – and so he raised her son back to life again (Luke 7:11-17). Jesus spoke out about the unfair treatment of widows by the synagogue authorities; he accused them of robbing widows of their homes. (Luke 20:47) Immediately he goes on to commend the poor widow for her sacrificial gift to the temple treasury.

Perhaps the most notable act of compassion towards the bereaved was the raising of Lazarus from the dead. This story is told only in John's gospel (11: 1-44). Jesus knew the loving hospitality of the home of these three single people. We are told of Jesus' affection for Mary, Martha and Lazarus. Jesus also knew that these two women were dependent on their brother. It seemed strange that he didn't respond the moment that he heard of Lazarus' illness, but Jesus knew that his Father had a deeper purpose than the healing of a friend. Jesus knew that Lazarus was already dead. He said to his disciples, 'Lazarus is dead and for your sake I am glad that I was not there so that you may believe'. Even although Jesus knew that he was being obedient to his Father, he could not disguise his compassion and grief when he saw the sorrow of the two sisters. Jesus wept with the others as he approached Lazarus' grave. Then, demonstrating his total dependence on his Father, he brought Lazarus forth from the tomb to the great joy of Mary and Martha. Many were brought to belief by this miracle of resurrection.

e. By demonstrating that men and women can relate together in fellowship and ministry

In addition to Jesus' friendship with Mary and Martha and their brother, there were other women with whom he had a relationship of fellowship as he journeyed around the country. There were Mary Magdalene, Joanna – the wife of an official at the court of Herod – and Susanna, and others who are not named. These women were helping to support Jesus and the disciples out of their own means (Luke 8: 2 and 3). These women remained loyal to Jesus even through the time of the crucifixion when most of the disciples had fled. They were there at the tomb where he had been laid. It was the women who found the empty tomb.

In a culture where women were only given any position when they became mothers, and where many women were simply used by men for sexual gratification, Jesus recognized them as people with dignity, spirituality, intelligence and ability. Jesus treated all men and women with respect because this was the creational intention of God the Father, Son and Holy Spirit.

2. *Jesus affirmed man and woman's creational difference in purpose and function by choosing men and not women to be his disciples.*

From the beginning of his ministry, Jesus made it clear that he had not come to destroy Jahweh's ancient rules for living given to his chosen people. Rather, he had come to make the teachings of the law understandable, and to demonstrate by the way that he lived his life – in attitude and action towards men, women and children – that the purpose of the law was to restore the shalom of creation. Instead of living in fellowship with God and with one another, most people lived their lives either imprisoned by man-made rules or in rebellion against God. The culture which had developed around the Jewish people in the preceding centuries was far from what God's desired. Culture and scripture were in conflict, so culture had to give way then as now. Jesus knew exactly what God's purposes for man and woman were because 'He was with God in the beginning. Through him all things were made: without him nothing was made that has been made' (John 1: 2 and 3). Jesus challenged every attitude and action that fell short of God's creational intention. Jesus reminded his disciples that God's standard is perfection (Matthew 5:48). In perfection God gave the responsibility to lead to the man. So when, as the only perfect human being that ever lived, he chose twelve men to be discipled by him for the leadership of what would eventually become the new Body of Christ on earth, He was not giving in to cultural pressure, but was conforming to the pattern of the perfection of creation – a pattern which had been continued down through the centuries.

In choosing these twelve men, however, Jesus did make a big break from the old covenant between God and his people. None of these men were priests or in the priestly line. They were very ordinary young men. In fact, in the book of Acts (4:13) they were described as uneducated, common men. Was it for this reason that Jesus chose them? They didn't have to unlearn all the man-made rules over which the teachers of the law spent years in argument. Jesus himself was their teacher. He spent many hours with these men explaining all that had been happening when they were with the crowds. Often he explained the spiritual significance of the parables and his dealings with people when they were alone together. He never hid from them what it would mean for them to stick with him. On several occasions he chided them for their spiritual blindness and deafness. The teachings gathered together in the Sermon on the Mount (Matthew 5 -7) were teachings given to the disciples' although not always in private. Jesus never gave them reason to believe that believing in him was an easy option. No young men have ever had a better theological education with theory and practice combined! Out of the twelve Jesus singled out, three – Peter, James and John – were especially close to him and they played a prominent part in the early church – Peter as a preacher, James as the first of the twelve to be martyred, and John as the writer of five books of the New Testament Scriptures (Gospel, three letters and the book of Revelation).

There were many others who also became believers and were committed to discipleship, but they were not in the band of twelve whom Jesus himself called disciples(Luke 6: 12-16). Luke's account at the beginning of Acts tells how Matthias was chosen (to replace Judas) because he was among the group who had followed Jesus from the beginning.

Jesus' last evening before he was arrested was spent eating the Passover supper with the twelve apostles. The Passover was normally a time of family celebration, but Jesus chose to celebrate this eventful Passover evening with only the twelve. He had very important things to say to them and very important instructions to give them about the immediate and distant future. The Passover meal was, and still is, very important to every Jewish family. This meal, which was right at the centre of Jewish faith and practice, was forever changed for these men when Jesus took the bread and broke it and gave them the wine to drink.

Messianic Jews believe that, in the process of this last meal that Jesus ate with his chosen twelve, some of the traditional mysteries of the Passover meal became clear – that what Jesus did at the last supper was a confirmation that he was the long awaited Messiah. This meal was the bridge between the Old and New Covenants; with this meal the New Covenant was sealed.

Jesus continued his teaching as they went to the Mount of Olives. He told them about the coming of the Holy Spirit, who would be more to them than he, Jesus, had ever been. They shared these very intimate hours with Jesus, and yet a few hours later most of them had fled in terror.

On the other hand, the women were there as Jesus carried the cross. They were there at the crucifixion. They followed as the body was taken to the tomb. They were there to anoint his body after the Sabbath had ended. They were the ones who carried the news of his resurrection to the unbelieving, fearful disciples. Jesus knew all they had done, and yet in his resurrected body he continued to teach the eleven who remained. He could have given fresh instructions. He could have suggested that Judas should be replaced by Mary Magdalene or even by his mother but he didn't because this had never been and would never be God's purpose for womanhood.

Jesus never saw the leadership of his new body – the church – as a matter for debate on the undifferentiated equality of male and female. He saw it as a redeemed continuation of the creational purposes of God in creating man and woman equal in value and worth but different in purpose and function.

7

How they brought the Good News from Jerusalem to Rome

Jesus' last words to the eleven apostles were words of command – 'Wait' and 'Go'. Wait until you have been empowered by the Holy Spirit and then go into all the world. Jesus had told them to start at home and work outwards. Only the eleven had seen Jesus ascend into heaven from the Mount of Olives. When they returned to Jerusalem to wait and pray, the women, including Jesus' mother Mary and his brothers, were also waiting there with the other believers – about 120 in all. This is the last mention of this group of women who had been so closely involved with Jesus. But they were there at Pentecost. They were filled with the Holy Spirit. They spoke in languages they had never learned and tongues of fire rested on them. They heard Peter refer to Joel's prophesy in which he said:

> I will pour out my Spirit on all people, your sons and your daughters will prophesy, your young men will see visions, your old men will dream dreams. Even on my servants, both men and women I will pour out my Spirit in those days and they will prophesy. (Acts 2:17 and 18 and Joel 2:28 and 29)

There is no doubt that these women would have been fully committed to spreading the Good News about Jesus and to being part of the praying, caring community of believers. But all the preaching and miracles came from the lips and hands of the apostles whom Jesus had chosen. After the day of Pentecost only Peter, James and John are mentioned by name, but the group of the apostles certainly continued to function in the leadership of the early church in Jerusalem.

These were exciting days for the early believers. J.B. Phillips in his preface to his translation of the Book of Acts says, 'Here we are seeing the church in its first youth, valiant and unspoiled – a body of ordinary men and women joined in an unconquerable fellowship never before seen on this earth.'

Down through the ages many believers have tried to emulate these early days of community living described in Acts 4 – and some have succeeded for a time. What is not usually noticed is that within a few years the believers were scattered by the persecution which followed Stephen's martyrdom, as 'Saul of Tarsus was still breathing out murderous threats against the Lord's disciples'. (Acts 9:1) In the second century AD a Carthaginian lawyer named Tertullian who, like Paul, began life opposing Christians, said that these early believers were 'constantly in trouble but deliriously happy'. Again like Paul he became a believer and a theologian. For Stephen and for the apostle James trouble meant martyrdom. The scattering of the believers meant that the Good News spread throughout Judea and to Samaria.

It is interesting to note that those who had been persecuted for so long for their loyalty to their God (Jahweh) had joined the ranks of the persecutors of those who had found a new level of relationship with that same God through the life, death and resurrection of the promised Messiah. The teachers of the law became even more harsh towards women – no doubt a reaction to the value placed on women by Jesus and his disciples.

Sapphira in Jerusalem (Acts 5: 1-11)

Sapphira is the first woman mentioned in this record of the beginnings of the church. Why did Peter react so strongly to the actions of this couple? Was it not the case that Sapphira, in acting with her husband, was being a submissive wife? Peter reacted in the way that he did because God's spirit is the HOLY Spirit. Ananias was not only lying to his fellow believers, but he thought that he could deceive God. His action would have tarnished not only his own witness but that of the whole group of believers. A wife's submission to her husband should never lead her into collusion with her husband's dishonesty. Peter confirmed her positive agreement with her husband's action before pronouncing on her the same punishment – death! Being part of the early church was an awesome responsibility as well as a wonderful privilege. As it was then, so is it now.

Mary – mother of John Mark (Acts 12:12)
Mary is the only other woman to be mentioned by name in the activities of the early church in Jerusalem. It was in her home that the believers had met to pray at the time when James the apostle was martyred and Peter was in prison. There is no mention of his father. Mary obviously was a strong influence in her son's spiritual growth. She had an open home where believers were welcome. Then, as now, the atmosphere of a home can have a profound effect on growing young people.

Dorcas (alias Tabitha) in Judea (Acts 9:36-43)
Dorcas and Tabitha are Greek and Aramaic forms of the same name. It means a gazelle – a graceful, gentle, small deer. This lady seemed to mirror her name. She was much loved in Joppa, a town near the border of Judea with Samaria, where she lived and earned her living as a seamstress. It is not known whether she was a widow or a single lady, but she was known for her care for women who were widows. She used her skills to provide clothing for those who were unable to provide for themselves. Dorcas is described as a disciple. The word used is *mathetra,* which is the feminine form of the word used to describe the twelve and the others who followed Jesus from the beginning. The word is not unique to Jesus' disciples however. It is used of

one who not only follows a teacher, but gives thought to what is being taught and follows through the teaching with some endeavour. Dorcas is the only woman so described in the New Testament. Peter needed no persuasion to go to Dorcas, although she was already dead. Those who went to bring Peter were also called disciples, rather than the more usual word believers used to describe the followers of Jesus. Perhaps Dorcas and the others had been amongst those who travelled with Jesus and Peter knew them well – but that is only speculation. At any rate, Peter obviously realized how much the lady was loved and needed among the believers in Joppa, where she demonstrated the reality of her faith – not in holding any leadership role among the believers, but in practical caring work amongst those with no power or influence. The scene that followed Peter's arrival is very reminiscent of that which Peter had observed some years before when Jesus raised the daughter of Jairus from death. Dorcas is never mentioned again, but she was a remarkable woman – a true servant and the first Christian to experience resurrection from death – what a contrast to Sapphira!

...to the uttermost parts of the earth

All of the area covered in Paul's missionary journeys was the Mediterranean land that had been captured by Alexander of Macedonia about 400 years before. By the time of the beginnings of the church they were under Roman domination. The ethos of these lands was quite different to that in Jerusalem, Judea and Samaria, where Jahweh had revealed himself to his people over many hundreds of years. When God sent Peter to take the Good News to the Gentile Roman soldier Cornelius, who was described as God-fearing, it was a confirmation that it had always been in the purpose of God to reveal himself as the one true God, the creator of every living being, to everyone. Paul quotes Isaiah 49:6 saying, 'For this is what the Lord has commanded us, "I have made you a light for the Gentiles that you may bring salvation to the ends of the earth"' (Acts 13:47). James the brother of Jesus quotes the Septuagint version of the Old

Testament (Greek translation) of Amos 9: 11 and 12 which says, 'The words of the prophets agree completely with this. As the scripture says '...And so all the rest of the human race will come to me, all the Gentiles whom I have called to be my own''(Acts 15:17 GNB).

Paul made it a practice to start testifying to the risen Messiah in the local synagogue wherever possible. God's purposes in scattering his people far and wide in earlier centuries can now be seen more clearly. Paul remained in the synagogue until he was forced to leave. By that time he had gathered a group of believing Jews around him to which God added Gentile believers. He soon discovered that it was not easy for faithful Jews and formerly pagan Gentiles to worship the same Lord together in perfect harmony!

Lydia of Philippi in Macedonia (Acts 16: 13-15)

Sometimes there wasn't a synagogue. This was the case in Philippi – chief city of Macedonia, named after the father of Alexander the Great. Paul knew where the local Jews were likely to meet for prayer, so he went to the riverside where he found a women's prayer meeting taking place under the leadership of a woman called Lydia, who was described as a 'worshipper of God'. She was a Gentile who (like Cornelius) seemed to know that Jahweh was the true God. She participated in Jewish worship as best she knew how. Paul had no hesitation or scruples about sitting down to tell these women the Good News of Jesus the Messiah. The Holy Spirit must have been preparing Lydia's heart, because there was an immediate response, not only from her but also from other members of her household.

Lydia was a prosperous businesswoman. She was a dealer in purple cloth – a luxury material only worn by wealthy people. She was a single woman – either widowed or unmarried, but was a woman of substance and influence. It is challenging to read that her immediate response to belief was practical action – the offering of the hospitality of her home to Paul, Silas, Timothy and Luke. Lydia was the first recorded convert in Paul's visionary call to Macedonia. Like Dorcas, she is never spoken about again, but it is more than likely that she went on telling the Good News about Jesus as she continued in her business life – gossiping the gospel, at which women have always been gifted!

Priscilla (or Prisca) in Corinth (Acts 18)

Priscilla, unlike Dorcas and Lydia, has several mentions in Scripture (Acts 18:2-3; 18:19,26; 1 Corinthians 16:19; 2 Timothy 4:19; Romans 16:3) but always alongside her husband Aquila. He was a Jew by birth, a native of Pontus in Asia Minor. Tentmakers were often employed to make tents for the Roman army. This may have been the reason that he had moved to Rome from Pontus. They were forced to leave Rome when the Emperor Claudius decided to rid Rome of all Jews. Paul, also a tentmaker by trade, met up with them in Corinth where they had settled and set up business again. Scripture doesn't actually say that Priscilla was a Jewess or that she came from Asia Minor. There are those who believe that she was a highborn Roman lady. This is one possible explanation of why, except in the Corinthian mention, her name always comes first, as this would be the accepted custom if this were the case. It is assumed that they were both Christians when Paul first met them. There was obviously an immediate rapport, which led to an ongoing relationship with Paul. Their home was an open one and when they moved with Paul to Ephesus, it became the place where the church met. Priscilla was obviously a very able and spiritually astute woman. Another reason given for her name being mentioned first was that she was more able than Aquila and was the leader of the partnership discipling other believers – even the brilliant Apollos, who hadn't got all his facts right! They illustrate well the complementary relationship in a marriage, which was God's intention. Their concern was that together they would be involved in building up those who were still shaky in aspects of their faith. In Romans 16:3-5 Paul greets them as his 'fellow-workers in Christ Jesus. They risked their lives for me. Not only I but all the churches of the Gentiles are grateful to them'. We only read of their work in Corinth and Ephesus (two difficult places to be based), but this greeting would suggest that they travelled even more widely in the cause of the gospel, eventually returning to Rome from which they had been expelled. It is never suggested in scripture that Aquila and Priscilla saw themselves as anything other than believers committed to helping others understand more clearly. Elders, who were responsible for shepherding and teaching the believers, were appointed in all the churches. Paul gave Timothy charge of the church at Ephesus for some considerable time. Others, like Aquila and Priscilla, worked alongside the elders in discipling and caring for the spiritual and material needs of those who were being drawn into the church.

In less than seventy years from the time that Jesus was born, the church had spread from Jerusalem to Rome. The persecution for which Peter prepared the church in his epistle began in Rome. Both Peter and Paul were executed there around AD65. In AD70 the Roman army destroyed Jerusalem and the temple. Jews and Christians alike were massacred in large numbers.

But the church continued to grow

A growing church – but not a perfect church. Paul, and every church leader since, most certainly could have identified with the song sung by a black slave in the Southern States of USA which says, 'Nobody knows the trouble I'se seen, nobody knows but Jesus'!

Paul must have felt very frustrated at times when he had spent many hours teaching new converts only to discover that, when he had gone on to the next port of call, disagreements and factions began to destroy the fellowship of the believers. Even before Paul's conversion, the Greek-speaking Jewish believers and the native Aramaic speaking Jewish believers quarrelled about the distribution of food, which was collected daily to provide for poor widows (Acts 6:1-7). Later on the question arose as to whether Gentile believers had to go through Jewish rites before they could become members of the church – a disagreement which necessitated Paul and Barnabas going back to Jerusalem to confer with Peter and the other apostles (Acts 15). Many of the issues that arose in the first hundred years of life of the church are still issues today – issues of morality, marriage and divorce, money, leadership and the position of women. There is truly 'nothing new under the sun' (Ecclesiastes 1:9). If Paul were writing to the churches today he would still be giving the same answers to the same questions because the purposes of God are, as we have seen over and over again, unchanging.

Women in the early church – in Jerusalem, Judea and Samaria

When the Holy Spirit came upon all the believers at Pentecost, spiritual gifts were given to both men and women. It would seem that it was the custom of the first believers to follow Jesus' example and attend the Sabbath synagogue service, where the women continued to be treated as unimportant observers rather than active participators. On the first day of the week, however, usually early in the morning or late at night because it was a working day, all the believers gathered together to pray, worship and receive instruction from one of the apostles. Presumably these early teachings from the apostles were the substance of what Jesus had taught the eleven in the days between the resurrection and the ascension. Many of the women believers in Jerusalem and Judea and some as far scattered as Samaria (?Dorcas) had heard Jesus teaching. They were, therefore, well grounded in the things that the apostles were teaching. Moreover, as daughters of Abraham, they had a firm foundational knowledge of Jahweh and his dealings with his people throughout their history. They had been set free from the ungodly, legalistic oppression that had been imposed on women in the preceding centuries by the teachers of the Law. They had no problems with the fact that their function in the body of believers was different from that of the men. Men and women had become brothers and sisters who were able to relate in fellowship together in a way hitherto unknown. Their united desire was to witness to the power of the risen Christ to make lives new. The fact that this group of men and women could work and worship together in moral purity was in itself a witness to a society where many men regarded women as possessions or sexual objects. They had been set free to express their womanhood as God had intended that it should be expressed from the beginning – nothing more, nothing less.

'and to the uttermost parts of the earth'

The situation in the churches planted in Paul's missionary journeys was quite different. Many of the believers in these churches had a totally pagan background. Few of them had any idea of the one true God whom the Jews had worshipped for two thousand years. The Pentateuch (the books of Moses, Genesis to Deuteronomy) and the teaching of the prophets were completely unheard of. The situation was very similar to that of people who are finding new life in Christ in our post-Christian culture today. The temptation is always to meld the ethos and customs of a godless society that is forever changing into the unchanging purposes of God for men and women.

There are two little phrases used in the account of Paul's time in the Greek cities of Thessalonica and Berea that are interesting. As a result of Paul's preaching in Thessalonica the scriptures say that a number of women described as follows in eight different translations became believers. Firstly in Thessalonica, they were leading (RSV), prominent (NIV), leading (GNB), chief (AV), rich (Jerusalem), influential (NEB), important (Living Bible), of social standing (J B Phillips); while in Berea they were – of high standing (GNB), prominent (NIV), high social standing (GNB), honourable (AV), from the upper classes (Jerusalem), of standing (NEB), prominent (Living Bible), influential (J B Phillips) (Acts 17:4 and 12). None of these adjectives was ever applied to Jewish women of this era. This suggests that there was a very different ethos abroad as far as some women were concerned in these regions where Paul's missionary journeys took him. It would seem that feminism had begun to emerge among Greek women.

Paul has frequently been labelled as a woman-hater because of his words of correction written about order in the Corinthian church, his advice about church leadership to Timothy and Titus, and his instructions on order in the home in his letter to the church at Ephesus (which is regarded by many NT scholars as a copy of a circular letter sent round all the churches). To understand these passages we have to look at the background against which they were written.

Corinth and the Corinthians

Geographically, Corinth was a very interesting place. It stood on a narrow isthmus of land which separated northern and southern Greece. All north/south traffic went through Corinth. Moreover East to West and West to East Mediterranean trade went via Corinth rather than face the storm ridden Cape Malea (now Matapan) round Southern Greece. Small ships used to be dragged on rollers across the isthmus. It was a major trade centre and therefore very prosperous. But Corinth had the reputation of being a very immoral, drunken and evil place. On a hill above the city stood the temple of Aphrodite, the goddess of love, from which one thousand priestesses descended to the city every evening to ply their trade as prostitutes. These women had a degrading effect on the whole ethos of this great city. Aphrodite and her priestesses had a powerful hold over Corinth by exploiting men's weaknesses. These were not downtrodden street women. They were women of power!

It was in this atmosphere of corruption and degradation that the Corinthian church was planted. Paul began, as usual, in the synagogue, but was soon expelled from there. The small nucleus of believers, including Priscilla and Aquila, was soon joined by many Gentiles. Paul spent eighteen months in Corinth teaching the foundational principles of the Christian faith, with his friends working with him caring for and encouraging these new Christians. However, the Corinthian believers soon 'allowed the world to squeeze them into its own mould' (J.B.Phillips' translation of Romans 12:2). It wasn't that they lost their faith, but they became high on experience and enthusiasm while they neglected the foundations that Paul had laid. They were more concerned to fit in to society than to stand out from it.

Paul wrote to challenge them to get their lives back into line with what they had been taught. He dealt with gross immorality, the error of getting involved in lawsuits with their fellow believers, the importance of Christian marriage, wrong behaviour at the Lord's supper, wrong use of spiritual gifts and the way in which women should conduct themselves in the church gathered for worship.

It is important to remember that these women had not the spiritual heritage that Jewish women had. However, it was the custom in all of this Mediterranean region that women wore a head covering. The prostitutes in Corinth had abandoned head coverings and some had had their hair cut short as a mark of defiance and rebellion. It would seem that this custom had spread to women who were not prostitutes. Paul is saying to women that they are not to adapt to the custom and attitude of the pagan world from which they had come. Their uncovered heads were giving a wrong message to unbelievers and to their own husbands. Paul uses this to reaffirm God's creational order (1 Corinthians 11:10-13). Whereas Jewish women had found new freedom in Christ, it may have been that some Gentile women were finding it hard to live within the creational order because they had already been 'liberated' from sexist oppression by adopting feminist attitudes. This was causing chaos in the worshipping community. Spiritual gifts were given to both men and women for the building up of the whole church, but they were to be used in an atmosphere of order and reverence. Whereas women were free to participate in prayer and prophecy at the appropriate time, they were not to interrupt the teaching or to participate in the official teaching time. This instruction is totally in accordance with everything that had gone before in God's relationship with his people. Paul says that this is the general practice in all the churches. He also says that he believes it to be the instruction of Jesus himself (1 Corinthians 14:33-39). Paul's overall concern was that women's attitude in worship should be in accordance with God's desires and not with local cultural customs. His concern was not to devalue women, but to preserve their dignity.

In Ephesus with Paul and Timothy

Paul was in Ephesus when he wrote the Corinthian epistles. Although Ephesus was not the evil city that Corinth was, it was a city dominated by the worship of goddesses. The temple of Artemis (or Diana), which was mentioned in Acts 19, was, as already noted, one of the seven wonders of the ancient world. The priestesses of Artemis had more authority than the priests. Also in Ephesus were the cult, of Cybele, with its mother Gods and the cult of Isis, which declared equal rights for men and women. The cult of Dionysus had similar attitudes. Ephesus was a place of philosophical debates and lectures, in which women took part. There were women in politics and in medicine in this part of the Greek speaking world.

Paul spent three years in Ephesus. During this time he lectured and debated every afternoon in the hall of Tyrannus (a local philosopher). He did this in the heat of the day because it was the only time that the hall was available. Doubtless he came across some of the aforementioned women. When Paul left Ephesus the young Timothy was left in charge. Paul wanted to make sure that Timothy understood clearly the position of women in church government in view of the ethos in which he was living (1Timothy 2 and 3).

When Paul wrote his letter to the church in Ephesus (and probably, as we have noted, to all the churches) he emphasized once more God's creational order for husbands and wives in marriage, comparing the relationship of marriage to that of Christ and the church – an awesome comparison which puts incredible responsibility on a husband for the care and encouragement of his wife.

In Crete with Titus

The Cretans had a reputation for being drunken, gluttonous and untrustworthy. Even the many Jews who lived in Crete had become infected with the evils of the Greek island. Moreover, it too was dominated by pagan priestesses. It seems that no man was allowed to be a priest on Crete!

Paul writes to encourage his 'true son in our common faith' Titus, who had been left there by the apostles to care for and appoint men as elders in the church. Paul is well aware of the enormous task that he has set this young man and how important it was that the right people were appointed. These men had to be worthy of their high calling. Belief had to be demonstrated in the way in which a man handled his family. A man whose family was in disorder was not worthy to lead the church family.

Paul also instructs Titus to be aware of the importance of older women in instructing younger women in the areas of homemaking and childcare. The older women are to show an example by life as well as by mouth, so that the younger women know their responsibilities in teaching and training their children. Believing women needed to be seen to be different from others.

Other passages relating to women

In his epistle, Peter addresses the difficulties faced by a woman whose husband is not a believer. This epistle was written to encourage all Christians who were facing persecution. He makes it plain that being a believer means being different from those round about. He challenges married women not to copy unbelieving women by concentrating only on outward beauty and adornment, but to concentrate on developing the inner beauty of a quiet and gentle spirit. This can only be done by spiritual growth, which in turn comes by concentrating on God's desires and purposes.

Widows continue to be a concern. Paul instructs Timothy to be sure that older widows are provided for if they have no family to care for them and if they have lived good and godly lives. Younger widows are to care for themselves or to remarry. It is clear from this passage that no woman should be leading an aimless life caught up in idle chatter and trivialities.

Last but not least......
At the end of his letter to the Christians in Rome there is a whole chapter of greetings to people who have worked alongside Paul in the gospel during his missionary travels. This epistle was written before Paul went to Rome. The first eleven chapters deal with foundational Christian belief – the sinfulness of mankind, and the salvation to be found only in Christ, the need to continue to grow spiritually, our total dependence on the Holy Spirit for this growth. The next four chapters are a 'therefore' – correct belief leads to correct behaviour. We are challenged not to give way to the standards of the world around us but to be completely transformed to God's way of thinking. This epistle was not written to address problems, but to encourage all believers, men and women alike, to understand more clearly God's, eternal purposes for all people everywhere.

In chapter 16 he names a whole host of people who have helped him in many different ways. Priscilla and Aquila are the only people mentioned elsewhere. Many of them were women who were faithful in their service to the Lord and who in some way have cared for him and worked with him.

All of these people, men and women, were part of the unfolding of the purposes that God had always had for his creation from the beginning of time. What he had begun in perfection, human disobedience had destroyed, and now because of the obedience of the Son to the Father restoration had been made possible. These early Christian brothers and sisters had learned how to love and serve one another in moral purity. This was the thing that amazed the watching world. They were people who had been pardoned, but who were not yet perfect. They had caught a vision of how they could go on being changed and so change a fallen world.

God's unchanging ways

This study of the unchanging God began in the perfection of the Garden of Eden where man and woman were created equal and different; head and helper to work together in caring for a beautiful world. Disobedience destroyed not only their relationship with God, but their relationship with one another. God has never given up. He chose one nation to whom he revealed himself and whom he preserved against great odds for 2,000 years, but his ultimate plan was the total restoration of what He began in perfection. He sent his Son to redeem and restore, to re-establish our vertical relationship with him and our horizontal relationships with one another. But in spite of all that God has done, that first foundational relationship has never been restored.

Do we really want it to be – that is, on God's terms not ours?

Part Three –
Relating God's Timeless Ways
to the Twenty-First Century

8

Introducing Mrs Proverbs

Proverbs 31:10-31

How could it be possible that this proverbial woman should have any relevance to the lives of women in the third millennium AD? She wasn't even real. She was a figment of someone's imagination. That someone wasn't a sexist man. These were the words of advice given by a loving mother to her son! Although Mrs Proverbs was not real in the sense that all the other Biblical women were, God has much to teach us through her. In fact she mirrors many of the virtues of these Biblical women who lived from the time of Sarah to the time of Priscilla – almost 2,000 years of changing cultures.

These verses show that God never meant women to be uneducated, uncared for, oppressed and helpless. This is the picture of a much-loved, highly intelligent, creative woman with great organizing ability who lived a happy and fulfilled life. This has always been God's desire for all women everywhere, whether married or single. Although it is the description of a good wife, these gifts and abilities are not specifically related to her wifehood but to her womanhood. Every woman begins life single and most women end life single – so there are lessons for all women to be learned here.

This picture of womanhood bears no resemblance to the lives of young women depicted in Victorian novels who frittered away their time on trivialities, waiting for the appearance of a suitable husband. Nor does it bear any resemblance to the young lady in the Nursery Rhyme which says:

> Curlylocks, curlylocks wilt thou be mine
> Thou shalt not wash dishes nor yet feed the swine
> But sit on a cushion and sew a fine seam
> And feed upon strawberries, sugar and cream.

These twenty-one verses of scripture were, however, written as a poem that goes right through the Hebrew alphabet. This explains why they seem to jump around a bit subject-wise. They speak of a woman's relationships, the organizing of her domestic affairs, her business acumen, her social concern and her spirituality.

All of these are still part of a woman's life today. There may be different emphases according to whether a woman is married or single, has children or doesn't have children, has young children or adult children, has ageing parents to care for, or has become an ageing parent. No matter how hard society may try to dictate otherwise, a woman's life is much more home- and family-orientated than that of a man, no matter how qualified or gifted she may be in other directions. There have always been women who have tried hard to deny their femininity, just as there have always been men who have tried to deny their masculinity. The current fashion to talk about personhood rather than manhood and womanhood contributes nothing but confusion to young people, and its ultimate result is to lead to a unisex society where same sex relationships increasingly abound. Male and female personhood are not the result of the fall, as some Christians would have us believe. Sexist domination and feminist retaliation are the result of our fallen nature. Masculinity and femininity were part of the perfection of creation. In a letter to *The Times* newspaper in 1990 *a propos* the care of the elderly, Dr Margaret Maison of Dorset said, 'Some blame must rest with modern feminism which has deluded women into false fantasies of fulfilment involving consumerism, male clone careerism, the pursuit of wealth and excessive independence, over assertiveness and absurd expectations of happiness. Residence in this cloud-cuckoo-land renders women incapable of meeting the varied needs of family life; it sends abortion rates soaring, produces a proliferation of broken homes and retirement homes and a general increase of bitterness and hardness of heart. Women should wake up, face reality and realize that there are wiser and more generous ways of life than those promoted by current feminist folly.'

Mrs Proverbs certainly did not live in cloud-cuckoo-land. I wonder how many women in modern society live their lives in balance as this woman did. She learned the secret of creating an atmosphere of Shalom around her in spite of living a full and active life.

Drawing lessons from this passage, I want to examine the three main areas where our Christian womanhood is expressed – the home, in society, and in the church.

9

A Woman in her Family as Homemaker

Some years ago I had the opportunity to speak on the subject of homemaking to a group of women in a church in Northern Ireland. In a discussion time afterwards, one young woman told how she had become weary of being patronized by sophisticated young business women when she accompanied her husband to his firm's social functions. On introduction she would be asked, 'and what do you do?' When she replied that she was a full-time homemaker by choice, the questioner would look at her with incredulity in her expression, say, 'Oh really,' and then, as soon as possible, turn to someone else. One evening when asked the inevitable question she said, 'I run a small family business.' There was immediate interest. 'What kind of business?' was the next question. 'My business is called a home – I am a homemaker.'

In 1975 Simone de Beavoir said, 'No woman should be authorized to stay at home and raise her children ...... Women should not have that choice because, if there is such a choice, too many women will make that one.'[10] Our society today is trying hard to make that pronouncement come true. The government (whichever is in power) proclaims the importance of family life and yet, held to ransom by the feminist lobby, makes it harder and harder for a woman to choose to be a homemaker as the main focus of her life. The steady moral decline in Britain in the past thirty years has made it necessary to shift the goalposts in the definition of family. The first move was to replace Judaeo-Christian as a description of family life in our nation with the word 'tradition'. Now family means any combination of adult(s) and children who live under one roof. There is now a great gulf between Biblical concepts of family and the concepts of our secular society. The Biblical family has at its heart a father, a mother and children living together in such a way that others are always welcome and shown loving care. Strangely enough this is an accepted pattern in many places in the world that have not been Christianized – because it is the blueprint embedded in human beings since creation. Such families are seldom fatherless and often include grandparents and other relatives as well. It used to be that young women grew up with a positive or negative attitude to homemaking based on their own experience of home life – which did not depend on material circumstances but rather on the attitude modelled by their mothers. Because of the frantic lives lived by most women today, it is hard for mothers to model and for young women to have something to follow. From every direction the role of a woman as homemaker is made to look foolish, unimportant and obsolete.

A friend attended her daughter's final school Speech Day, where the headmistress made much of the academic achievements of a few of the girls. The guest who came to present the prizes extolled the wonderful career opportunities open to young women today. Not once was marriage or motherhood mentioned, far less the possibility that some might find fulfilment in being full-time homemakers. Schools, books, magazines and TV all join with Simone de Beavoir in belittling the importance of the home. The Bible never suggests that role reversal is an option. Men and women both have important but different responsibilities in the building and functioning of a home, but these responsibilities, in normal circumstances, are not interchangeable. Yet many Christians happily concur with the idea of the house-husband as a commendable alternative lifestyle. This has everything to do with feminist belittling of manhood. It has nothing to do with Biblical masculinity. The other extreme is that the man of the house has no involvement whatsoever in the daily routine of home life. There are some who believe that real men don't wash dishes – but that has nothing to do with Biblical masculinity either. It has everything to do with the sexist belittling of womanhood.

As always, the truth lies at neither extreme. The attitude that says, 'It's your turn to wash up or do the hoovering or change the baby's nappy,' has no scriptural basis whatsoever. It is true that Mr Proverbs did not seem to contribute much personally to the running of his home – although he did make sure that his wife had adequate assistance. Perhaps his lack of involvement has something to do with the attitude that says clearing the kitchen, visiting the supermarket or putting the children to bed is nothing to do with me. The man who takes his role seriously in the home will always lead by example, remembering that the King of Glory stooped to wash dirty feet and, in his resurrection body, cooked fish for his weary disciples' breakfast. The example shown by Jesus wherever he went was that of servanthood. In fulfilling their God-given functions in the home – men and women should remember that they have a wonderful opportunity to model servanthood to a rising generation.

For forty-four years I have shared my life with a man who has never seen it beneath his dignity to roll up his sleeves and do whatever needs doing when he has seen me struggling with children or chores. But on the other hand, he has never done anything out of any 50:50 attitude – nor has he ever neglected his own work to do so. It has often meant he has forfeited his own rest time. I have come to realize (not without a struggle in the early days of our marriage) that my response as his helper is to make it as easy as possible for him to respond in full to the call of God on his life to pastor and teach the people of God. This has, at times, meant a great deal of loneliness and a giving up of some things that I could have done. But God is no-one's debtor and He has more than compensated for any sacrifice He has called me to make.

These verses in the Bible were never meant as fodder for either feminist or sexist views on where responsibilities lie. They are about the impact that a woman can have when she devotes her abilities to serving others without seeing self-fulfilment as her primary aim.

Running the Small Family Business

Good housekeeping is a solid foundation in transforming a house into a home. Mrs Proverbs did not do all of her housekeeping herself, but she organized it and made sure that it was done. Help can come from other members of the 'family business' – including junior members – or from others employed to help. For many years I had the help of one of our church members, who did two or three times the amount that she was paid to do because she saw it as part of her service to God. Madge became and has remained a dear friend to all of us and was also a wonderful, trustworthy confidante to me. She knew about many of the pressures of manse life, but her lips were sealed. Apart from human help, we have a multitude of gadgets and much advertised cleaning products to assist us. It was in this area that the TV adverts of thirty years ago were so demeaning to a woman's intelligence. It is interesting that this same means is used today to proclaim the message of role reversal and make men look like simpletons – all in the cause of political correctness. Gone are the days when a homemaker like my mother (and many millions like her) had only her hands and a few unsophisticated hand-operated tools to use in keeping the home and its occupants clean. The irony is that the results achieved were often far above those achieved by our sophisticated gadgets. The latter don't move furniture around to clean behind and under. Fitted carpets can't be rolled up and hung over a rope to be beaten before being carefully shampooed. Nor can the floor underneath the carpet have an annual scrub! Dust mites never had a chance to multiply (not that they had been heard of). Windows are only cleaned now when we discover that it isn't the outside window cleaner who isn't doing his job properly! My mother's cooker top and oven were always sparkling. My future intentions are good every time I get round to cleaning the oven, but. And that in spite of the fact that I am convinced that a clean oven produces better results and makes a kitchen smell differently!

Housework needs to be done by someone. Some people really enjoy it, and I admire them for it. For me it is done for the finished result rather than the enjoyment of the process. Scripture songwriter Dale Garnet wrote a book called *The Pleasure of Your Company*. In it she describes her early chaotic attempts at housekeeping when she married. Every corner of their home was covered in clutter for which she had never bothered to find an appropriate place (probably the dustbin!). When anyone came to visit she had always to move a pile of papers or unironed laundry to vacate a chair for the guest to sit on. One such guest said to her one day, 'Dear, I have always lived by the saying "Don't put it down, put it away"'. This had a deep effect on her – as it did on me when I read it. Another homespun piece of advice that came from this book is, 'Clean the corners and the room will take care of itself.' I had been married for thirty years when I read this book – it's never too late to learn.

As homemaking is more than housekeeping so is housekeeping more than housework and laundry which tend not to stretch the mind as much as the muscles. Budgeting, however, is quite different especially when resources are limited and a little has to go a long way. Time, thought, ingenuity and planning are needed. When a visit to the local supermarket is not thought out in advance it is inevitable that unnecessary items land in the trolley. At the time when our family's food consumption was at a maximum and housekeeping money was at a minimum, someone suggested that I should make out menus for the week and only buy what was necessary to make the chosen dishes – always making allowances for unexpected guests. I asked each member of the family to give me a list of their favourite meals and then combed my less exotic cookbooks for fresh inspiration. Equipped with these suggestions, I made out menus which did not include chips with everything (as some would have liked) but did include an occasional extravagant choice. This required an investment of time to set it up but did make a difference to the size of the weekly bills. I was also able to buy store cupboard ingredients that were necessary rather than picking up things that just might be useful. There was much less wastage. The menu was posted every week on the fridge door and was usually met with a mixture of approval and groans! I realize that such measures are not necessary for everyone, but it is always good to remember that we are all meant to be good stewards of God's provision for us in time and money.

In terms of housekeeping, Mrs Proverbs believed in forward planning in order to feed and clothe her family and in the general organization of her household. Much stress today could be avoided by following her example. There are those who almost take pride in the disorder that their busy lives create. I have heard women use the story of Mary and Martha to defend their lack of organization at home. Their interpretation of the story is that Mary was the spiritual one and Martha wasn't. It is evident however that Jesus appreciated Martha's gifts of hospitality; he was rebuking her for her poor-little-me attitude to her sister. Martha had lost sight of why she was doing what she was doing and had become critical of her sister. But it was Martha, not Mary, who some time later recognized who Jesus was. 'Yes, Lord, I believe that you are the Christ, the Son of God, who was to come into the world' (John 11:27). It is not a choice between spending time attending Bible studies or prayer meetings and keeping order in the home. Both have their place and are important! God is a God of order. But God is also the creator God and He has bestowed creative gifts on each and every person.

A Woman's Creativity in the Home

There are few women who can equal the creativity of Mrs Proverbs, who not only made bed-quilts and garments but spun the thread to make her fine linen and rich purple cloth. She grew her own food and the grapes for the wine.

Not everyone has the same creative gifts. Not everyone can draw or paint, and yet every house is like an empty canvas waiting to be made into a home by the creativity of the homemaker. The poorest home from the point of few material possessions can be transformed by careful choice of wall colour and soft furnishings (which may well have been inherited or acquired at the local charity shop), by framing birthday cards or children's drawings in clip frames and hanging them in groups on a wall; by converting a wooden crate into a piece of furniture by covering it with a piece of cloth and topping it with a plant or family photographs, by bringing life into a room with greenery from the garden with or without flowers – all of these put a personal imprint on a home which is like a signature at the bottom of a painting. It's the little things rather than the lavishness, or otherwise, of the furnishings which make home home. There are those who have special gifting in the area of interior design. There are those who have outstanding artistic ability. There are those who have the ability to make beautiful patchwork quilts and cushions. These gifts need to be encouraged and used.

Most of us, however, need encouragement to develop hidden creativity. Formal flower arranging is definitely not my gift. I have watched demonstrations which have made it look so easy. I have been challenged as others have worked with great artistry with flowers in preparation for weddings – but oasis and I seem to be completely incompatible! Then I discovered that, if I forgot about oasis and simply concentrated on filling small containers – not necessarily vases – and went round the garden picking greenery and flowers appropriate to the container I could produce an arrangement that brought colour and life to a room. My early experience with pot plants was a disaster area – but I decided that I would learn from others and from books where I was going wrong. To my amazement plants began to survive and even to thrive!

During the years since our family has left us to build their own homes, it has been my privilege to travel a little bit with my husband and to receive hospitality in homes all over the British

Isles. I have been fascinated by the differing expressions of creativity that are really expressions of the personality of each individual homemaker. This has been especially true in the manses where those who have responsibility to set the pastor's salary do not always mirror the generous heart of God! There are many women in such circumstances who work miracles to transform houses in which they are required to live into welcoming and attractive homes – not by spending money that they don't have, but by digging deep into God-given gifts of creativity.

The preparation and serving of food is another area in which creativity can be expressed. Choice of bread, addition of a few salad leaves and a sprinkling of parsley can transform even a plate of modest sandwiches into a work of art. Cooking doesn't need expensive ingredients or exotic recipes to be good to the taste buds and pleasing to the eye. I have always enjoyed cooking. My mother was an excellent cook of plain everyday food but could rise to the occasion when the occasion required something more. Her girdle scones and pancakes (or drop scones) hardly had time to cool before they were consumed! Her sponge cakes were as light as the proverbial feather. She passed her love of cooking on to me, but her abilities with the pancakes have alas eluded me! I enjoy experimenting with food which would have been unknown to her. This doesn't mean that I greet the prospect of cooking day in day out with unchanging enthusiasm, but it would certainly be a chosen area of creativity. In the days when the budget was really tight, I really used to enjoy the challenge of making a meal out of left-over bits and pieces.

Unfortunately, cooking has become, for some women, a lost art, a drudgery, which they have happily handed over to someone else – be it the man of the house or Marks and Spencer. Admittedly the feeding of a family of ravenous children can sometimes feel like feeding time at the zoo where the food is consumed without any appreciation of the time spent preparing it. It is much easier to resort to fast-food that is received daily without comment – but it certainly doesn't train the palates of a younger generation to appreciate different tastes, nor is it good for their health.

The multiplicity of cookery programmes on TV is having some effect on stimulating interest in the art of food preparation. Thanks to Delia's most recent series I can now guarantee myself a perfect boiled egg!

Another area where TV is having an encouraging effect on creativity is in the area of gardening. For a very long time I regarded the areas beyond the front and back doors of our home as the responsibility of the men in the household. I hated the thought of gardening. Some years ago I was asked to take part in some seminars which spent one whole morning on challenging others to take seriously the God-given responsibility to care for His world. I realized that I could not take part in this seminar with any integrity unless I changed my own attitudes and actions. I resolved to take recycling seriously (bottles, cans, paper) and we acquired a compost bin – a modest start, but at least a start. Reluctantly I realized that caring for the part of God's world immediately round our house was as much my responsibility as it was Jim's. I resolved to learn from books and from those who knew about these things as I had done with indoor plants. I didn't buy a field and plant it, but I do try to weed and plant the patch over which we are stewards – and I have come to enjoy doing it. There's something very satisfying in seeing seeds and bulbs that have been planted growing into flowers. There is an added bonus that the products of one's labour lasts a little longer than the products of kitchen creativity!

A Woman's Presence in the Home

My husband's mother died when he was nineteen years old. She was a woman who lived a very busy life. She went out to work early in the morning during most of Jim's childhood life. She did this, not by choice but from necessity, because the grocery business that they owned had failed during the years of the industrial depression in the 1930s. There were debts to be repaid and she chose to play her part in doing so. After work she called at her parent's home to tend to her mother who had cancer. Only then was she free to go back to care for her own home and be there when her sons came from school. Jim's memories of his childhood are of a well-organized, fresh and clean home where people were always welcome. She was a very creative person – dressmaking, knitting, embroidery, baking were all activities that she enjoyed. She was a happy and fun-loving person. When she was found to have advanced breast cancer it came as a tremendous shock to her husband and two sons. She continued for as long as she could – and probably longer than she should have – to do what she had always done. For some time she was confined to bed in their living room so that she was still in full contact with family life, organizing it rather than doing it, but eventually she had to go into hospital. I can remember going with Jim to his home soon after she had died. It was like a different place. It was still clean and tidy, but it was a sad house. It was as though the home had died – not just the homemaker. It was never the same again.

My father died as the result of a road accident. I flew up to Scotland on the morning he died. Of course it was strange not being greeted by my dad. We were all very sad and tearful. Part of my mother seemed to have died too for a time – but the home was still my childhood home and continued to be so as long as my mother lived. When she died, it became my sister's home and is still a welcoming place, but I find it hard to associate this same house as the one which was my home until we married. My sister has put her own unique stamp on it. When we go there it is because it is her home and not because of childhood memories.

Very recently one of our daughters-in-law went to her aunt's funeral. When asking her about it she talked about the service at the church and then about meeting up with her relatives back at the house. Without my asking, she said that the house seemed empty although it was full of people. We began to talk about it and I asked her 'Do you think that it was as though the home had lost it's soul?' She said that that described it very accurately. The house was there, but the homemaker had gone.

Because of the current attitudes to homemaking, I think that few women realize how their presence or absence affects the atmosphere of their homes. Unfortunately this works negatively as well as positively. Many years ago I began to realize that the general atmosphere in the family in the evening had a great deal to do with me. If I had had a bad day and one of the children or my husband had had a bad day as well, the chances of tensions and disagreements around the family meal table were considerably increased. I began to realize that my bad days were not really the fault of the broken down washing machine, or the difficult phone call, or a difficult situation handled in a counselling session, or even unbalanced hormones, but something much more fundamental than that. At some point during that day I had lost my inner peace. The unrest within me met the unrest within other family members, and gradually everyone was drawn in. My mind went back to the lessons I had learned from Roy Hession's book 'The Calvary Road'. I thought about the perpetual state of unrest I had caused in the family home in these early days because of my inner struggles. I went back to the book and read these words: 'There is one simple but all inclusive guide the Word of God gives to regulate and walk with Jesus and to make us know when sin has come in. Colossians 3:15 says, 'Let the peace of God rule in your hearts' (AV). Everything that disturbs the peace of God in our hearts is sin, no matter how small it is, no matter how little like sin it may first appear to be. This peace is to 'rule' our hearts or (a more literal translation) 'be the referee' in our hearts. When the referee blows his whistle at a football match the game has to stop, a foul has been committed. When we lose our peace, God's referee in our hearts has blown his whistle!'[11] A few lines further on he says, 'We do not lose our peace with God over another person's sin.' It seemed that I had forgotten the impact that that last sentence had made on me when I first read the book. No matter how hard or frustrating a day I had had, whether with people or with gadgets, my inner peace had been lost not because of what had happened or had been said or done, but because of my wrong reactions of frustration, or anger, or sheer self-pity. I found that if I took time to allow the Holy Spirit to show me my cause of unrest within before the first member of the family came home, I was able to react very differently to their frustrations and disappointments or to rejoice sincerely with them over the good things that had happened during their day. Of course, every member of the family needed to assume responsibility for their own wrong reactions, but that was always made easier for them if the peace of God was being allowed to rule in my heart.

Although order at home and using creative gifts are important, the creation of a welcoming atmosphere is much more important. There are many women today who go though life resenting the fact that they are women. They have been so brainwashed by the fallacy that men have always had the best of life, that they reflect the idea that it is impossible to find fulfilment anywhere other than out in the big wide world. It is impossible to create an atmosphere of Shalom at home when the lack of personal peace is not just to do with the day's happenings but is rather to do with a deep discontent – a discontent that comes from a feeling that somehow life is passing by and all that has happened thus far is of no significance. But to whom is it of no significance – to society, to the family, to God? I really believe that there is enough time in our lives to do everything that God has purposed for us to do. Some of us want to run ahead of God and do it all now. Others want to lag behind. When society is constantly belittling and mocking the job of homemaking by suggesting that it is a non-job and the least important part of a woman's life, it is easy to come to believe what is being said. Most young women today enter into marriage and family life having been indoctrinated by such views. When I came through my own struggles in the early 1960s and surrendered my training to God to use as He willed, I didn't really realize the full significance of what I was doing. However, what I do realize now is that, at the time, a deep contentment came into my life and I knew that God could be trusted with my future. This has stood me in good stead when Satan has tried to tell me otherwise. Contentment in our circumstances is the starting place for building an atmosphere of Shalom around us which, as I have discovered over many years of enduring ear-splitting music, has little do with lack of noise!

When a woman is on her own

Homemaking is not the prerogative of the married woman. A woman becomes a potential homemaker at conception when by God's choice the two cells that joined to become one cell contained the data necessary for a female child to be born. In an article in the *Independent on Sunday* published on 28 June 1998 under the headline, 'What men and women do best,' it says, 'For years women have insisted that anything men can do they can do better. Now new research into the workings of the brain reveals that the sexes are simply differently hard-wired. Men, it seems, are strong on spatial and mechanical skills (i.e. building treehouse) and women are good at domesticity and childcare (i.e. keeping treehouse). It's all rather troubling.' The German astronomer Kepler who lived in the sixteenth century said, 'Science is thinking God's thoughts after Him' – how true!

Until recently women who live alone were either single because they had never married, or because they had become widows. But now there are many different reasons for women being alone, some with children, some without. Single or married, widowed or divorced, our 'hard-wiring' is all the same. For a woman to deny any potential for homemaking is like ignoring the hard disc with which every computer comes equipped. As computers can have added software, so can we. Which explains, I think, why I understand things mechanical and electrical much more easily than my husband does and why one of our sons finds great enjoyment in cooking. It's why I come to conclusions about certain situations by intuition and feeling while Jim comes at them by a long reasoning process. It's not that I don't think and he doesn't feel or have insights and perceptions, but we just come to the same conclusion by a different process.

Older women who have never been married are often the ones who have had responsibility for ageing parents. They have continued to live in the family home when other siblings have left to set up their own homes. They have earned their living but have never had the choice of creating their own home. Many such women have been in their late fifties or have even reached retirement before they have faced the privileges and responsibilities of running a home for themselves. Some choose to go on living as before, changing nothing, denying their homemaking abilities and, after retirement, lead solitary lives. Others rise to the challenge of making the family home into their own home. They change the furnishings and put up the pictures that they like. They suddenly discover the freedom of having a kitchen where they can cook what they want when they want. They can have friends come to visit when it suits them. They can come and go as they please. It's not that they don't value the memory of parents who have now gone, but they are now free to express themselves at home with the freedom that they had enjoyed in the workplace! The hard-wiring finally comes into action.

My sister comes into the latter category. The home and garden of my childhood has gone. Instead there is the home that my sister has built within the same four walls. A beautiful garden of trees and shrubs has replaced my father's very tidy, productive, but regimented garden! When my sister went into hospital I flew up to Scotland to be near her. For the first time ever I lived in her home on my own. It was then that the realization of what I have just written came to me. The house seemed very empty, not now because my mother wasn't there, but because my sister – the homemaker – wasn't there.

It is unusual these days for a single woman to remain in the family home. Employment often takes young women away to other areas. Some just decide to have their independence. For many the career is the important thing in life and the functional flat is where they retire exhausted every evening to eat and sleep. Property is acquired as an investment rather than a place to build a home. But others allow their hard-wiring to spring into action, going against all the modern trends and resolving to build a home which will welcome them back after a hard working day.

There are many women today who have been uprooted from the homes that they loved because an unfaithful husband has deserted them. Their whole world seems to have collapsed around them and it all seems pointless now. They are suffering from bereavement without a death having occurred – except of course the death of their marriage. There are many widows who have had to leave the houses that they made home because the death of their husband has brought reduced circumstances financially.

But whatever the reason for being alone, the hard-wiring is still there waiting to be tapped into. Many women today want to ignore the presence of their hard-wiring and live on software skills which seem much more attractive because they have nothing to do with the gentler arts of homemaking. For those who live alone, it is worth remembering that the home where Jesus, who was single, found refreshment in his earthly life was at the home of three single people – Mary, Martha, and their brother Lazarus. We are not told why they were single – an unusual thing in their cultural setting, but we do know that it was a hospitable home.

The possibility of 'entertaining angels without knowing it'

If the end product of a woman's homemaking efforts is to produce a home which looks like something from the pages of a glossy magazine, or if the home is run with such efficiency that its occupants hardly dare breathe in case they mess it up, then all her efforts are pointless. But if the aim of homemaking is to create an atmosphere which is orderly but relaxed and welcoming, a place where family, friends or strangers feel comfortable, a place where stress begins to be dissipated, a place where people feel they can talk or be silent as they will; a place that can be filled with family noise and still be a haven of peace; a place where the smell of cooking (fresh not stale) stimulates the taste buds – then all of the efforts will have been worthwhile and bring great satisfaction, even though the actual results may fall short of the ideal some of the time.

Throughout scripture we are exhorted to share our homes with others. The Bible knows nothing of the tightknit little family with no concern for those outside of it. Hospitality is a much greater thing than simply inviting friends for a meal, although that is certainly a good start. It is an attitude that displays a willingness to serve others, an openness to meet the needs of others, a realization that we are but stewards of everything we have. God is the owner.

Not everyone has the privilege of entertaining angels as Abraham and Sarah did (Genesis 18:1-8) – although sometimes we have wondered if we might have done! Abraham immediately sprang to action to make these visitors feel welcome. There was nothing mean and grudging about the way that they were cared for. They were served the best veal for meat and the best flour in the bread. Hospitality was a joint effort between husband and wife. The guests were made to feel that it was a privilege to serve them and provide for them in abundance. Abraham was a rich man, so this was no problem to him.

Abraham gave out of his plenty, but the widow at Zarephath gave to Elijah out of her poverty. This woman was alone and struggling to make ends meet. By responding to the request of the prophet, she found that God provided all that she needed – and more. God brought great blessing into the lives of all three as a result of their response to those who needed food and care.

This would be our testimony over the years as we have welcomed people from many parts of the world into our home. Often our understanding of the scriptures has been deepened in times of talking together. Often we have been deeply challenged by the way in which they live their lives, and their desire to serve rather than be served. Sometimes we have had the privilege of ministering new hope to some who have been going through dark valleys of one kind or another. Occasionally we have had to cry out to God for His love and grace to flow when we have become weary and our patience has worn thin! But God has taught us lessons about ourselves on these occasions – lessons we might not otherwise have learned.

The giving of hospitality is one of the areas where the giftings of a husband and wife can flow together in making people feel welcomed and appreciated. And yet many times we have received wonderful hospitality from those who live alone. None of us is excluded from Jesus' exhortation to give the cup of cold water in His name.

In another chapter in Dale Garret's book, she gives an account of their family's experiences of hospitality given to them as they travelled around the world. She tells of the many blessings that they received, but she also had some horror stories to tell – of people who had offered the Garret family accommodation but didn't actually have a room to give them, so the guests had to wait until the host family had finally switched off their TV and vacated the living room. They were then free to unfold the sofa bed while the children slept on the floor; of unwashed sheets and empty larders in houses they were given to occupy, of people who insisted on showing their latest holiday videos when the travel weary guests were longing to sleep. Unfortunately, experiences like these are not unknown to some of our friends, but thankfully they are very much in the minority. It is important, however, to think of the needs of the people who come into our homes. Hospitality is not a ministry that should ever be entered into when stressed or over busy. The stress of the household can very easily be passed on to a guest, who then feels guilty at simply adding to family tensions. A woman who is holding down a full-time job outside the home and raising a family is probably not the best person to extend the offer of hospitality to strangers – especially travel weary preachers! Towards the end of his letter to the believers at Rome Paul says, 'so that I might come to you with joy and together with you be refreshed' (Romans 15:32).

Paul is expressing his anticipation of meeting up with these people. If you are not in a position to bring refreshing to those who come to stay in your home, then stick to the offer of a meal, or even a cup of coffee – or change your lifestyle.

We are constantly amazed at the kindness and thoughtfulness shown by those who receive us into their homes, and have indeed been refreshed in every way by meeting other members of God's family.

Hospitality is both a natural and a spiritual gift. Many people who have no Christian belief have very hospitable homes. As believers, we have the opportunity to add another dimension to caring for others – whether it be a neighbour who drops in to share a coffee or someone invited to share a meal. The guest may be a visiting preacher or a missionary who has come to speak in our local fellowship. On the other hand the guest(s) may be friends of our children who have just appeared on the doorstep, as they tend to do! There was a time when most of the meal-time hospitality of our household was extended to the teenage friends of our children – a very important group of people. Often during school holidays our doorbell used to ring about fifteen minutes before our 1p.m. lunch hour. At first I used to grumble and suggest that they tell their friends to come later in the afternoon. Then it occurred to me that perhaps a better attitude was to make sure that I made enough soup and had defrosted enough rolls to cope with one or two extra. Our household was unusual in that not only was I around at lunchtime, but so was my husband. A family meal table was infinitely preferable to a lonely lunch. It was a wonderful way to get to know these young people.

We need to remember the words of Jesus: 'whatever you did for one of the least of these brothers of mine you did it for me' (Matthew 25:40). Caring for others, whoever they may be, is an opportunity to demonstrate our willingness to give 'our utmost for His highest'.

10

A Woman in her Family as Wife

The vehemence with which a young woman journalist, appearing on a TV programme in June 1999, decried the fact that Sophie Rhys-Jones chose to include the word 'obey' in her marriage vows to Prince Edward was interesting ,but hardly surprising in today's egalitarian climate.

The concept of marriage is certainly not on the priority list for many people today. An increasing number of people who enter into marriage have already been living together, or at least have slept together. The word 'marriage' is often equated with the word 'wedding'. The wedding day is now not necessarily the day on which two people leave their family homes to be joined together in marriage. The wedding day can now take place, if indeed it does take place, at any point in a couple's relationship – often after the birth of one or two children. Weddings are big business and often have little to do with the beginning of a marriage. Sometimes the act of making a definite commitment to one another lifts the relationship into a deeper level, especially if the decision to marry follows an encounter with God and a commitment to follow Jesus.

Jewish marriages certainly included a great deal of celebration in Biblical times – celebrations which could last for several days. The actual wedding day came after a substantial period of betrothal, which – as has already been noted – was as binding as the actual marriage. The creational description of marriage given to us in the last verses of Genesis 2 requires the leaving of one set of relationships to enter into a new relationship with a person of the opposite sex. The King James translation of the Bible uses the word 'cleave' to describe the joining together of two people in marriage. It literally means that they are glued together – with glue more powerful than superglue – and so cannot be separated without doing damage to both. What God meant by marriage is much more than two people based in the same house who sleep together and possess a piece of paper which makes the relationship legally binding. God's intention for marriage is a fusion of two lives in a way which is beyond our understanding but can only be fully experienced by keeping to the instructions of the Maker. God's blueprint for marriage requires chastity before marriage and fidelity in marriage. That marriage was never intended to be the means of stifling a woman's gifts, abilities, or spiritual growth, is well demonstrated in Mrs Proverbs.

'and they lived happily ever after'
Someone has said that 'marriage is total commitment to an imperfect person'. Someone else has said that 'marriage is one of the ways that God uses to make us into the people He wants us to be'.

No one prepared us for marriage. Our much-loved minister talked to us about the wedding service, but that was all. It was assumed, because Jim was a minister and I was a doctor, that we knew it all. The trouble was we thought that we did! It was not even the custom for the officiating minister to address the young couple in Scottish wedding services in those days. In fact is was thought quite strange that we wanted to repeat vows to one another instead of just saying 'I will' and 'I do'.

During most of our seven-year courtship we dreamed of the day that would end all our separation – the day which would be the beginning of our 'happily ever after'. Those seven years were far from easy. Jim's mother was dying of cancer when our relationship began. She died at the end of our first year at university, just before the beginning of the second year autumn term. His father married again within eighteen months. Jim had not yet come to terms with his mother's awful suffering and the gaping hole that her death had left in his life. This led to an enormous crisis of faith. I felt totally inadequate to help him. He found the traditional trite words of evangelical Christians were a hindrance rather than a help to finding God in the midst of his grief and emotional turmoil. Separation was the pattern of our life during term-time. We seemed to be constantly catching buses going in opposite directions. Our studies were very demanding. When we met up at weekends we frequently spent Saturday side by side in the Mitchell Library in Glasgow, or in the sitting room of my parental home surrounded by textbooks. On Sundays Jim was usually preaching in some church in central Scotland – a requirement of the Baptist College.

We knew from the start that we would marry one day – but we also knew that there were other considerations than our desire to be together. My 'career' was the big one. Should I go on and do postgraduate study or not? It wasn't necessary in those days but would have given more options in the future. I was very conscious of the sacrifice my parents were making for me. I was sure that I should be studying medicine, but we were equally sure that God had brought us together. There was no-one we could talk to. We were caught up in the early days of a major cultural change, where more and more young women were being encouraged into professional training without much thinking ahead into postgraduate years. At one extreme the feminist ridicule of traditional roles had taken root and was growing, and at the other extreme was the viewpoint that said that a woman's place was in the home. Many of the young women who were my contemporaries were, like myself, trying to find out where they fitted in. There were one or two definite career women in our midst, but not many. The prevailing attitude to medicine among the women students was a desire to care for people. I can't think of one woman student who saw medical training as the gateway to making vast sums of money. The same could not be said of some of the men.

Another ongoing struggle that we had was in dealing with what Elisabeth Elliot describes as 'the natural and human hunger for marriage'[12], which was raging within us. There were no books written on relationships in our student days. Amongst evangelical Christians sex was a taboo word. It was as though not speaking about it or acknowledging the existence of such desires was to deal with them. I can remember a student conference in our fourth year of study where it was made plain that any show of affection between undergraduates who were not officially engaged to be married, was unacceptable behaviour. We were rebuked for holding hands! It only served to make us feel guilty that we, as Christians, had such feelings for one another. Our respect for our parents and our basic knowledge of God's standards kept us in times of temptation during these years.

Although I could never recommend a seven-year courtship, there was a very positive side in that the deep companionship that we have known throughout our marriage was nurtured and developed during those years. We walked a lot and talked a lot because neither of these cost money!

Our wedding day and our honeymoon in Guernsey were everything we dreamed of – and more. (We returned to the same hotel to celebrate our Silver Wedding and our Ruby Wedding.) It seemed that 'happily ever after' had come!

Two weeks after we had returned from honeymoon I caught Asian 'flu – not a good start. My first attempts at housekeeping were a little better than Dale Garret's – but not much. I began to learn just how much hard work my mother had put in to make our family home the welcoming place that it was. Helping at home was very different from being the homemaker! In the ten months of Jim's first full pastorate before we were married, the congregation had got used to his total availability as a single man. I found myself at home every evening except Tuesday (when I went to a women's meeting), Wednesday (when we both went to the prayer meeting), and Sunday (when we both went to church). I was not accustomed to being at home alone. In my growing up years there was always at least one other member of the family around; in student years I lived in digs with others where everything was done for us; in hospital there were people everywhere. My loneliness, compounded by the constant nausea of the early days of pregnancy, made me wonder where all our dreams of our life together had gone. In fact I was rapidly moving from the fairy tale world of 'happily ever after' to the real world of living out marriage vows with a real person who wasn't quite as perfect as I had thought him to be (and he was making the same discoveries about me). Someone has said that four people not two are involved in a marriage. There is the grown man and the grown woman plus the little boy that was and the little girl that was. The little girl in me had become an expert at getting her own way. The little boy in Jim responded to conflict by withdrawing into silence. This had increasingly become his way of handling conflict in his relationship with his father and stepmother. Neither of us had any regrets about marrying – far from it – but growing into our marriage vows was not as straightforward as we had imagined that it would be.

Our understanding of Christian marriage in those days was more cultural than biblical. I can remember , as a girl, asking my mother why we did or did not do certain things, the response was: 'because your father says so' or 'because your father has decided not to'. When I asked my mother 'Why?' She would say, 'because your father is head of the house'. I related this to Victorian attitudes rather than to Biblical principles. The church that both families attended was evangelical but dead (but thought it was alive). Week by week the minister preached sermons from texts. Until my student years, when I attended Inter-Varsity-Fellowship Conferences, I had never heard any real solid Bible teaching – but no-one taught about marriage because we were not meant to focus on that! It wasn't until after we were married and we had our late night discussion sessions with the faithful deacon Robin (mentioned in an chapter 2) and his wife Betty, that I began to realize that the Bible contained some very clear instructions about marriage, which, until this point, I was not willing to hear. Headship and submission were not, as I had thought, Victorian ideas with no relevance to the marriage of highly educated modern young people (as we were then).

From that time on I accepted that headship and submission were part of the biblical pattern of marriage, but my understanding of these words were still derived very much from an orthodox evangelical culture rather than the Scriptures themselves. When God touched our lives in the 1960s first of all by taking us back to Calvary and then on to a personal Pentecost, it was as though, like Paul when Ananias prayed for him, scales had been lifted from my eyes. This, of course, was not an outward and physical blindness, but it was as though light shone into my soul and so many parts of God's word suddenly came into focus. This affected every part of my being. The same was true for Jim. Our good marriage moved into a new dimension of closeness as we were drawn together by a new hunger to understand God's purposes for our lives together, and as individuals. In 1971 a book by an American Lutheran pastor called Larry Christenson, entitled *The Christian Family* was published in Britain. How I wished that this book had been written fourteen years before when we began our marriage. Perhaps I wouldn't have been ready to benefit from his exposition of Ephesians 5:22-24 at that point. In revisiting the book recently I am amazed at how far society, Christian society included, has moved away from the scriptural truths as expounded in this book. My own testimony has been that bringing our marriage under scriptural order has been for me a very liberating experience, even although it is as different as chalk is from cheese from the feminist view of what it means to be a 'liberated woman'.

Headship and Submission – the heart of the matter
When these two words are bound up with law instead of grace, they become a prison house where harshness and resentment flourish — a battleground where sexists and feminists fire salvos

at one another; insuperable barriers to the development of Godly masculinity and femininity whether it be in the home, in the church, or in society. I have chosen to look at these two words in the context of marriage because that is the main scriptural setting for them. If they are properly understood in the context of marriage – God's perfect foundational context – then there will be no difficulty in understanding their application elsewhere.

There are two differing and opposite forms of legalism in the context of marriage. The first is the fruit of the disobedience of the man and the woman in the Garden of Eden. It has to do with the attitude to the woman, which God told her would be the consequence of her disobedience. It has nothing to do with the purposes of God, but rather has its roots in the man's fallen nature. It is the legalism that interprets headship as the right to rule the household with unquestionable rigidity – a loveless authoritarianism. It is the legalism that imposes servility on a wife (and children) that ultimately leads to loss of personality and passivity – or else to a build up of brooding anger and resentment, which, if it doesn't eventually explode outwardly in rebellion and defiance, will produce many kinds of emotional and physical dis-ease.

The second kind of legalism found in the context of marriage today comes out of an attempt to sidestep any form of leadership in a marriage – a relationship which is founded on a 50:50 sharing of responsibility. It is the legalism which says, 'If I do the shopping, you do the cooking: if I do the cooking, you do the washing up; if I clean the car, you clean the house; I did the ironing last week, so you do it this week.' It is the legalism that draws up a pre-marriage contract in an attempt to avoid conflict in the marriage or make it easier when the marriage ends in divorce.

These are the extremes, and there are many positions between these two extremes, none of which bear any resemblance to God's creational blueprint for the relationship that we call marriage.

The secular feminists of the 1960s decided that marriage was a product of male chauvinism and so decided that they would do everything they could to undermine marriage and their aim would be its eventual destruction – an aim which they might have achieved by now if marriage had been a purely human institution. Christians who would call themselves feminists, while strongly upholding the sanctity of marriage as part of God's plan for a strong and stable society, would nevertheless deny that leadership in marriage has been given to the husband. This requires a degree of reinterpretation of the parts of the Pauline epistles and of 1 Peter, which give direction to husbands and wives. The claim is that mutual submission in marriage is what Paul teaches in the passage in Ephesians 5, which is probably the most quoted passage about marriage in the scriptures. In the early part of the chapter Paul is instructing believers in the way that they should behave as 'children of the light' and how they should relate to one another. In Ephesians 5:21 he says, 'Submit yourselves to one another out of reverence for Christ'. This is in line with other 'one another' instructions given to believers throughout the Pauline epistles (e.g. love one another, be kind to one another – and many more). In Colossians Paul also deals with the relationships between believers before he focuses in on his instructions for good order in individual households. In 1 Peter 2 the same is true. Peter speaks about general behaviour and attitudes among believers before focusing on wives and husbands. In all these three passages the instructions are the same. 'Wives submit to your husbands.' There is never anywhere any instruction for husbands to be submissive to their wives. It is also true, however, that nowhere is a husband instructed to force his wife to submit to him. The submission of a wife to a husband has been described as a 'voluntary yielding in love'. The submission of a wife to her husband is out of respect for the one to whom God has given the responsibility to lead, in a relationship of two people who are equal in creation and in redemption. Paul compares the response of a woman to her husband with the attitude which the church has to Christ, who is its Head.

But Paul goes on to charge husbands with the immensity of the sacrifice that Christ made in order to become Head of the church. Being the head of the household demands the same attitude of sacrificial love. The Greek word for head (*kephale*) has become the focus of much attention for feminist theologians, many of whom have written papers in which they set out to prove that this word translated 'head' should actually be translated 'source' – and therefore it does not in any way imply leadership or authority. In fact it is unusual to find feminist writings (whether by men or women) where this meaning of *kephale* is not taken for granted. An American theologian (Prof. Wayne Grudem) has also done much research into the meaning of this word. He studied 2,336 examples of the use of this word in Greek literature from the New Testament period and did not find one occasion where the definitive meaning was 'source', whereas he listed over forty examples where the meaning had unquestionably the sense of leadership and authority. At the conclusion of an article written in response to the writings of several well known feminist theologians, he says, 'After all the research on this word by myself as well as Cervin, Payne, Bilezikian, Kroeger and others there is still an unanswered question: Where is there even one clear example of *kephale* used of a person to mean 'source' in all of Greek literature before or during the time of the New Testament? – If there is still not one clear example before or during the time of the New Testament then how can so many writers go on saying that this is a 'common' meaning at the time of the New Testament? Or even a possible one? Perhaps such examples will be forthcoming, but until they are it would seem appropriate to use much more caution in the statements that are made about 'source' being a common or recognized meaning at all.'[13]

It would seem that 'source' has been accepted among feminists in the same way that the theory of evolution (i.e. in the sense that man is descended from the apes) is spoken of amongst scientists. Without any intention of undermining the work of those who undertake such research, one is left wondering why one word in Scripture should cause such a theological storm. Is the reason for the storm a determination to prove the position of undifferentiated equality between man and woman that is at the heart of feminist theology? It would certainly appear to be so.

Theology needs to become practice

It is easy to read some words of Scripture, but how does it work out in practice? Many women would subscribe to the theology of submission but in practice would demonstrate the opposite! There is the story told of the man who was asked at his Golden Wedding celebration how he had managed his household over the years. 'That's easy,' he said, 'I make all the major decisions and my wife makes all the minor ones – there have been no major decisions thus far.' I can remember many years ago being in a company of women where one of the group was complaining about the unreasonable (from her perspective) behaviour of her husband. An older woman who had been listening to the conversation said that she understood what was being said and had no doubt of the fact that it was hard to cope with, but she went on to say, 'But that's his problem, don't make it yours.' In other words the wife's complaining to others wouldn't change the situation but would only make it an opportunity for Satan to sow seeds of self-pity and criticism in her own heart, which would become a barrier not only between husband and wife but also between the wife and God.

During more than forty years of pastoral involvement with people, we know how much anguish there can be in Christian marriages where God's blueprint has been ignored or distorted beyond all recognition. It is also true that we have seen wonderful restorations in marriages where both partners have committed themselves to live according to God's instructions. We have also seen the truth of the apostle Peter's advice to women with unbelieving husbands bear fruit (1 Peter 3:1-2). Several years ago I was involved with other leaders' wives in praying for the unconverted husbands of church members. One evening we felt that God was telling us to pray for the wives rather than the husbands, along the lines of the above scriptural reference. We prayed that these women would be the wives that God wanted them to be even though the going was tough. One month later when we met to pray again we were able to rejoice that three husbands had become Christians!

Sometimes a woman's over-spirituality can be the biggest hindrance to God being able to work in a husband's life. Mrs Proverbs was a wife who feared the Lord and that was, no doubt, the source of her motivation in all that she did. But she didn't see caring for her husband, family and others as a hindrance to serving God but rather that this was her sphere of service – a means of worshipping God and serving Him. This would seem to tie up with Paul's instructions to the believers at Rome when he tells them to present their bodies as living sacrifices – 'This is your spiritual act of worship. Do not conform any longer to the pattern of this world, but be transformed by the renewing of your minds.' (Romans 12:2) Paul goes on to give very practical ways in which this worship is to be worked out in the function that God has given each one of us. This has particular application within the marriage relationship.

God's function for a wife is not the same as God's function for a husband. The arithmetic of marriage that $1 + 1 = 1$ is not just a reference to physical union, important to the health of the marriage as that is, but there are other unions of soul and spirit which take place over the years when each is giving to the other in the way that God intended. This does not mean that each becomes a lesser person as an individual – the opposite is the case. A man's masculinity is increased and a woman's femininity is increased. God's multiplication as well as God's addition is a mystery.

A husband's leading in headship has nothing to do with getting and demanding, but everything to do with giving in sacrificial love. The Greek word is *agape* – a quality of self-sacrifice and devotion which was introduced to the world by Jesus. It is out of *agape* that a husband's leadership in marriage flows – a responsibility to provide for, protect, guide, direct and sometimes correct; a responsibility to encourage his wife and care for her body, soul and spirit. With these attitudes not only the wife but also the children will develop into the people God wants them to be. An atmosphere is created where respect flourishes naturally between husband and wife and is communicated to the children, without any need to command it.

A wife's giving in submission is also rooted in *agape* love and is a response of respect. It is interesting to note that it is to the wife first that Paul speaks about headship and submission – not to the husband. There is an interesting parallel in this with the words spoken to the woman (not the man) in Genesis 3, where God tells her that the result of her disobedience is that the man will rule over her. In these verses it would seem that Paul, in addressing the wife first, is stating a return to God's original purposes, made possible by the death and resurrection of Jesus.

In her book, *Let me be a Woman,* Elisabeth Elliot says, 'Acceptance of the divinely ordered hierarchy means acceptance of authority – first of all God's authority and then those lesser authorities which He has ordained. A husband and wife are both under God but their positions are not the same. A wife is to submit herself to her husband. The husband's 'rank' is given him by God, as the angels' and animals' ranks are assigned, not chosen or earned. The mature man acknowledges that he did not earn or deserve this place by superior intelligence, virtue, strength or amiability. The mature woman acknowledges that submission is the will of God for her, and obedience to this will is no more a sign of weakness in her than it was in the Son of Man when He said, "Lo I come to do Thy will, O God!"'[14]

'this crazy little thing called love'

These were the words of a song that was top of the pops sometime during my childhood years. We have only one word in English to describe many different kinds of love. We say we love ice cream, our pet animals, our homes, our gardens, our leisure pursuits, our children and our husbands. It is a good demonstration of the poverty of our language. The sad thing is that often the word is used when the word lust would be more appropriate! In Greek there are four words for love – *philio, storge, eros, agape*.

Philio is the word used for the bonding relationship between friends. It is the emotion that is at the root of concern for other people in society. It appears in words like philanthropy – defined as love for humankind, practical benevolence. The city of Philadelphia established in USA by the Quakers literally means 'the city of brotherly love'.

Storge is the word used in closer family relationship. It is the emotion between parents and children and brothers and sisters. Both of these words have an attitude of loyalty and respect built into them – the attitude which was in God's heart for His relationship with humankind when He created us.

Eros is the Greek word for romantic love – a love also created in purity right back at the beginning of time. It is the love which God intended to be expressed between a man and a woman joined in marriage. In any other circumstance it is degraded into little more than animal passion. *Eros* was intended by God to be a source of joy and fun as well as a deep unfathomable union of two bodies, which symbolizes the much deeper union that has already been described. It has been suggested that the place of the sexual relationship in marriage is like the sparking plug of a car. It's a small part in proportion to the size of the car, but without it the car won't go! In the early days of marriage that probably wouldn't be an adequate proportion, but as the pressures of family life increase, there is sometimes the tendency for a wife to forget that the sparking plug is necessary – but as has been said already, without it the car won't go! Later in the same book by Elisabeth Elliot which was quoted earlier, she says, 'The essence of sexual enjoyment for a woman is self-giving. Give yourself wholly, joyfully; hilariously...neither husband nor wife should withhold this pleasure from the other except by mutual agreement for a limited time. His body belongs now to you and yours to him. Each has 'power' over the other's each holding the other's in holiness and honour under God. You will find that it is impossible to draw the line between giving pleasure and received pleasure. If you put the giving first the receiving is inevitable.'[15] These are the words of a mother written for and to her daughter who was about to be married. As the years go on the passion of *eros* may quieten a little, but, still has the same importance in the deep oneness of marriage.

When *storge, philio* and *eros* combine there is a quality of commitment that can be found in any good marriage. But there is another word for love that Jesus introduced into the world – *agape* – that brings a new depth into every relationship between Christians – including marriage.

Agape has been defined thus by William Barclay. 'It is the spirit which says, "No matter what any man does to me I will never seek to do him harm. I will never set out for revenge. I will always seek nothing but his highest good."'[16] And 'Christian love is unconquerable benevolence, invincible goodness. It is not simply a wave of emotion; it is a deliberate policy of the life; it is a deliberate achievement and conquest, and victory of the will. It takes all of a person to achieve Christian love – not only the heart but the mind and will as well.' This is the sacrificial love of Calvary which Paul speaks about in 1 Corinthians 13 and which is so often read at weddings: 'Love is patient and kind, never jealous or envious, never boastful or proud, never haughty or selfish or rude. Love does not demand its own way. It is not irritable or touchy. It does not hold grudges and will hardly ever notice when others do it wrong. It is never glad about injustice, but rejoices when truth wins out. If you love someone you will be loyal to him no matter what the cost. You will always believe in him and always expect the best of him, and always stand your ground in defending him' (Living Bible Translation of verses 4-7). I wonder how many couples really listen to these words. When difficulty or disillusionment come into a marriage, when sickness devastates one of the partners, when unfaithfulness is uncovered, when income doesn't match expenditure, the only brand of love which can be relied upon to weather the storm is *agape* love.

Mrs Proverbs' many attributes were appreciated by her husband and family; but this is not always the case. The promises that are made before God have no 'unless' or 'if' in them. They are promises of unconditional love and loyalty. The fact that one partner has disregarded them does not absolve the other partner from keeping them. Society has made it very easy for marriages to be dissolved, but we have to remember the words of Jesus when the Pharisees were questioning him on the subject of divorce. 'So they are no longer two but one. Therefore what God has joined together let man not separate.' What society means by marriage in these days and what the Bible teaches are two different kinds of relationship. Secular society sees marriage as a legal contract between two equal persons who desire to commit themselves to each other at this point in time. Biblical marriage is a joining together of two equal but different people, a man and a woman, in a mystical union only to be ended by the death of one partner. Often, when reading the instructions for some new household gadget, the instructions will say, 'For best results follow the instructions of the maker.' If this is true for home gadgets, it is even truer for marriages.

There are those who may not have even known the 'Maker's instructions' and who have experienced the tragedy of being involved in marriage breakdown. With God failure is never final. He accepts people just as they are. God's requirements to begin again are simple – entering into His forgiveness can follow repentance for failure. A friend of ours who became a Christian after being divorced, told us that she had not only repented before God for her part in the marriage break-up but she had also gone on to ask the forgiveness of her ex-husband, her children, her parents and her in-laws. She said that it was at that point that she really knew the reality of God's forgiveness and was released to go on with living her life as God would have her do. But knowing God's forgiveness does not cancel the consequences of ignoring God's blueprint for the relationship between man and woman. Deep wounds leave scars and sometimes disablement. Scars are a reminder of something that happened – but in themselves, they should not cause problems. Disablement might mean that certain areas of life are restricted and that nothing is as straightforward as it once was, but life is still there to be lived. There is no experience of life that God cannot use when it is put into His hands. God spoke to the prophet Jeremiah and told him to go to the house of a potter and watch him at work. He watched as the potter took a piece of clay that had been damaged and rework it into another pot (Jeremiah 18:1-4). God is able to do that with a damaged life put into His hands.

The Wife of the Third Millennium AD

No matter how the world has changed over the years the principles that governed Mrs Proverb's life and the principles governing wives of the twenty-first century are the same. The fundamental principle of her life was giving – of her love, her time, her talents, her whole being, for the enrichment and support of her husband first, and then of her children, and all the others whom her life touched. Through her the lives of others were enriched. Contentment, and the approval of those she loved, was her reward.

11

A Woman in the Home as Mother

Parenting is the politically correct term that includes motherhood and/or fatherhood. It is a term that has evolved with the breakdown of the Judaeo/Christian pattern of family life. It is a unisex term for the person(s) responsible in a household for the rearing of children. Parenting is a non-judgmental term that covers every kind of 'family' unit in our secular society today. It removes any suggestion of gender-related roles that are so deplored by feminists.

The One-Parent Family
There are many reasons why children are being reared by single parents – mostly mothers. Some women are single mothers because of the death of the husband/father of the family. Forty years of being involved in people's lives have meant being caught up in the pain of such bereavements. I have been challenged many times by the courage shown by young widows in taking on double responsibility in such circumstances. Some have eventually remarried, but others have not. Instead they have found employment to fit in with the care of children. Many have had to move house or even locality to cope with financial restraints, or to be near family support. Similarly there are fathers whose wives have died and have managed to raise their children well and still continue to earn a living. But death is no longer

the main reason for children being reared by a mother or a father alone. Thousands of children have been deserted by their father – or sometimes their mother. Desertion by a spouse is another form of bereavement that is handled with great courage by some of those in this position.

There are many young girls who are not promiscuous but have become pregnant through one much regretted act. Forty years ago, having a child 'out of wedlock' was considered a major disgrace and so many such girls found themselves being dispatched, some against their will, to a home for unmarried mothers. Not all of these homes were the dreadful places described in recent TV programmes but, nonetheless, were often the place where a young woman's motherhood was brought to an abrupt end within days of giving birth. But the removing of an infant after birth does not end the deep bonding which normally takes place between mother and child during nine months of pregnancy. Many of these children were raised in good, loving, stable homes with adoptive parents. This, however, has not removed the yearning in the hearts of many of these mothers to know where their child is. For those who didn't allow their child to be adopted there was often a hard road ahead, knowing that the child would bear the stigma of illegitimacy.

Many years ago one of our church members, a single lady, found out that her parents had never been married. She was distraught. 'I am illegitimate,' she said, 'how can God love me?' It was at that time that I believe that God showed me that there is no such thing as an illegitimate child – it's the parents who are illegitimate in God's eyes. Every child is fully acceptable to God no matter who the parents are or what may have been the circumstances of their conception. Many children have grown into adulthood with the stigma of illegitimacy constantly in the background (even when parents have eventually married), and have spent their lives trying to prove their worth to themselves and to anyone who knew of their birth circumstances. Others have gone through life with the words, 'I'm sorry,' constantly on their lips, as though they were apologizing for being born. For an illegitimate parent, God's forgiveness is no less freely available and complete for moral sin repented of than it is for any other form of sin.

The current moral compromise of society has removed the stigma of illegitimacy from children and parents, but that does not alter the fact that God's standards of morality have never changed. The vast majority of children being raised in one parent families or in step-parent families are in this situation because we live in a society which prefers to encourage people to do what feels right for them, thus stifling the moral law which God has put into the conscience of every human being. As the family of God, we have a responsibility to care for and encourage those who are legitimate single parents and those who have received God's forgiveness for a moral lapse, but we need to be very careful not to condone or even encourage the continued immoral behaviour of others. Jesus held compassion and righteousness, grace and truth, mercy and judgment, in perfect balance in his dealings with people (e.g. John 4). He freely forgave sin but never condoned it. He loved sinners, but condemned their sin and challenged them to change their way of living. We need to pattern our compassion on the example of Jesus and not on current social standards. Tolerance is seen as the top virtue in our society. There is no Calvary in tolerance. Grace on the other hand has everything to do with the price paid by Jesus on Calvary to deal with our sin and make forgiveness possible. Grace deals with sin – tolerance overlooks it.

Are fathers necessary?

The government's ideal is good parenting. The Bible's ideal is that every child should know the loving care of a father and a mother. Every child ever born has been born to parents who are far from perfect. It is a sad fact that the perfect Fatherhood of God has been marred for so many people because of the inadequacies, or (increasingly common) the absence of an earthly father. The constant error is to see God in the image of an imperfect earthly father, instead of seeing how far the earthly father falls short of the perfect image of the Fatherhood of God.

In an article entitled 'Where is dad?' an American pastor says, 'Real men do not just make babies. Real men take responsibility for the physical and spiritual care of the children they beget – and for those begotten and deserted by others. Responsibility lies at the heart of fatherhood as it was intended to be.'[17] As husbands and wives have equal and different roles, so do fathers and mothers. Both have a part to play in the development of a child in body, soul and spirit. Fatherless children need to see role models of Godly fatherhood – fathers who are unashamedly the leaders of their households but who are also deeply involved in their children's lives. The pastor who wrote the article quoted above goes on to draw attention to the passage from the end of the prophecy of Malachi which says these solemn words: 'See I will send you the prophet Elijah before the great and terrible day of the Lord comes. He will turn the hearts of the fathers to their children, and the hearts of the children to their fathers; or else I will come and strike the land with a curse'(Malachi 4:5 and 6). In line with the ethos of our post modern inclusive society the word 'father' has sometimes been changed to the word 'parent' in some translations of scripture. But in God's eyes a father is a father and a mother is a mother. If God had desired that children should be 'parented', He would not have chosen to create two separate beings – as we have already noted. He could have done it that way, but He didn't. As Christian women we need to encourage fathers to take their God ordained role of fatherhood seriously by demonstrating attitudes of respect and deference instead of trying to mould them into a role of surrogate motherhood.

Motherhood – *what is it?*

Motherhood is not a temporary interruption in a woman's real life. Motherhood is a privilege and not a right. Motherhood changes the whole course of a woman's life. Becoming a mother gives a woman the opportunity of nurturing and playing a major part in the moulding of the next adult generation. Much of the stress related illness in women today is caused by trying to live life in a pre-motherhood mode with pre-motherhood (and often pre-marriage) priorities. This creates real tension and eventually something has to give. I have to confess that I have never understood why women who have declared themselves desperate to have a baby are willing to hand the total responsibility for care of that child over to someone else for most of his/her waking hours. Motherhood not only brings privileges but it also brings responsibilities. The privileges cannot be fully experienced without bearing the responsibilities. A child is radically so much more than just another possession. In normal circumstances no one can give to a child the care, the attention and sense of security that the one who conceived and carried the child in utero can give – not even a loving father. Being a mother brings some restrictions of choice into a woman's life, but it opens up many new avenues of opportunity to grow as a person in learning to deny self and care more for others.

So little attention has been given to motherhood as the main calling in a mother's life that I am going to look in detail at what it means. Motherhood is not something that fits into a slot somewhere in a woman's life – it is a life-long commitment. Shakespeare wrote of life as consisting of seven ages. With apologies to Shakespeare – One mother in her time plays many parts, her acts being seven ages!

1. *Pregnancy*

The confirmation of a pregnancy produces a multitude of reactions – from overwhelming joy to unbelief and distress. It all depends on circumstances. The wife who has almost given up hope of ever bearing a child reacts very differently from the young unmarried woman who regrets giving way to her natural instincts in the wrong circumstances. The woman who was hoping to become pregnant again will react very differently from the woman who thought that her childbearing years were over and family life had settled into a gentler phase. For some it seems that the timing is all wrong and the pregnancy is an inconvenient interruption to plans and aspirations. For the older woman the thought of going back into nappies, night feeding and teething can be quite overwhelming. During the first pregnancy there is always (even in those who've read the books and delivered babies) an apprehension about the actual birth – which may be even greater in the second pregnancy because of a bad experience first time round. But in every case there is one basic fact – that this new and previous life has begun by God's say-so even if not by human intention.

For some, pregnancy runs smoothly with no problems. For others, pregnancy is fraught with problems of abnormal sickness, heartburn, varicose veins, or backache. For a few, serious complications arise with blood pressure or bleeding from an awkwardly positioned placenta, or latent physical problems may come to the fore. For most the last month seems unending and is a mixture of excitement and growing apprehension. Every woman has niggly fears about the health of her child and a concern for safe delivery. For some, pregnancy ends before nine months. For most, pregnancy ends with the birth of a healthy child. For a few, pregnancy ends with tragedy and loss of a little life. Sharing in the joys and sorrows of young couples has been part of pastoral life. I can still feel the pain of one situation when the beautiful and much wanted little daughter of our assistant pastor and his wife died after heart surgery when only a few days old. I would have done anything to be able to give back the child whom that young mother longed to hold and to suckle once more. A heartbroken father also ached for his little girl and struggled to cope with their joint bereavement. I never see a life size china doll but I remember that little one as she lay in a tiny white coffin. One year later they welcomed twin boys into their home who are now fine young men, but I sense that part of their hearts lies buried in a village somewhere many thousands of miles away from where they now live. Others have come to terms with having a little one who needs special care because of some form of mental or physical disablement. God always seems to give special grace to such parents – and also to the siblings of such a family. Sometimes a disabled child brings great heaviness, but many times over such a special child brings unique joy which others find difficult to understand. It seems that such families have learned to take nothing for granted and have developed a deeper sense of what is and is not important than those of us who have never worn their shoes.

But some have become mothers by adopting a child. Here is the story of one such mother –

We had been married for eight years when the doctors told us that it was unlikely that we would have children. We had seen our friends starting families, many of them having had two or three children already. It hadn't worried us unduly when we hadn't succeeded at first to start a family as we were enjoying being by ourselves and had a very busy life. But there comes a time, especially for a woman, when she feels that she will not be fulfilled until she has a child. So when the doctors told us that we were unlikely to have any children there was a time of bereavement for the family that we could not have. After a few months we began to talk about adoption, as we had seen a Christian adoption society advertised in a Christian magazine.

Having decided that we would like to adopt, we applied to the Adoption Society. We were asked to come for an interview and the Society sent someone to inspect our home. We were informed that the decision would be made at their next board meeting as to whether we were suitable people to adopt a child. The letter duly arrived to say that we had been accepted. The first hurdle was over. We knew from the interview that even after being accepted there might be a long wait –anything from one month to two years. They had informed us that many things were taken into consideration when placing a child – the physical characteristics, education and social background among others. The Society was a Christian organization, which meant that the mother had requested a Christian home for the placement of her child.

Six months later a letter arrived to say that there was a baby boy the Society thought suitable for us and could we pick him up in two weeks time? We were so excited. We had two weeks to get ready, so there was a scramble to buy all the equipment needed (we hadn't dared buy anything sooner just in case they changed their mind). Our families were excited too. We had told them that we were expecting a child, but we didn't know when it would arrive, after the Adoption Society had accepted us! They were all very supportive.

On the day we picked up our son there were feelings of elation and apprehension. Would we bond with the baby? What would he look like? Would we be able to cope, as we had not gone through the normal antenatal classes? We were shown into a small room with a baby in a cot and were left to ourselves to get to know him for a few minutes. There was an immediate bonding, as though the child were our own.

The baby immediately became part of our family, but we knew there were still some hurdles to overcome before he was officially ours. A few days after we picked him up we had to write officially to the authorities to say that we intended to adopt this child. We would then be given a date for a court hearing. We already had the consent from the baby's mother to take the child but she also had to sign a consent form for the adoption, and during the three months before the court hearing she could change her mind at any time. It was a difficult time, knowing that however much we loved him he could still be taken away. At the court hearing all the paperwork was in order and the judge signed the forms declaring that officially and in all respects our son was ours.

After the adoption went through we were encouraged to write and send a photograph of the baby to the mother through the Adoption Society, because she was not allowed to know who we were. We wrote of our delight in being able to cherish her son and to tell her how much we loved him. We received a lovely letter back from her saying how glad she was that he was part of our family.

Two years later we went through the same trauma, but this time with a beautiful baby girl. We often pray for the mothers of our children, particularly at birthdays when we know they will be thinking of them. Even though they will probably have families of their own, they will never be able to forget their first child.

Both our children knew from the first that they were adopted. As we sang and talked to them in their first months and years they were told the story of how they came to be part of our family and it became 'their special story'.

2. Early Infancy

I (and my husband) have a deep respect for, and maybe envy of, those who produce babies easily. Only one of our children's births could be classified as a normal delivery. One would have thought that the old adage that 'practice makes perfect' would have come into operation, but alas it was not so. It was as though I was working my way through the abnormal labour section of my obstetrics textbook, because each time the problem was different! But in the end, each time, a healthy baby was born. The hours that had gone before soon faded into insignificance. I don't regret any of these experiences because they have made it much easier to empathize with others and help them get things into perspective.

Those early days are a strange mixture of euphoria and weariness. The constant thing about babies is that they have a unique gift of turning a fairly orderly home into a scene of complete chaos. (Perhaps this was even more so in the days before disposable nappies, automatic washing machines, tumble driers, and central heating.) The first few days of coping on one's own with this tiny scrap of humanity who has the power to decide when (or even if) his/her parents eat and when (or even if) parents sleep can be quite daunting. It is very difficult to come to terms with the fact that there is no time off twenty-four hours a day and seven days a week – 'Will I ever survive for a month never mind for a year? What have we done? I just want to sleep. Perhaps an only child isn't such a bad idea after all!' – Those are all common thoughts in these first few, usually tearful, weeks of motherhood. There never seems to be any time between feeds. Housework passes into history and this week's dust piles on last week's dust, while the laundry basket reaches mountainous heights – unless someone comes to the rescue. There is always the tendency to feel that one is a hopeless mother and 'everyone else copes much better than me' – which is of course not true. Mothers who have easy deliveries probably regain strength much sooner than those of us who don't because they haven't known the prolonged physical effort, but they still have crazy hormones to cope with.

A baby's first smile somehow makes one feel that there is a response of approval – and an overwhelming pride in what has been achieved, which is out of all proportion to the event, sweeps over the mother – and father if he is there to witness this milestone! The household begins to settle into a new routine. One night the infant sleeps right through until morning and an anxious mum leaps out of bed convinced that a terrible tragedy has occurred. On discovering that all is well a thought comes that it would have been nice to know in advance so that one could fully appreciate the luxury.

Some children produce teeth with the minimum of fuss. Others, like ours, don't. I can remember feeling very annoyed on being assured by a female doctor on TV (who turned out to be single and childless) that teething was a natural process that didn't involve coughs and tears and nappy rash and soaking wet jumpers!

The great temptation in the first year of a first baby's life is to think that if only he/she was sitting up; on solid food; able to feed self; standing; walking; talking, then life would be much easier – because other little ones who do these things seem to be much easier to cope with. But crawling babies have a wonderful ability to find things that might hurt them and pull things over as they try to stand up. Babies who have started to pick up their own food have an uncanny habit of finding small things to put in their mouths other than food! It's better to learn to be content with the stage that your child is at. Every stage has more positives than negatives and every stage passes quickly (honestly!).

An editorial article in *US News* and *World Report* (August 97) emphasizes the importance of speaking to a young baby. The number of words that a child hears stimulates the development of complex connections in brain cells. The first three years of a child's life are vital in this process. Touching and holding, especially by the mother, are also vital in a baby's development. It is important to remember that the child listened to the mother's heartbeat and heard the mother's voice all the time while in utero. It is very important for a baby's security that a mother spends quantity time, not the 'quality time' so often spoken of, with her child. During such times a mother begins to sense if something isn't quite right in the baby's hearing or seeing or movements. Most of a mother's anxieties are groundless, but they still need to be eliminated. In these early days too, a baby begins to learn by the tone (not the volume) of a mother's voice the early ground rules for acceptable behaviour. It is very important that a baby is constantly affirmed, but it is also important that a baby who is about to become a toddler knows where the boundaries are. Eventually every charming child looks a parent straight in the eye and says, 'No'. This is the vital time for parents to agree on a code of discipline to which they themselves must be disciplined to adhere. Threats should not be made which are not followed by the promised action. Sometimes, towards the end of a tiring day, it can be easier to give in than to persist. Sometimes, towards the end of a tiring day, it is easier to sit and say 'no' than to get up and divert a child's attention away from a forbidden pursuit. The word discipline comes from the same Latin root as the word for a disciple – a pupil, a learner, a follower. Discipline should consist of more positive teaching than negative restrictions – but this takes time and patience and effort. A child learns more by example than by words alone.

3. *The Pre-school Years*

Until the 1960s these pre-school years ended with a child's fifth birthday. Now most children have begun in playgroups or nursery school by the time that they are three. By that time it is more than likely that the mother is back to 'ages' one and two with child number two! This is where life begins to get more complicated, but it's usually much easier second time around.

The pre-school years are what we mothers decide to make of them. I don't think that there are too many women who find these early years the most fulfilling stages of motherhood. It's such hard work to keep up with everything that needs doing, especially if sleep is in short supply. But the development of speech and motor skills that takes place in these years is miraculous, even although some are slower than others. It is probably easier to appreciate this as a grandparent with time to take note! Scribbles begin to become circles which gradually become people with eyes, nose, mouth, hair and ears. Arms issue from under the ears and legs are usually below the mouth! The volume of works of art that come home from playgroup onwards must be a benefit to the paper industry, but I sometimes wonder how many trees were sacrificed for our children's artistic endeavours!

These pre-school years may seem long with a first child, but the bonding which takes place in these years is irreplaceable, and the sense of satisfaction in knowing that all the early achievements of a child are largely the result of your input into their young lives makes being there with them and for them more than worth while.

4. *Early School Years*

When a child officially starts school, it's the first time that a mother and child are separated not by choice but by law. All of a sudden the five-year old who seemed so big, when compared to little brother or sister, seems so small and vulnerable. Some start school without any problems. For others it is a tearful separation. This only happened to us with one out of four. We wakened in the morning to floods of tears, we ate breakfast with tears, we drove (because of the tears) to school with tears, and we separated with hysterics! This went on for several weeks. It was all the result of his first introduction to the school's headmistress some weeks before, when the said lady took one look at our son and informed him that he wouldn't be allowed to come to her school in long trousers. At the time, unknown to us, he had thought, 'so I won't come!' For some reason he hated short trousers. There was no question of negotiation. When Miss—— spoke, her word was unbreakable law akin to the law of the Medes and the Persians! We had heard of her reputation before we got there, but since our son was normally a happy, friendly child we foresaw no problems. It was a complete personality clash that was awesome to behold! Fortunately, his first teacher was the daughter-in-law-to-be of my wonderful home help. Eventually, a state of uneasy truce prevailed and peace reigned in our household.

It's quite incredible to see the change in a child over these early months at school. Playground humour pervades the tea table, much to the amusement of younger members of the family. 'My teacher' becomes the final authority on everything! From then on it's a round of reading books and spellings, tables to be learned, parents' evenings and Christmas performances (for which costumes need making). By the time we had four children at four different schools (three of whom were very much performers), it took a great deal of organisation to fulfil all the church and school demands around Christmas.

Some mothers find it hard when the last child starts 'proper' school. For me it was the end of fifteen years of pre-school children. The daytime hours became an opportunity to become involved in a host of other things that had been on hold for many years. But by then we had two teenagers in the family!

5. *The Teenage Years*

This is the time when one is tempted to think that it was much easier when one's children were in bed by seven o'clock.

Memories are short! By God's grace, with much prayer, the co-operation of very committed youth leaders and an ability, at times, to see the funny side of things, we survived the roller coaster years of four teenagers. This is an emotionally draining time more than a time of physical effort. By this time endless food consumption and piles of laundry have become a way of life. This is the time when the telephone is permanently in use, bedrooms look like disaster areas with mouldy coffee mugs under beds and on window sills. It's the time when romances come and go with the resultant emotional upheavals into which everyone is drawn. Our oldest son once thanked us for allowing all of them 'to have their little teenage rebellions'. I suppose that compared with what some parents have gone through, they were very little, but they didn't seem so little at the time. When the first two had emerged into being stable young adults and were firmly rooted in a personal Christian commitment, we thought that we knew all there was to know about teenage years. When the younger two lads began to spread their wings, we realized that we were mistaken. Even the older two were appalled at the way things had moved on in the space of a few years. Every morning during these critical years I used to spend time in their bedrooms praying in the prayer language God gave me when I was baptized in the Holy Spirit some years before. When I prayed in English I found that I always ended up telling God what I thought he should be doing in their lives. When praying in tongues, I was able to commit them daily to God's care and protection, so that He would be able to do in them what He wanted to do. All four of our children were baptized as believers in their early teens. For our daughter, that meant a pretty straight course ahead in spiritual growth. Our sons never went away from God, but they did go off Christians who put spiritual pressure on them as sons of the manse. They all went through times of severe testing, or as our older son put it, 'their little rebellions', but by God's grace emerged much stronger in their faith.

Through these years their dad made sure that he concentrated on major issues as far as discipline was concerned. Major issues were to do with truthfulness and obedience. These were the non-negotiable areas laid down in their early years. Minor issues were things that we didn't like but, as another dad put it, 'didn't injure their health'. Things like clothes, length of hair, untidy bedrooms, taste in music came into this category. We knew that they crossed the boundaries in areas like under age smoking and alcohol consumption at times. I tended to get very upset and anxious, but Jim kept a very even keel and dealt only with known facts and not with the hearsay that some people regularly fed to us. The important thing was always to guard relationships and keep lines of communication open, even at times when they were skating on thin ice as far as the church fellowship was concerned.

Music plays a very important part in most young people's lives – a fact which my generation finds very hard to understand. When our daughter began going to a friend's house every Thursday night to do her homework, I discovered it was so that she could watch Top of the Pops. At that point I made a decision that I would watch it with her, and then with her brothers, and I continued to do so for many years. I reserved the right to say what I thought but was also prepared to hear why they liked certain bands. I read the words of the songs on record sleeves and expressed concern about some of the moral tone of these songs and the lifestyle of the people who sang them. It was, however, pointed out to me that composers like Chopin and Mozart didn't lead exemplary lives and Wagner was deeply involved in occult practices. I didn't appreciate the decibels issuing from bedrooms – especially when they were doing homework – and said so. I have to confess, however, that there were one or two tracks that I came to have a liking for as they were played evening after evening when they came in from school! This has continued to be the music of the younger generation, and to continually condemn it outright without trying to find out why they like it is not liable to help in building relationships.

Some of this music is evil and used for immoral and occult purposes. But some of it is completely neutral. There are Christians who are trying to break down the monopoly a godless society has on music. They do it by striving for excellence in musical performance and morality in lyrics sung. They need encouragement.

Teenage years are years when a mum being at home after school is so important. Teenagers may seem very confident and sometimes arrogant on the outside, but school is sometimes a very difficult and even dangerous place to be these days with strong peer pressure, a climate of low morality and easy availability of drugs. They tend to build a tough protective shell around themselves for protection. Home needs to be a place of safety and acceptance, a place of welcome and affirmation – but bricks and mortar don't do that at four o'clock after a difficult day. It's not usually until adult life that they get round to expressing their appreciation of a mother's presence. I can remember often the door opening and a voice calling 'mu-um'. When I replied 'yes, what do you want?' – 'Nothing, I just wondered where you were'. Many young people these days come home to a list of chores to be done instead of a welcoming cup of tea. I am not suggesting for a moment that young people should not have a regular part in household chores but it shouldn't be because mum is absent by choice, rather than necessity. On several occasions I have had young adults unburden themselves about how much they hated being 'latch-key' children. In none of these cases was it a case of necessity. They loved their mothers and had never told them how they had really felt. Their mother's employment certainly brought material advantages, but they would rather have had her presence.

It is very important in the years when young adults are emerging that we co-operate with God in the building of mature adults. Sometimes we try to be God in their lives and this is rejected. It is often better to feed them what I call digested Scripture instead of quoting scripture verses. What do I mean? A mother bird takes food and grinds it and feeds the young birds with half digested food. We need to take scripture and model its truth in our own lives and attitudes. They need to know that we pray for them when they don't want us to pray with them. A friend of ours once said, 'You can always talk to Jesus about someone when you can't talk to someone about Jesus.' I can remember being very challenged when I read in a book that we pray for our children and yet the minute they go out the door we almost expect them to walk into Satan's grasp. We need to learn to trust God and dismiss Satan's negative whisperings in our ears. Of course young people do silly things and stretch the boundaries, but then so did their parents. Some young people make a real mess of things and bring real heartache. It would be very unhelpful of me to make dogmatic statements about how to cope in such a situation, because I have never gone through the pain of such circumstances, but I do know that God does hear prayer even although His answers don't seem to come when or how we want them. Many people have given testimony to God's breakthrough into their rebellious lives because their parents continued to pray for them.

For parents this is a period of learning to begin to let go. The constant tendency is for young people to want their independence too soon and for parents, and particularly mothers, to want to hold on too long. But the letting go should be a learning process for teenager and parents. I can always remember being with a friend (also a minister's wife whose children were a little older than ours) when her son rushed in from school very excited. He said that ALL his friends were going to see a certain James Bond film and could he go too (in the 1960s a 'what would people say' thing for a son of the manse to be allowed to do!). My friend didn't say, 'Indeed you cannot', - which would have been my response! Instead she said that when his dad came home the three of them would talk about it. He was allowed to join his friends, but not until the reasons for their hesitations had been openly discussed. Many years later I was reminded of this when our teenage sons were very keen to watch a film on TV about the Vietnam war. We were in a houseparty with other Christian leaders (whose children were much younger than ours) who were opposed to the teenagers in the group being allowed to watch this film. Jim and one of the other parents suggested that the two of them would go to another room with the teenagers to watch the film – which was certainly very gory and contained a considerable amount of bad language but was true to life concerning a horrific war. About midnight that night our sons came to our bedroom with coffee cups in hand (as teenagers tend to do) to talk about war. Was there such a thing as a just war? Was pacifism the proper stance to take? They had real fears in their hearts that one day they would have to go to war – (it was just after the Falklands war). If we had not allowed them to see the film, as some of our colleagues thought, we would have lost a golden opportunity for them to voice their very real fears. If I hadn't had a flashback to that other manse kitchen when the question of watching this film arose I would probably have been part of the say 'no' group. Many times we had similar deep discussions in our bedroom at midnight when we were longing to go to sleep. It's all part of the process of bringing older young people to the place of making good decisions for themselves.

Our daughter and our oldest son were tremendously helpful in the teenage years of their two young brothers. Sometimes they showed wisdom far beyond their years in the way that they handled them. I can remember on several occasions being given good advice by them because they were much more aware of what was going on in the youth culture surrounding their brothers since they were now involved as leaders themselves. They had reached young adult years.

6. *Young Adults*

Young people are officially adult when they are eighteen. By this time they can drive cars, get married, go to war, and vote in elections. And yet they are still very vulnerable. This is a hard stage in mothering for many women. The vast majority of young adults in the area where we live go off to university at this age.

When the oldest child reaches this important stage there is a sense that an era of family life has come to an end. I found it harder to release our daughter into this stage of adult life that I did with her brothers. Perhaps it was because she is our only daughter. For me this meant that I was now the only female in the home for most of the year. Table-talk was now almost exclusively about sport, guitars, drums, and cars. As I have said earlier, I found it really hard to go into her empty bedroom. Edinburgh was a very long way away and we could not afford the train fare for mid-term visits. There was a sense that we weren't complete any more. It was with a great sense of relief that we heard that one of the first people she met in her hall of residence was a Christian, the daughter of missionaries in South America – their friendship has continued since then. I found it really hard every time we saw her off on the train to Edinburgh. It was just as well that I didn't know at that time that she would never really come back to live at home again. I am sure that she had her moments of homesickness, but she coped well. None of our sons went further than Nottingham and tended to come home for weekends from time to time, loaded with dirty laundry and with ravenous appetites and going back with clean clothes and half my store cupboard! It wasn't that they were any less loved or valued, or that it was any easier for them to adjust to being away from home; it was just that the first letting-go was the hardest.

One of the things that we learned very quickly was that they were not quite the same people that they had been when they came home for the first vacation. They tended to try to live their newly discovered adult independence within the family set-up. A new kind of consideration had to be learned (by both parent and offspring). Occasionally a fatherly word of correction still had to be spoken.

7. *Married Children*

The gradual process of letting go which began in teenage years must now come to completion. Another person now comes first in the adult child's life and that must be fully accepted. The old adage about losing a son and gaining a daughter, or for that matter losing a daughter and gaining a son, is absolutely true. Evelyn Christenson wrote a book called, '*Gaining through losing*'. It's a good Biblical principle – losing life to find it and giving up in order to gain. In relationships with married children, the old relationship must be given up in order for the new one to flourish. When a child is born the umbilical cord is cut soon after birth, and the child's life independent of the mother's body begins. When a child marries there is an emotional umbilical cord that has to be cut in order for the new relationship to grow and mature. In doing so the gains far outnumber the losses. Maternal love can flourish towards two instead of one, but must never be a possessive, controlling love but a true *agape* love – a love devoid of self-seeking.

When all is well in children's marriages it is easy to stand back, but if a marriage is under stress the mother's heart feels the pain of that unhappiness. But parental interference doesn't help in such situations. We always need to be there for our children in times of crisis, not to take sides but to be a catalyst for healing. I knew before I married that my mother would not be a listening ear for any complaints I had about my husband, but I knew that she would always be there for both of us in times of crisis.

It never gets any easier to cope with a child's illness, no matter when it occurs. It's hard when they are little, but it's just as hard when they are adult and are no longer living at home. There was one memorable day when I was in our daughter's home in London looking after our three-year-old granddaughter because her mother was in hospital with little sister, who was suffering from an undiagnosed illness that caused her to lose consciousness quite suddenly. The phone rang. It was our son who was living alone two hundred miles away. He was obviously in need of immediate medical attention. All I could do was to instruct him to phone for an ambulance! I felt torn apart. Needless to say I made another phone call to my husband who, as soon as it was possible, got in his car and headed northwards.

'Once a mum, always a mum' is the conclusion I have come to. Being a mum is a whole range of differing relationships that continue through life. Being a mum is character building. Being a mum can bring deep sorrow but also great joy. Being a mum is hard work most of the time, but brings great rewards. Why does society try to rob women of the importance of the God given task – and then wonder why there are so many juveniles involved in crime when mum is absent from the home?

P.S. – *What about grandchildren?*

Becoming a grandmother is an enormously exciting event. Grandchildren are a wonderful bonus and a great source of joy and fun – but one soon understands why God, in His wisdom, set a time limit on child bearing years. My father used to love to see all six of us arrive, but his pleasure on our arrival was far exceeded by his pleasure on the morning of our departure! We now know how he felt. It was a question of 'peace, perfect peace with loved ones far away' – to misquote an old hymn!

Our responsibility to our grandchildren is to love them and pray for them and provide the little extras. All other responsibility belongs to their parents, as it once belonged to us for them. The relationship between a child and grandparents is a very special one and should be treasured.

What is meant by a 'working mother'?

It has already been noted that we are all, men and women, meant to live full and useful lives. But is a mother only a working mother when she earns money? According to government propaganda and media hype it would certainly seem that this is so. There has been more than a little inference from recent government statements suggesting that a woman who chooses to devote most of her time and energy to home making and child-rearing is a drain on the nation's prosperity. Such women are not regarded as working mothers. I certainly don't feel that I have never worked! In actual fact Jim has always regarded his earnings as our earnings that we both work for in different ways.

My part has always been to free him to do what God has called him to do, but at the same time fulfilling the purposes of God for my own life in, and out, of the home. No account is taken of the unpaid commitments undertaken by homemakers which have benefited society and which have involved caring for others, especially the old, the young and the vulnerable. This work is still carried on in church and community by an ageing few. For this reason there is an increasing financial burden on the state to carry out the work once done by good neighbours and friends, who managed to do it without books of regulations and yards of red tape.

It's not that there is anything inherently wrong in earning money – far from it, but what it may be right to do when children are older is seldom the best choice when they are young. There are some important questions that need to be asked before launching out into work outside the home.

Why do I want to do this or indeed why am I already doing it? Is this the right time in my family's life? Will this bring added pressure to my husband's work life? – (perhaps not a popular consideration today). What is my motivation for doing this? Pressure to conform to a secular society's demands? Economic pressure – real or perceived? Fear of falling behind on a career ladder? Purely for self-fulfilment? Is it really going to benefit family life – not just economically?

But the most important question of all – Is this what God wants me to do at this particular time? If you are sure that the answer to that is 'yes', having taken note of all the other questions, then no-one will suffer and everyone will benefit. This was the key to Mrs Proverbs working life – everyone – not just she – benefited by her home-based business.

1. *The Pressure of Society*
Many young mums have been indoctrinated, if not directly then certainly indirectly, by American feminist Betty Freidan's pronouncements on women who choose to be homemakers – 'brainwashed by femininity' and 'not fully human'. The

constant inference which has been taken up by many others in public life is that those who choose to be at home while their children are young are bound to suffer from boredom, low self-esteem and atrophy of brain cells. If this is believed then it may well become true. My personal experience was that, in the days when all our children were in bed by eight o'clock, I did more reading and thinking than at any time since. Jim was out most evenings and when he came in from his evening's work he was frequently bombarded with questions – mostly theological – and issues for discussion. I think that sometimes he wished that my brain cells had atrophied! This whole idea stems from research on a woman's IQ when going through the early years of child rearing. Evidently some research has shown that a young mother's IQ tends to drop during this time because of lack of stimulation. Maybe my IQ did drop – I don't know – but one thing that I am sure of is that my wisdom increased greatly. I don't think that God is too concerned about IQ, but He is certainly concerned that we grow in wisdom and in knowledge of Him. When all around are suggesting that the job you are doing is unimportant and undemanding of course self-esteem will suffer. A very interesting statistic has recently emerged that there are more nannies than car workers in Britain! It seems that to look after other people's children has no effect on self-esteem, but looking after one's own children has! Don't give in to secular society's opinions. Instead realize that the job that you are doing in nurturing and moulding your children is of vital national importance. Only God knows what plans He has for each child in the future – every person who has made a real impact for good in society was once a child. How can this job be unimportant? Boredom comes from lack of realization of the importance of these early years in a child's development. Being willing to read the same story for the tenth time is of value in brain development, so stick with it!

Our labour saving gadgets do release a lot of time that homemakers of a previous generation did not have. This has been highlighted by the recent TV programme about life in a late Victorian household. Housekeeping then was certainly labour intensive. The programme demonstrated very clearly the inability of a twenty-first century, highly intelligent woman to cope with what was the daily routine of people like my mother who, I am sure, did not go around all the time with a glum face, and whose culinary achievements were probably very much superior to those of today. But if less effort and ingenuity is needed in modern housekeeping, there is no less time and energy required in looking after young children. Indeed the opposite may be true in a society where young children have to be constantly supervised for their own safety.

A few months ago I was in a company where a young mum was heard to say that, since her youngest child had started school, it was time that she found a job. Why did she feel that this was a logical conclusion to come to? It could, of course, have been a right decision in her case, but I tend to feel that society's pressure more than any other reason led her to this decision. She was already using her free time well in being available to other young mums and as a listening ear to people with problems. The pressure of society alone is not a sufficient reason to opt for paid work outside the home. Immediately paid employment begins, a tension of loyalty is created. A woman is caught between the contractual requirements of an employer and the emotional and physical requirements of the family. The danger is that family always has to take second place –'he who pays the piper calls the tune'.

2. *Economic Pressures*
There are two kinds of economic pressure. They could be summed up by saying 'greed not need' and 'need not greed'.

a) Greed not need – or the pressure of materialism
TV adverts and glossy magazine pictures of clothes, home furnishings, gadgets, cars, holidays etc. come to us daily without

stepping outside the home. Every year there is a bigger and better shopping mall somewhere. Not a week passes but another offer of a credit card or a bank loan comes through the letterbox. Every one is an enticement to get into more and more debt. Luxuries are portrayed as necessities. Children as well as adults are targets.

When we were setting up home the parental advice that we were given was to 'cut your coat according to your cloth'. Jim went to his first pastorate just after we had both graduated. He had saved what seemed to us a large amount of money by saving most of what he had earned in summer jobs during his student years. We had, in our imaginations, completely furnished the manse that was to be our first home with these savings. When we came to the wonderful day of going out to spend this money, we found that there was a large disparity between the coat we wanted and the cloth we had! In actual fact we were able to furnish one room; buy a carpet and curtains and four dining room chairs for another; buy a bed and curtains for the main bedroom; buy a kitchen cabinet for the totally unfitted kitchen; and a carpet for the stairs. That left one bedroom and the study (except for a pile of books) completely unfurnished! We had to swallow our pride and gratefully accept everything that anyone was willing to give or lend. One year later wedding presents made a great contribution to the necessities and comforts of the household. In fact towels, tablecloths and teaspoons we had in abundance! Looking back, we are both thankful that neither easy terms nor credit cards were an option. When there was no money in the bankbook, there was no money. We never lacked food or warmth, but we never had anything left over at the end of the month.

If the economic pressures are due to a drive to spend beyond your means, then it is highly unlikely that a mother's earnings when there are young children to be cared for will solve the problem, because you will be forever raising your sights to another level. The fact that a mother's earnings make it possible to buy outrageously expensive trainers, or video games, or new bicycles (as opposed to second-hand) is merely passing on your own acquisitiveness to the next generation. It is not doing a child a favour to put a TV and/or a PC in his/her bedroom. The effect of this is another way of splintering a family that already spends little time together. It is very hard for children when parents cannot provide what some of their friends have (beware the blackmail of 'everyone has one but me', whatever that 'one' might be). On many occasions we had to say 'no' to our children and sometimes it really hurt us to have to say so. On other occasions we went on to say that even if we could afford it they still wouldn't have whatever it was that they wanted. Our middle son was about ten years old when he decided that he wanted to learn to play the drums and could he have a drum kit! It's not difficult to discern what our response was. It was a frequent item in his prayers at night. He regarded it as a direct answer to his prayers that Roy Castle, who with his family had recently come to worship in Gold Hill, invited him to play his drums in his practice room behind his garage. Roy recognized that John had indeed a real natural talent that he began to develop. At this point we agreed with the lad that for every five pounds he could save we would add five. From that moment on he started saving pocket money, birthday money and every other money gift that came his way. He stopped spending money on sweets on Saturdays – a major miracle! After a few months Roy heard of a bargain drum kit, which he volunteered to buy and store for us (unknown to John). Eventually we decided that the savings had reached a level where we could negotiate the snare drum, then the base drum and high-hat cymbal. One day he came home from school to find a complete starter drum kit set up in a back room in the manse. That was a moment to remember for both him and us. The look of absolute delight on his face was unforgettable. We have no doubt that that drum-kit meant much more to him than it would if we had gone out and bought it for him a year or more before.

Never be pressurized by a child's emotional blackmail. In the long run your child will realize that your presence in the home was of much more value than this year's latest (but next year's discarded and out of date) video game or other toy.

b) Need not greed – providing the necessities
Young couples today face enormous financial pressures which have nothing to do with keeping up appearances but have everything to do with keeping a roof over their heads and feeding and clothing their children without getting into debt.

We never had to face the pressure of mortgage repayments when our children were young because the house came with the job. Our problem arose from the fact that the kind of house we lived in was completely out of proportion to the salary we were paid. When we lived in Scotland we were expected to meet the total cost of heating and lighting. A large proportion of our monthly salary went on keeping a large stone built house warm –without central heating. We made the mistake of following the custom of the people who lived around us in that we ran up monthly grocer's, butcher's and milk bills (before the supermarket era had arrived). This was very convenient. Meat ordered by phone by 9am was delivered by 10.30am at the latest. Our grocer collected our weekly order on Tuesday and it was delivered on Thursday. Greengrocer's and fish vans came round weekly. It meant that I never had to carry heavy shopping. My daily outings (on foot) with the children were for fresh air and exercise rather than shopping. Two hundred yards away at the end of the street was a little Post Office, where I cashed my family allowance and made extra purchases when necessary. But bills have a habit of catching up. By the time the monthly bills had been paid and money put aside for coal and electricity and our Sunday offerings, there was very little left for clothes for the children. Clothes for ourselves didn't come high in our list of priorities, that was not easy for either of us. We had a wonderful children's clothing exchange programme in operation with another manse family who lived at the other side of Scotland. I made most of our daughter's clothes and some of my own. My parents and sister often bought extra items of clothing for the children.

We were dependent for anything else like household equipment and holidays on extra money Jim managed to earn.

One evening we went out for supper with some church members of our own age group. There was an American couple present who were speaking about tithing their income (giving God 10 per cent). A Scots woman said that they could never afford to tithe – a statement with which we could identify but didn't say so. The American wife said, 'We couldn't afford not to'. This really struck home to both of us. We began to talk together and pray about the way in which we handled our finances. The first thing we did was to lay aside a tenth of our next salary before paying any bills. The amazing thing was that we made ends meet without cutting down on anything! Shortly afterwards, while in hospital recovering from an emergency Caesarean birth, I read a biography of Hudson Taylor, the great missionary to China. More challenge was to come. Not only did he tithe, but he sometimes gave away almost all that he had when he met someone whose need was greater than his! We learned that tithing is only the beginning of giving. Hudson Taylor had learned that God is no man's debtor and that He (not a human employer) is the provider of all our needs. We resolved that from then on we would not run up bills. We would never buy anything that we could not afford to pay for there and then. We would honour God with our resources and look to Him as our Provider according to His promise in scripture which says that, 'God will supply all our needs according to His riches in Christ Jesus' (Philippians 4:19). Our responsibility is to be good stewards of all that He gives us. Every so often we would go through a period of having to count every penny. Sometimes, especially when our lads were growing up, I had to spend the last week of the month's food money on unexpected expenses, and yet when it came to the time we still had food on the table. At these times we always had a lesson to learn – had we been ignoring the Holy Spirit's prompting about some area in our lives or had we not been as generous as we might have been towards others? In the midst of these times, however, we always knew that God keeps His promises and can be trusted to provide what was needed. At other times we have felt like God's spoiled children when we have had unexpected gifts or holidays and outings – but most of all in the provision of our own lovely home. It is important to note, however, that we have both been willing to work hard in the work that God has called us to do.

It seems as though many Christians have never realized that God is our provider, not just for pastors and missionaries, but for all who are in the place of God's appointing – including the professional and business world – doing what He has purposed for them to do. Real financial pressure is certainly a good motive for working outside the home, but the timing might be wrong. Unless there is good family support in caring for little ones it will only add to the burden instead of removing it. Sometimes, however, circumstances can change with dramatic suddenness – literally overnight – redundancy, death of a husband, failure of a business venture, a broken marriage, a disabling illness. All of these bring not just economic pressure but complete upheaval of the lives of everyone in the family.

Here are the stories of two women, one of redundancy, the other of the tragic death of a much-loved husband.

Linda's Story

'Steve was made redundant without warning on 21 July 1992. At that time, Mark was nineteen and had just completed the second year of a three year course at university; Nick was seventeen and coming to the end of his Lower sixth year at school; Andrew was nine – at the end of Year 6. I was already working eighteen hours a week over three days as a physiotherapist in the NHS.

Initially, my feelings were of shock and deep sadness for Steve. The next day we took stock. Financially, we could manage for probably three months. As we sat outside on the grass in a numb, bewildered state, we became aware of several sparrows flying around and into a nearby bush and making a lot of noise (Matthew 10:31). From that time on we were very aware that the Lord would provide for our family and us. I considered working full-time, but Steve would not commit himself to being a house-husband. He committed himself fully to finding another job and taking any work that came his way. I did not feel capable of doing two full-time jobs and so did not increase my hours. I felt it important to keep the home running as smoothly as possible.

The boys were all aware of our situation and were very supportive emotionally and in prayer. We told them about the job applications as they were made, and also when the rejection letters came back, and later the interviews. To me, work was an escape from the situation at home. I had tremendous support from my colleagues. It was also an aspect of my life that had not changed. I found it very hard to have Steve at home on my non-working days. My routine was thoroughly disrupted and I had to make many adjustments. Steve had no problem with my going out to work as we were thankful for the income it provided and he too was working, at finding a new job. There were times of fear about the future but then the sparrows would appear again. There were times when I felt low and would find support from a close friend because it would not be fair to expect support from Steve.

The Lord was faithful to us as a family all through the two years that Steve was without full-time employment. We supported each other and put our trust in the Lord. Our church family were fantastic in their support in prayer, in acts of kindness and words of encouragement.'

The way in which this whole family handled these two very difficult years brought great challenge to those of the church family who knew them – and gave honour and demonstrated clearly the faithfulness of God the provider to all of us, not just to them.

Ruth's Story

'I was told that Steve had died following a second heart attack at 4am on 8 February 1996, the day before he was due to return home'.

Ruth's immediate reactions were numbness and nausea, of unreality and inability to cry at first. These were followed by feelings of bewilderment about what to do first. Steve ran a removal business. There were people who needed to know that he was no longer there to fulfil the promised contracts – other firms to be contacted.

Ruth had held down responsible jobs in her profession of nursing before she married Steve and before Daniel was born in 1988. She had helped Steve to get his struggling business going and had to come to terms with a considerable drop in financial resources. She had never regretted this. But now Steve had gone and with him the business and their income – what was she to do? She tells of being overwhelmed by the caring and generosity of the church family in those early days – food, flowers, cards, companionship were all freely given. Gifts of money, help with sorting out the mortgage, selling the business, filling in endless forms, sorting out tax, was all willingly given. Other fathers came alongside Daniel to do the things he had done with his dad. Willing volunteers did odd jobs. In the end, though, she had to make decisions for their long-term future. She decided not to go back to her demanding profession. She says, 'I had no desire to work long hours to afford luxuries which I could do without, as it would mean paying other people to look after Daniel, which I wanted to avoid. Motherhood is the most rewarding job in the world.' Instead she chose to use her musical gifting in playing her harp at wedding receptions – and she became lollipop lady at the local school. These have brought in enough to meet their needs at this time.

These are only two of the circumstances that overtake people unexpectedly, but they do illustrate that God is faithful. These two women faced their circumstances with great courage. Neither of them allowed themselves to wallow in self-pity and say 'Why us?' or 'Why me?'. Both had very good excuses to return to their profession full-time, but both of them chose to hold fast and keep family security as a top priority.

3. What about my career?
Circumstances have changed a lot since I was asking myself that question. Now it is much easier for women to tailor their professional commitments to family life. Retraining programmes and refresher courses are available when (and if) the right time comes.

But what do we mean by this word career that is dangled before young people now? For many years doctoring, nursing, teaching, the ministry, missionary work and administering the law were regarded as vocations into which people went with a desire to serve and care for others. But now almost all of these are seen as careers among many others, which demand higher, and higher financial rewards as people climb the career ladder. The word 'my' seems to fit in well with the career concept. There is a sense of personal aggrandizement rather than a desire to be of service. Young women (as well as young men) are indoctrinated at school with the necessity of finding a career. The equal opportunity concept almost forces young women to think that if they are not really interested in being 50 per cent of the student body and then 50 per cent of the workforce they are letting the side down. The message given by society is that self-esteem and self-worth depend on a person's goals and the achieving of these goals. Success is measured by kudos gained and finance accrued. Little attention is paid to the price a family has paid in broken relationships in the process.

The Bible has a different message to give. A person's self-worth and self-esteem are found in understanding who we are in God, what Jesus has done at the cross, and our response of obedience. God is more interested in 'why' than 'what' we are doing. He has a broad plan for each of our lives. There are some basic features common to each one of us but different for man and woman because he has 'hard-wired' us differently. Each one of us is, in another sense, completely unique with gifts and abilities which God has given us to use in a way which is glorifying to Him and will bring blessing to those around us. As we have already noted, God is more concerned with growth in wisdom, which is related to knowing God's heart, than the acquiring of knowledge, which can bring good or evil. God needs His people in all walks of life and it is certainly His purpose that His people should be represented at the top of their professions, in boardrooms, in government, in industry, in the media and in sport, but this should never be at the expense of neglecting children or other family responsibilities. Neither should it be for pure self-aggrandizement. The Bible teaches that God's evaluation of success is very different from ours. No matter what we do in life, we should be there because that's where God wants us – to be salt and light in society.

The fact that a woman has done professional training does not mean that the main focus of her life should be any different from a woman who has had no such opportunity. Marriage and motherhood mean that such training will be used differently from the woman who has no children and who has never married.

When I handed 'my career' back to God to use as He wanted, I knew that, from then on, it didn't matter what people thought. The word 'my' was removed from the whole issue. All I had to do from then on was to listen to what God was saying. It is highly unlikely that God would work it out for everyone in the same way as He did for me – as I have already said, each one of us is unique. But I have known several women who have persisted in going on in professional life regardless of the stage of family life they were at. The result has been added stress for everyone in the family and a weakening of family bonds in later life. I also know many women who have waited until the time was right and have given many profitable years in a professional capacity without adding stress to anyone in the family. God's timing is always perfect. We have already noted that to run ahead of God or to lag behind Him does not bring peace. A friend once said to me that what a person has to fight to get, they have to fight to keep – and this would seem to be confirmed over and over again in observing families where a woman persists in putting personal fulfilment before the needs of her husband and her family because she feels she has won the right to do so.

But there are some women whom God wants out in society, either on a voluntary or earning basis, who are not willing to be moved out of their comfort zone. We all need to be open to God to change the direction of our lives. I can think of no better person to be teaching children with learning difficulties than a mother who has agonized over her own son's dyslexia. Women who have reared children and have experience of life have much to contribute to the nursing of sick people. A friend of mine decided to return to nursing part time after her children went to university. She did so with fear and trembling, even after attending a refresher course. She very soon realized that she had much more to give to patient care than she had had when she was young. She was often appalled by the cavalier attitude of some young nurses as they dealt with patients. They had plenty of head knowledge and were exceedingly efficient, but lacked the understanding which is gained by being a patient and also by being involved pastorally in families whose loved ones are sick and have eventually died. A university friend came back to this country with her husband after a lifetime of service in a missionary situation. They could have 'retired' to some idyllic spot, but chose instead to settle in a city area where they are surrounded by the Asian people whom they had served for so long. My friend has given many hours to these people whose language she speaks as she works in a local G.P. surgery. Both became school governors to represent the people amongst whom they had worked.

There is no more secure place to be than in the place of God's appointing, fulfilling His purposes. If at this time His place for you is at home nurturing some of those who may become future leaders in church or state, or who will become ordinary citizens upholding standards of good behaviour, don't despise that calling.

A Woman in the Family –

In concluding these chapters on a woman in her family I want to quote the observations of three women of different ages, two American and one Irish.

Mary Kenny

Mary Kenny is an Irish journalist who has written articles for *The Daily Telegraph* and the *Express*. In the article quoted she updates an article that she wrote for *Good Housekeeping* magazine twenty years before. This article appears in the 75th Birthday edition of that magazine (*GH* October 97).

'I now look back on my children's babyhood with such a sense of nostalgia and yearning, but I know at the time I was often too busy rushing around trying to organize a busy, busy working life in London with motherhood to actually enjoy them. I understand working mothers who say, 'Oh, my children are much better off with their nanny/mothers help/child minder/at the crèche' because I said these things too. My kids don't seem to have sustained any lasting damage – fingers crossed – from the chaos of their upbringing (my younger son recently described his childhood quite cheerfully as chaotic but loving) but I think I lost out.

Sometimes I wish I had some of these hours back again, lovely summer days with babies round me in my mother's garden in Ireland – days I would break off to fly to, say, Manchester for some dumb TV programme that everyone has long forgotten. I now see that I overestimated the value of work and independence and I understand more important things, love, family life, how children grow. This came to me when visiting a graveyard touched by the number of graves that remembered devotedly 'The best mum in the world – always in our thoughts', and struck by the notion that seldom is one lovingly remembered for being chief executive or a brilliant sales rep.'

Later in the article she goes on to comment on 'the Pollyannaish' plans of the present labour government for support of working mothers as no solution to a 'dilemma which won't go away' because it's a human problem of choices and relationships. 'Choice was the big word in our generation, but choice means consequences, and if you choose one thing, you reject another. We have to understand that and stop the wishful-thinking fantasy that, with just another trick of the loop, society can somehow make it possible for us to have it all. You cannot have it all – that is the human condition.' She goes on to commend the educational opportunities open to women and the opportunities that that brings, 'but I am saddened to see so much energy being given over to the problem of how mothers can, in effect, get rid of their children. The focus of nursery schools is often down to that, yet young children only benefit from short periods at nursery school and it's no substitute for the continuous love of one particular person in their lives who does not abandon them....Some forms of childcare employed by career parents I now see as actually cruel – crueller than the moderate smack child experts recommend making illegal.'

Meghan Cox Gurdon

Meghan Cox Gurdon is a young American journalist. She was brought up by a feminist working mother and was well indoctrinated by Betty Friedan's view on homemaking. She describes how she and her college friends laughed at the whole idea of being a homemaker – to them it was 'embarrassingly retrograde'.

In an article in the *Women's Quarterly* (Spring 1998) she writes, 'Well now, how to admit this? Reader, I grew up and became a housewife.' In her lengthy article she describes her life in the early days of marriage and motherhood when she worked full time as a foreign correspondent for radio while her daughter was cared for by a full-time nanny. It was when she was six months pregnant with her second child, when she got caught up in a nasty riot situation between Protestants and Catholics in Ireland, that she began to think that maybe there was another way to spend her life. "This is no place for you," a policeman in riot gear called out to me looking pointedly at my figure of six months and counting. There was a time when I would have resented such paternalistic meddling but not that day. Sudden images of broken glass, plastic bullets and weeping children began flashing through my mind. What on earth was I doing? Another bottle splintered near my head. I made a loud joke about needing a maternity-style flak jacket and scuttled away to safety. That day marked the beginning of full-time-wife-and-motherhood for me although it was not until my son was born later that fall that I finally stopped being a foreign correspondent.'

The transition from being a full-time professional woman to being a full-time wife and mother was not an easy one. 'It was bleak midwinter and we were living in hotels' (because her husband's new job had taken them back to the USA from England), 'my husband was preoccupied with his new job. My son was still tiny and my figure consequently, was still dumpy. All these factors contributed to unexpected feelings of aimlessness and envy. It hurt my pride to push a pram along streets crowded with striding, purposeful, briefcase-wielding women my own age. So awful was my sense of diminished social status that I began to put a spin on my activities. "Oh, I'm a radio journalist", I'd say "on extended maternity leave." Then there was the practical challenge of using up time I would ordinarily have spent on the phone, at the computer, on a deadline, or on a plane. I found myself compiling absurd lists of chores (buy milk, do laundry) so that I could have the pleasure of striking them out, one by one, thus stimulating the sense of progress which enlivens a working person's day. I hadn't bargained on the boredom – or rather what initially felt like boredom – of spending all day with small volatile people who are not interested in foreign affairs and need a lot of feeding. But slowly – shock of all shocks! – with dawning happiness I began to learn how to be wife and a mother, not just during an hour of 'quality time' after work but all the time...Of the two dozen housewives I know best, all but one has a minimum of a bachelor's degree. Most of us left successful professional careers after our children were born, and most of us are in our thirties.

During our coffee mornings – yes we do meet for coffee – we talk politics as much as we do infant feeding schedules.' She goes on to describe the incredulity and criticism of some of her friends – and her mother who feels that her daughter is now left 'by the wayside'. 'We new housewives have to get that idea out of people's heads. We are not on the periphery of society. We are at the centre of it. It's ludicrous to believe that an educated woman is less interesting and somehow marginalized because she doesn't bring home a paycheck. It took feminists just two decades to destroy the public pride and the private satisfaction that many women used to draw from the domestic sphere. It wasn't men who reproached women for 'giving up' or who purse their lips resentfully at the very mention of our occupation. Let's stop this nonsense. We have nothing for which to apologize and a great deal with which to exult ... We need to show our daughters how admirable and richly rewarding it can be not to spend all day at the office.'

Dorothy Patterson

Dorothy Patterson is a theology graduate of New Orleans Theological Seminary who continued to study Greek and Hebrew and earned money part-time while completing a Masters Degree although already married. She continued to hold down a full time job while still breast-feeding her first baby because her husband had not completed his studies. She says, 'I can see that my first and freshest energies were devoted to professional pursuits away from home. When we moved to Arkansas a void in my life came to the forefront. My theological training seemed a waste for the task of motherhood before me. In the midst of this frustrating time I turned to the Lord. I determined in my daily quiet time to read through the Bible systematically with a new purpose: to determine God's message for me personally as a woman, a wife and a mother. This experience became the catalyst for my life and ministry.'

At the end of a lengthy essay entitled, 'The High calling of Wife and Mother in Biblical Perspective', she sums up the challenge of full-time home making in these words. 'Home-making – being a full-time wife and mother – is not a destructive drought of usefulness, but an overflowing oasis of opportunity; it is not a dreary call to contain one's talents and skills but a brilliant catalyst to channel creativity and energies into meaningful work; it is not a rope for binding one's own productivity in the market place, but reins for guiding one's posterity in the home; it is not repressive restraint of intellectual prowess for the community, but a release of wise instruction to your own household; it is not the bitter assignment of inferiority to your person, but the bright assurance of the ingenuity of God's plan for the complementarity of the sexes; especially as worked out in God's plan for marriage; it is neither the limitation of gifts available nor stinginess in distributing the benefit of these gifts, but rather the multiplication of a mother's legacy to the generations to come and the generous bestowal of all God meant a mother to give to those He entrusted to her care.'

Dorothy Patterson says of the Book of Proverbs, 'No other book is more saturated with home and family and the relationships therein. No other book has more to say to women specifically.'

12

A Woman in the Family of God

What lesson could we possibly learn from Mrs Proverbs about the role of women in the church today?

She is a reminder that God began with a family. Worship was a family activity before people were gathered together to worship, and this was obviously a worshipping family where God had his rightful place. It was known in the community where she lived that she was a woman who honoured and feared God, a woman who was wise and who gave good counsel. She was a woman who brought honour to her husband by her attitudes and her actions. She was a helper par excellence. But she could never have been the woman she was if her husband had not also been a man who treated his wife in a way that brought honour to God. This little cameo is, I believe, a picture of man/woman relationships as God intended them to be. Each played a different part that brought benefit not only to their own family but to the community. There is no evidence here of domination and defiance, of a competitive spirit, or of role reversal. This man had not allowed the tendency to sexism that is part of a man's fallen nature to have any part in his attitude towards his wife. He brought out the best in her and she in turn behaved towards him with Godly deference.

A great deal of political energy has been deployed in the Western world in the latter half of the twentieth century in an attempt to stamp out sexist attitudes and actions towards women. But all over the world sexism still exists. No matter how many laws are passed it will continue to exist because it is a symptom of manhood's fallen nature. No law has ever succeeded in changing that – not even the laws given by God through Moses. Wherever men try to dominate and crush there will always be a reaction by women who have been the victims of such attitudes. Sadly what is true in the secular world is also true in the family of God. Many God-fearing men have been taught by example and instruction that it is their God-given right to rule over women. The result has been that, in many sections of the family of God throughout history, women have been undervalued and their natural and spiritual gifts have been suppressed by arrogant and dominating men. Although they profess to have been made new men in Christ, they have continued to behave towards women with the same attitude that exists in secular society. As I have noted more than once before no such instruction was given to the man whom God created perfect. God only warned the woman that it would be so as a consequence of her part in disobeying God's instructions.

At the other end of the scale there are Christian men today who have taken up the feminist cause and spend a significant amount of time and energy apologizing for being men, thus abandoning their God-given leadership to appease the aspirations of women who are reacting against the tyranny of sexist domination.

And so the pendulum swings from one extreme to the other, while somewhere in the middle lies the truth, which is not a compromise of extremes but is, in fact, the narrow way spoken of by Jesus (who is the Truth) and demonstrated by him when he lived on earth. In a world of compromise and tolerance, Christian men and women should portray a different way of thinking and behaviour instead of blending like chameleons with their surroundings.

One of the passages of scripture which has constantly confronted me over the years of thinking through this whole vast subject of what it means to be a woman is at the beginning of Romans 12, where I have been challenged not to be conformed to the pattern of the world but to be transformed by the renewing of my mind. The Greek word used for transform is *metamorphoo*, the word from which we get the word metamorphosis. This describes the change that makes a tadpole become a frog or a caterpillar become a butterfly. It is not a superficial, patch-up repair, but a complete transformation. I have been part of a congregation more than once when the preacher has issued the challenge to be a butterfly and not a chameleon! The mind change that is being spoken of is the same mind change as that written in the letter written by Paul to the Christians at Philippi which, in the King James (AV) version of the Bible says, 'Let this mind be in you which was also in Christ Jesus.' In these passages we are not being challenged to change our opinions about certain things but to be willing to undergo major mind surgery so that we have the same attitude to people and situations that Jesus had. To use another metaphor, it is as though an old tape recording has been completely wiped clean, so that the mind is ready to record 'the mind which was in Christ Jesus'. A more modern translation says, 'Your attitude should be the same as that of Christ Jesus' (Philippians 2:5 NIV).

What is the mind of Christ?

Many years ago now an American theological college lecturer, whom we met as a result of an exchange programme in which our church was involved, gave several lectures on the subject of 'The mind of Christ'. He said some things which the Holy Spirit has brought back to the forefront of my mind during times of inner conflict or when there has been conflict amongst God's family – the church.

The first challenge is in the area of wisdom. The Bible teaches that there are two kinds of wisdom (James 3:13-18). The world's wisdom has its root in selfish desire and selfish ambitions (an outcome of Genesis 3 where the forbidden fruit was eaten?), and leads ultimately to the mind becoming a battleground where envy and strife flourish and the Truth is replaced by our own perceived truth, or the Truth is even denied. Sadly this is not an unusual happening in the lives of individual Christians or in churches the world over. By contrast, the wisdom that 'comes from heaven' is characterized by the absence of conflict. All the qualities that come from receiving God's wisdom are totally compatible with each other: love, joy, peace, patience, kindness, goodness, faithfulness, gentleness, self-control all flow in perfect harmony. Peace, like all the other qualities, is a positive quality – not just a lack of strife.

There have been three major occasions in my adult life (and many minor ones) when I have known deep inner conflict which has led to looking to human wisdom rather than to God. I have written about two of these, but the third was much more recent. When Jim stepped aside from the main leadership role in Gold Hill and the word 'retirement' was on everyone's lips, I thought that life was going to be very different. The pressure of pastoral concerns and church politics, the mounting awareness of the responsibility of teaching the Word of God on a Sunday morning which meant that his concentration was focused elsewhere for most of Saturday, meetings on six nights out of seven (which only occasionally involved us both together), the phone which always rang just as we were about to eat (in spite of an ex-directory number) the burden of accepting responsibility for all that went wrong – all this was at an end.

In the months that followed, Jim kept rehearsing all these differences to me, but all I knew was that I was at home alone even more than I had been during the children's growing up years, and for longer periods of time – most weekends and sometimes during the week too. When he withdrew from local leadership we both felt that it was right that I withdrew from all the local church ministries in which I had been involved. I suppose a form of bereavement had set in. The old enemy of self-pity settled on me once more. It just wasn't fair – why couldn't Jim just retire like others had done. I had thought that we would have more time to do things together, not less. The fact that we spent most evenings together when he was at home; or that Saturdays were now very different, was no consolation to me. I sought, and got, support from family and friends. When I tried to persuade him to my point of view I only ended up more miserable than ever. He was always very patient with me, which only made me more frustrated.

One day, as I sat complaining to God about how disappointed I was and how I hated being alone at night, I began to realize that there was a war raging inside me which, until that point, I had convinced myself was completely justifiable. But where had peace gone? Again, most of the time I had learned to wear a mask that disguised how I was really feeling when I was with others – except when they asked how Jim was enjoying his retirement! The resolution of this inner conflict did not come immediately, but gradually I began to realize that God was using Jim's teaching gifts even more than before. People kept saying that his preaching and teaching seemed to have an added power. I realized that I was actually in danger of opposing the purposes of God for his life. I had been operating on the world's system of wisdom based on human rules about retirement, which is seen as a cessation of active participation in a life-time's working habits at the age of sixty-five. Jim's withdrawal from leading the fellowship was certainly right, but his calling to teach and preach had taken on a new sense of urgency. A new anointing of the Holy Spirit had been given to equip him for a renewed call. I began to realize that my unhappiness had been making it even more difficult for him to go away from home. His natural preference has always been to be at home with his family. Over the years I had learned to release him to get on with the job that God had called him to do, but now I was finding it really hard. It is so easy to justify reliance on human wisdom and almost to enjoy the conflict when self-pity and all its accompanying negative attitudes convince one that the conflict is right and justifiable – but only for a time because human wisdom knows nothing of the positive peace that is beyond human understanding.

Now we can have honest and open discussion about the preaching programme and we can pray together about each event as it approaches. Jim knows that I am once more in full support of him doing what God wants him to do as part of these 'retirement' years. Almost immediately after I accepted the fact that I needed to release him into this new phase of service in his life I was given the go-ahead to write this book. This was something that God had put on my heart some years before but, until this time, the doors had remained firmly closed. Now I had the time to build on the foundational material which I had gathered over many years; the time had come to go through the Scriptures, the time had come to read, to listen, and to observe the trends of a secular society in more detail; the time to weigh up and analyse the impact that these trends were making on the family of God.

The other aspect of the teaching on 'the mind of Christ' which has continued to make a deep impression on me is to do with the Christ-like quality commonly known as the fruit of the Spirit, which is listed as nouns in Galatians (5:22 and 23) and as adjectives in James (3:17) and also mentioned in shorter lists in Ephesians (4:2 and 3) and in the first letter of Peter (3:4). The fact that really impacted me at the time that this teaching was given is the fact that all of these Christ-like qualities not only have opposites which come from Satan's influence, but they also have perversions or compromises which, I suppose, are fleshly rather than anything more sinister – but they do distort the original meaning. Thus it is possible to deviate from the meaning in two directions. We have already looked at the unique quality of *agape* love which, on the one hand, is the opposite of hate, but, on the other hand, bears no suggestion of permissiveness or over indulgence. The opposite of the adjective pure is impure or tainted or, in the moral sense, lustful. The perversion of the word is puritanical – which is how society interprets Christian purity, especially in terms of sexual behaviour. The word pure is to do with being able to bear the scrutiny of a righteous God. In fact the meaning of all nine flavours of the fruit can be better appreciated by coupling them with the word pure – e.g. pure love, pure goodness etc. As Christians we don't have too many problems with recognizing and turning away from the opposites of all these qualities, but we do have problems with recognizing their perversions.

We confuse earthly happiness that focuses on circumstances, possessions or even spiritual highs, with joy. Don't misunderstand me I have often known pure joy in the presence of the Lord in a worshipping community of God's people, but I have also been caught up in situations where joy has been replaced by an empty exhilaration which leaves behind a sense of emptiness rather than peace. Joy and peace are intertwined and both are able to be experienced in spite of circumstances. I believe it was C.S. Lewis who once said, 'Joy is peace dancing and peace is joy resting.' In situations even of deprivation and torture believers have testified that they have known the joy of the Lord in the deep places of their hearts.

Gentleness is perverted to weakness, when in actual fact it derives from a word used of a wild horse that has been tamed to the point where it accepts the bit in its mouth. It carries the idea of controlled strength. A gentle person is one who has ceased fighting inside, who is teachable, considerate and submissive (voluntarily unselfish). The opposite is one who is self assertive, always fighting for rights – in other words straining at the bit. The picture of Jesus in the old hymn 'Gentle Jesus meek and mild', is an example of how the meaning of these words have been perverted. They have denuded the human Jesus of his perfect manliness.

Patience literally means long-temperedness. The word is most often used in the Bible in relation to God's long-suffering attitude towards us as sinners, but it is not an attitude which overlooks wrongdoing. Instead it has, as God himself has, the ultimate desire to bring repentance and change. Leniency and over-tolerance are its perversions.

It is so easy to take these passages of scripture which challenge us in the area of our character and then behave as if they were options rather than necessary changes in our lives. It is not unusual to hear people excuse their attitudes by saying that they are just like Peter – impetuous and sometimes thoughtless – but they fail to notice that it was the same Peter (whom Jesus rebuked on more than one occasion) who, later in his life, wrote powerfully about how we should behave even when persecution comes. The fruit of the Spirit growing in his heart brought radical change to the way that he spoke and the attitudes that he had. If we allow the fruit to grow in our lives – and that is our responsibility – it will affect the manner in which we exercise the gifts which God gives us. It will ensure that we are more likely to allow God's unchanging wisdom to control our thinking instead of paying heed to the world's forever changing wisdom. The world's wisdom only brings more stress to already stressful lives.

Throughout this book thus far my aim has been to show that neither feminism nor sexism are compatible with the narrow way that we have been called to walk. Attaching the word Christian to the word feminism does not sanctify it any more than attaching the word Christian to the word sexism would! The same attitudes and arguments are heard among the people of God as are heard in our secular society. If what scripture says about the difference between worldly wisdom and the wisdom that comes from God is to be followed through, we still have a great deal of soul searching to do before we come to a place of peaceful agreement rather than what is, at best, an uneasy truce and at worst a continuing strife and conflict in the family of God on the issue of gender.

Before embarking on a study of the role of women in the family of God we need to think well about these words quoted in an earlier chapter, 'Be aware of your own bias and assumptions and you will be less likely to baptize them with scripture'. It is incredibly difficult to divest our thinking of all perceived truth that has been impressed on us over the years. When, that day in Portugal, I asked God to deal with my prejudices I really didn't think that I had many! But slowly over the months God showed me that I had gone from a completely egalitarian viewpoint to a legalistic set of rules about what a woman should or should not do. It is very easy to ascribe truth to ways of doing things which we personally like and are accustomed to - and error to ways of doing things which we personally dislike and are unfamiliar to us, without having any biblical basis for our likes and dislikes – our own bias and assumptions. This is a constant challenge to me as an older woman in a fast changing world. We need to separate these lesser issues from the main controversy which is, 'What are God's unchanging purposes for us as women in the family of God at the beginning of a new millennium in the history of that family, the church?' From time to time it will be necessary to revisit and draw together some of the issues already dealt with elsewhere.

1. Women have equal opportunities with men in society so why should there be discrimination against them in the church?

It must be very difficult for a woman who has risen to a high position in a profession or in the business world to find that her abilities are not appreciated or are even undervalued or ignored in her local church family. This becomes even more difficult when such gifting and ability are lacking in the men who are in leadership positions. This is further compounded if the woman is single and has total responsibility for managing every area of her life. A church that ignores and undervalues its women members is not a true representation of the New Testament church.

The argument raised in the question seems logically sound, but there are very good reasons for suggesting that it is not a logic that is applicable to the church.

Firstly, there is the assumption that because equal opportunity is the current policy in society then it must be right. There needs to be an awareness that the decisions and dictates of a secular no-faith and multi-faith society are not appropriate as guidelines for church practice. Throughout the history of his people going back to the time of Abraham, God constantly warned against allowing the standards of surrounding society to influence and water down his instructions for right living. When God gave Moses his rules for living these instructions became even clearer. When the Jews ignored God's instructions disaster befell them. Jesus, in the Sermon on the Mount, reaffirmed the principles laid down in the Old Testament when he challenged his disciples to become salt and light in society (Matthew 5:13-16). The salt that Jesus spoke about here is not the salt that is added to food, but rather the chemical that was used to disinfect the dung pile and to fertilize the ground to produce good crops. Disciples of Jesus are those who challenge sin and wrongdoing and who encourage healthy growth. We are to bring light in dark places. In his discourse with the eleven just before he was arrested, Jesus warned them that to follow his teaching would make them very unpopular.

It was just after my time of crisis in Portugal, which made me wonder if I was completely adrift in my thinking, that I suddenly realized that there was definitely something wrong when the church was willing to take its lead from an increasingly godless society in its attitude to gender related issues in church leadership. Just recently I discovered that Francis Schaeffer said these words shortly before he died in 1984: 'Tell me what the world is saying today and I will tell you what the church will be saying seven years from now.'

Secondly, the church is a living organism (the new body of Christ on earth), not an organisation, it is a family with a God-given order, not a business organized according to boardroom structures. Leadership of the church is very different from management in business, where there is a ladder of promotion to the highest position. The calling of God to lead his people is a call to servanthood according to the instructions given in the Bible. Human qualification and ability are not the top priority in God's eyes. His most important requirement is the desire to serve and to do so in obedience to Him. In society certain jobs have more kudos than others. In God's family every job that needs to be done is equally important to him, as described in 1 Corinthians 12. In the church family of which we are a part, the senior pastor and the church housekeeper are both members of the church staff. Both attend staff meetings along with the other pastors and the administrative staff. They have very different roles, but without the presence of either one of them the church family does not function as effectively as it does when both are there and functioning in their own sphere.

Thirdly, the way in which society views male and female is different from the biblical viewpoint. Society does not accept that we are created beings but rather that we are the end products of an evolutionary process. There is no sense of divine purpose behind our differing genders. Maleness and femaleness are accidents of birth. If both are educated equally and indoctrinated into personhood then all distinctions will eventually disappear into history. Society in general and some politicians in particular are trying hard to make that happen.

2. What about the part that women missionaries have played in carrying out Jesus' command to 'go into all the world'?

There are those who would argue that many women have gone abroad as missionaries because there seemed to be no way in which they could fulfil God's calling on their lives at home in a local situation. If there is any truth in such an assertion then it is an indictment on the way in which the church has operated under the pattern of the 'one man ministry'. On the other hand, God's order laid down in the scriptures does not change with circumstance or location.

Women have played a huge part in carrying the gospel to the far corners of the earth. It would seem that women have always responded more quickly and readily to missionary appeals for reinforcements than men. Women's heart response comes first followed by a confirming head response. Men's response tends to start in the head and work its way down to the heart. It's all to do with different hard-wiring again. It is very often easier for a woman who is single and without responsibilities for others to make that initial response. Even if he is single a man has to think deeply about making a decision which would affect not only himself but those whom God may give him to provide for. There are married men who have genuinely felt called by God but have been held back by an unwilling wife.

Single in heart and purpose
Only eternity will reveal the full impact of the thousands of single women who have responded to God's call to go in His name. Some have felt a definite call to remain single for the sake of the work God called them to. Others have come to terms with their singleness after much struggling. Gladys Aylward, whose work with Chinese orphans was portrayed in a film called '*The Small Woman*', said in conversation with Elisabeth Elliot that she had asked God to send her a husband from England. She said, 'I believe God answers prayer. He called him – but he never came!' – which may well have been true.[18]

Every Scottish child attending Sunday School during my childhood knew the story of Mary Slessor of Calabar. She was a Dundee mill-girl who knew that God was calling her to work in Africa. She resolutely refused to be put off by those who felt that she was not strong enough in body or equipped enough intellectually to be a missionary. She persisted and in 1877 set sail for Nigeria. The journey to get there was daunting enough without all the hazards of the African interior where she insisted on working. She went alone into unexplored territory despite attempts to stop her. She argued, 'a woman would be less of a threat to native tribesmen than a male missionary would be and therefore safer'. She worked there for thirty-eight years. She became engaged at one point to a missionary who, because of his health, would not leave the coastal region where it was much healthier. She broke off her engagement and worked on until she died in 1915. She was responsible for building churches and schools and acted at one point as a local magistrate on behalf of the government.

Gladys Aylward, already mentioned, faced similar opposition when God called her to China. She left London alone, unsupported by any missionary society, with all her belongings in a small suitcase. Hundreds of Chinese children who were orphans were cared for and educated because of her responding to God's call.

Amy Carmichael, the eldest child of a prosperous Irish Presbyterian family, had already served her apprenticeship in evangelism amongst mill girls when she responded to a missionary call. She spent fifty-three years working abroad, first in Japan, then in China and Ceylon. The last twenty-five years were spent in Dohnavur in India, where she founded a community where children in moral danger could find care and protection. During that time she never had a furlough. Amy Carmichael was a woman who knew that she was called to a life of singleness. She found complete fulfilment in the work God called her to do.

In the last twenty-five years of the twentieth century Jackie Pullinger knew that God wanted her in Hong Kong. She, too, went out alone because no-one confirmed her call. Countless numbers of young Chinese men and women have found deliverance from drug addiction and have entered into new life in Christ because she did what she knew God wanted her to do.

Some single women have been martyred for their faith. Some have gone through experiences of physical danger, deprivation and torture when caught up in tribal and other war situations.

Some have worked alone in remote places. Many people all over the world have the scriptures in their own language because of women Bible translators who have worked on, unhindered by family pressures. Others have taught people to read in their own language so that they can read the translated scriptures for themselves.

Many of these women have been, and are, known only to their own families and a few prayer partners who support them in their work, but all of them are known personally to God and he knows the work they have done in obedience to him.

God's call always needs to be worked out in accordance with scriptural guidelines. Were people like Mary Slessor and Gladys Aylward being unsubmissive in their determination to go abroad? We have already noticed that submission is not blind obedience. Each individual is answerable to God and each individual has direct communication with God since Jesus died on the cross. These women were not going against scriptural guidelines in answering the call of 'Go ye, therefore'. But the same Biblical restrictions apply to women wherever they serve God. His call never contradicts his Word. If some of the women (e.g. Mary Slessor) did get involved in ministries that God has reserved for men the exception doesn't cancel out scriptural teaching. God knows the circumstances and the attitudes of the individual heart. He certainly blessed Mary Slessor's work in the middle of the Nigerian jungle. In personal conversation with Elisabeth Elliot she related how she worked person to person with young South American Indian men to teach them the Scriptures (perhaps like Priscilla) so that they could teach the emerging church on a Sunday morning. She saw that it was very important that a church got it right from the very beginning. She also said that on many occasions she could have preached better herself but she did not do it.

Workers together for God

For the most part the role of married women in overseas mission has been different but no less valuable. This is inevitable. As we have already seen, marriage and motherhood bring new boundaries into the use of a woman's time and energy. No matter how much help is available, she is still where the buck stops in creating and running a home and in caring for its occupants.

Some women have heard God's call to go overseas while they were still single. They went to do missionary training, went out to the place in the world where God had called them to go, and became established in their area of work and service. Then they met, and chose to marry, their husbands. Like many women who are not missionaries abroad, they carried on more or less as they had done before marriage – until God blessed their union with a child. It was and still is incredibly difficult for such a woman to come to terms with the physical and emotional change that a child brings into her life – as it is for some at home. But a woman missionary has often had the added pressure of feeling that she is now no longer meeting the expectations of those who sent her out to be a missionary. Somehow she is a different breed of woman. In years gone by – hopefully it is changing now – the mission and/or the sending church (and sometimes the woman herself) has seen the work of the mission as a higher priority than the care and nurture of children and the building of a Christian family.

Some women married and had children before God's call came to them as a couple to go overseas. The call which comes to a wife and mother can never involve the same level of commitment which the call of God on a single woman's life does. Some women have found this hard to acknowledge. They have felt that somehow being a wife and mother who has been called to work alongside a husband in his calling doesn't have the same kudos. There are others who have fully acknowledged this reality and have been more than content to regard themselves as facilitators, encouragers, envisioners and prayer partners to their husbands. Many have been used as listening ears and wise counsellors to those around them.

Married women have often faced times of life threatening dangers, as their single sisters have done. One of our own missionary families with two young children had to take refuge in the hallway of their African home while government and rebel forces fired mortars at one another over the roof of their home! On another occasion this young mother was alone at home with her two children when young men broke in and held her at knife-point on the floor. Suddenly footsteps were heard and the robbers ran away – but no-one else appeared! Such experiences take a long time to recover from and inevitably leave scars that God alone is able to deal with.

Perhaps it was the great evangelical emphasis on personal belief and the service of the individual that laid down a pattern for missionary workers in the nineteenth and twentieth centuries that led to lack of recognition of just how powerful the witness of Christian family life could be as a tool of evangelism. Instead it would appear that the call to world evangelization was often an instrument for the neglect of the importance of family life and relationships, leading to loss of faith for some of the children of these families.

The cost of being a disciple? (Luke 14:26)

Over the past twenty years Jim and I have had the privilege of visiting missionary situations in several Far Eastern countries. In 1980 we spent six weeks travelling from Hong Kong to Thailand, Malaysia, Singapore, the Philippines and back to Hong Kong. Since then we have added Indonesia, Taiwan, Korea and Japan to the list. But 1980 was my first experience and was my first exposure to the realities of every day living to which missionaries have to become accustomed – the sweltering humid heat (and it wasn't the hot season!), the bugs, the strange food, the even stranger smells, the ever present possibility of meeting up with snakes (my pet phobia at the time, which never actually happened although there were some near misses in Thailand), a stomach that was never really happy, the frequently primitive sanitation – all of these made up my first experience of real culture shock! It was the first time that I had ever been away from our family home for more than a week or two at the most (and even that had happened rarely). Our two older children were at university but were only a telephone call away. The younger two were in the early years of secondary education. But now there was no means of contact. I didn't know what was happening from day to day.

It was against that background that I became a neutral listening ear to missionary mothers who felt that they could pour out their hearts about their concerns for their children. None of them doubted that they were in the place where God wanted them to be. All of them had a deep desire to see people come to a living faith in Jesus. None of them wanted to turn their backs on God's call – but most of them were finding it difficult to reconcile the commitment to the mission with the demands of being a wife and a mum. Often it was necessary to leave their children in the care of local women employed to help them in the home (who weren't necessarily believers). This was probably more of a concern to me than it was to them, because I had encountered the results of such a situation in the course of pastoral counselling. Their real concern was the fact that their children would have to go hundreds or even thousands of miles away to be educated. Some were already going through the pain of that separation. Few, if any, of these parents would have chosen a boarding school option for their children if they had been in their home countries. I had no solutions to offer. I felt rebuked for my concern for my own children, who were being very well cared for. There were no easy answers. I listened and I prayed for them and I wept in my heart for them. For me it was the other side of a story which had troubled me from late teenage years.

The summer before I began my medical training in Edinburgh, I spent two weeks as part of the domestic staff at a missionary summer school in the north of Scotland. I shared a room with three girls who were all daughters of missionaries, and whose parents were in various parts of the world. One of them had spent time in a Japanese internment camp when the school which she and her brother and sister attended in China (1,000 miles away from parents) was captured in 1941. Their parents had escaped to Taiwan. These three children were separated from one another in different dormitories and hardly saw one another. Life in the camp was not as horrendous as others camps were. It was in the same camp that Eric Liddel the Olympic medal winner died (probably of a brain tumour). The camp was liberated in August 1945 and it was not until December of that year that they were reunited with their parents. Their father returned to China in 1947, followed later by their mother. Before long the parents were behind communist lines and when I met M she did not know where her parents were. This was in August 1950. Mercifully they were both safe and finally came back to Britain in 1951. During my years at university and throughout our years living in a manse we had met and got to know many other missionary children who barely knew their parents.

All through these years I had harboured some criticism of these parents. But now as a parent myself I was experiencing the pain from the other point of view. What must that mother have gone through, knowing her three children were in a Japanese prison camp? She had no idea how they were being treated. The questioning that had started in my heart so many years before at that summer school came back to the forefront of my mind. What was actually meant by the words spoken by Jesus, 'If anyone comes to me and does not hate his father and mother, his wife and children, his brothers and sisters, yea, even his own life he cannot be my disciple' (Luke 14:26). Who was Jesus speaking to? He was speaking to the crowds who were following him. He wasn't speaking to his disciples. He was speaking about the cost of turning away from dead religious practices to follow him. He was making it plain that to be his disciple would mean a separation from family and friends because those nearest and dearest to them would try to persuade them that they were mistaken. Loyalty to Jesus and his teaching must supersede all previous loyalties.

This point can be illustrated by the story of a young Muslim woman who became a follower of Jesus. From that moment on she had no choice but to put her loyalty to Jesus above all family loyalties. For many years her life was in danger as her family tried to find ways of forcing her back to her native land and her old beliefs. She continued to love them and pray for them, but for many years there was little contact. When she obtained British citizenship she began to ask God to let her visit her family so that she could show them that she still loved them and honoured her parents. Eventually she went to visit them on holiday, but when they discovered that she had no intention of returning to her old beliefs she was cruelly treated. Every year she chooses to return to her family for a few weeks where she bears a gentle witness to Jesus, and her loyalty to him has never wavered. Many of the young Koreans whom we have come to know and love live daily with the cost of putting their obedience to Jesus above loyalty to family ties and expectations.

The challenge of this verse is the challenge that every missionary brings to the people to whom they have been sent. But can this verse really be applied to the painful separations that parents and children alike have experienced in missionary situations? The children aren't opposing their parents' loyalty to Jesus. The whole of scripture supports the idea of family and the responsibility of parents to care for their children and train them in Godly ways.

Can it be right that a woman, whose parents were missionaries and who sent her to boarding school when she was three, sums up her childhood by saying that she was a child of a 'no parent family'. She loved her parents and has a great respect for the work they did. She cared for them in their old age in a highly commendable way. She still has a great love for the land of China where they were missionaries. She never saw her parents during the war, she was in a boarding school in Britain where one of the punishments was to deny children their parents' letters! She and the other woman whose story I have told have weathered the storm of these separations – but many others have not. Many have gone through a similar emotional and psychological trauma to that of the children of divorced parents. I believe that those held responsible before God for such trauma will not, in most cases, be the parents, who did what was expected of them, but those in churches and missionary societies who put these expectations on parents as part of their call to missionary service.

It would be wrong not to pay tribute to the many good schools for missionary children and to the work done there by teachers and houseparents who try to fill a huge emotional gap in children's lives. We were privileged to visit one such school and were very impressed by the whole atmosphere and the complete dedication of those who worked there.

But times are changing...

The whole missionary scene is changing rapidly. Many missionary parents are now opting to come home for the main educational years of their children. Many have returned to carry on when children have reached adulthood. Some have successfully educated their own children to GCSE level. In some places it is possible for children to be educated locally.

Tent-making has become a necessary way of reaching people in certain countries. Being a mother in a tent-making situation affords opportunity for building natural relationships with other young mothers. This is not an easy option, since great wisdom and caution are needed. The gospel is demonstrated by attitude and action and the living out of Christian family life. To get to this point there are the same preparations as in traditional missionary situations – language learning, understanding the culture, the giving up of many of the freedoms to go out and about which we consider normal in this country, dressing differently, coping with the attitude of men towards women, coping with heat and flies, concerns about children's health and education.

Now, too, we are seeing missionaries come to the needy west from those countries that have heard the Good News and are in turn responding to the challenge. But this would never have been so if others had not responded to the call to 'Go and make disciples'. From our own experience in Korea, the majority of those responding to the new missionary call in the East, at any rate, are women.

3. Does God not want to use a woman's gifts - natural or spiritual?

My early memories of Sunday mornings were of church bells ringing and the main street of our home town being busy with people going to their various churches – rushing to get there before the bells stopped ringing at 11.30am!

The pattern of worship in most of the churches – mainly Church of Scotland, Congregational, Baptist, Methodist – was more or less the same. The minister called the people to worship, perhaps the choir sang an introit, a hymn or metrical psalm, followed by prayer, a children's talk, children's hymn, offering, prayer, hymn, sermon, prayer, hymn, benediction, home. It was the liturgy of churches that, especially in Scotland, would pride themselves on a non-liturgical heritage. Christian Brethren and Episcopalians would be the only ones who did not follow this basic pattern in timing and form of worship. But the Episcopalian rector and the minister of the other denominations mentioned were responsible for all the components of the service. They were assisted in leading worship by their organists and the choirs. For a large number of the people who went to church on Sunday morning they had done their religious bit for the week.

> They do it every Sunday,
> They'll be all right on Monday,
> It's just a little habit they've acquired.

Evening worship, which in our church was traditionally an evangelistic service, was attended by the more committed members of the congregation.

The minister was expected to be a good preacher, a fiery evangelist, a caring pastor, and a good visitor! In the Baptist system of government he was the only elder. He was assisted by a varying number of deacons, one of whom was church secretary and another church treasurer. The secretary handled all church correspondence and administration. The treasurer was responsible for banking Sunday offerings, keeping accurate accounts, paying the salary of the minister and church caretaker, paying bills for coal, gas and electricity, and negotiating with local contractors on behalf of the deacons for repairs and redecoration. These two were regarded as the minister's right-hand men.

There were others, men and women, who faithfully taught in Sunday School and ran other youth organizations. There was a faithful group of women who ran the Women's Meeting. Women also sustained missionary interest for the most part. A few of the men were lay-preachers who went around mission halls and small churches. During the minister's summer holiday (always one calendar month) these men conducted the prayer meeting held on a Wednesday evening. There were those with a heart for evangelism. One of these was my future father-in-law who, with a few others, used to go to Saturday night evangelistic meetings in churches and mission halls. It was on one such occasion that my husband made his preaching debut!

I wonder how many people of my age have similar memories of how 'church' was done! What a contrast to the living, vibrant relationships of the church when it was born. In these mid-twentieth century years it seemed that the church nationwide was asleep. There was no concept of the church members being part of one living Body – the body of Christ on earth as described by Paul in his letter to the Corinthian church (1 Corinthians 12:12-31). Many natural gifts apart from singing and playing the organ and piano, lay dormant in the church setting. There was no expectation that God wanted to impart spiritual gifts to ordinary church members – men or women.

These were the years when liberal theology, which questioned the Scriptures, was rampant. But as in the inter-testamental period for the Jews, there were those who kept firmly to the authenticity of the scriptures and prayed. Their prayers began to be answered when Billy Graham came to England in 1954 and Scotland in 1955 – the flame was rekindled. Ordinary people, male and female, young and old, were trained as counsellors or became part of the enormous choir. From that time things began to change. The church was being roused from sleep. The scene was set for a renewing work of the Holy Spirit.

'Your sons and your daughters will prophesy'
These words, quoted by Peter on the day of Pentecost, (Acts 2:17) come from the prophecy of Joel (2:28). There seems to be no agreement among scholars about when Joel lived. But it is probably true that many Jewish male eyebrows were raised when

he went on to prophesy that, 'Even on my servants, both men and women, I (God) will pour out my Spirit in those days' (Acts 2:18). Peter, speaking under the anointing of the Holy Spirit, acknowledged that 'those days' had come. It would not be surprising to Peter, or the other apostles, because they had seen that Jesus treated women in a completely different way from many of the priests and rabbis. He knew that men and women were equally valuable in God's eyes, and that women are spiritually very receptive and eager to be taught. He had also seen that Jesus never blurred the gender differences when it came to who was in charge. The believers were already a band of brothers and sisters committed to spreading the Good News in ways appropriate to their manhood and womanhood. The promised Holy Spirit had come to equip them for that task.

The Holy Spirit still comes today, not only to lead people to Jesus, but also to equip men and women for the task of making the Good News known to others. The work of the Holy Spirit in the life of the believer is to enable him or her to reproduce the character and conduct of Jesus.

Jesus' character portrayed as the fruit of the spirit is allowed to grow in a believer's life. It is a process of dying to self and becoming alive to the Spirit's prompting in our lives (Galatians 5:16-26). It is an ongoing process throughout the rest of a believer's life. Paul instructed the church at Ephesus to 'be filled with the Spirit'. The tense of the verb used says, 'be being filled' – a recognition that we have, in our humanity, a tendency to be leaky vessels. Growth in Christian character is not an option but rather an imperative – 'Be!' not 'it would be desirable that...'.

Jesus' conduct is portrayed by the use of spiritual gifts. The gifts bestowed on the believers by the outpouring of the Holy Spirit at Pentecost are sometimes spoken of as charismata – gifts of the grace of God. [This word charisma is also used of the gift of salvation (Romans 6:23).] There are those who believe that these gifts were only given for a period of time and are no longer available to believers today. They are gifts, and gifts can be received or refused. When my birthday comes along my family still bring me gifts. They have been purchased and wrapped and are given with the intention of enriching and enabling me in the days that lie ahead. I could decide that I am too old and mature now to receive such gifts – that it would be childish to expect to receive gifts at my age. I could decide to leave them unwrapped and so never discover their usefulness – but I don't. I receive them with gratitude and use them in the way that the giver intended them to be used. This is a trivial and imperfect illustration of the gifts that God has made available through the outpouring of the Holy Spirit on the lives of believers since the day of Pentecost.

These gifts are given to equip us in the work that God has called us to do – they do not in any way alter our status before God or people. Some men and women have misused the gifts that God has given. Sometimes the flesh rather than the Spirit has been in operation. Satan can counterfeit every supernatural gift. That does not alter the fact that these charismatic gifts are real and available to men and women alike, and are given to equip the people of God to care for one another and to reach out to those who have not yet been made new in Christ.

In western society the 1960s was the time when the nation's turning away from God changed from a slow moving stream to a river in spate. Those whose Christianity was nominal stopped keeping up the pretence. It was the time when John Robinson's book '*Honest to God*' was published; 'God is dead', became the assumption of many people. But, as I have already said, there were some who had come to faith in the Billy Graham Crusades and others who had a deep longing to see God move in power in an increasingly unbelieving nation.

It was this longing in our hearts that took Jim and I back to a new and deeper understanding of Calvary in the early 1960s. which led us on to experiencing a personal Pentecost in 1968. Our whole concept of what 'church' was about was turned upside down. During most of that decade God brought many people into our lives who were living their Christian lives in a dimension that was, until then, outside our experience. Some of them were

Presbyterians but most of them were Anglicans. It was from our Anglican friends that we first caught sight of what is meant by the new body of Christ on earth. In the gospels Jesus in his human body was confined to being in one place at one time. In the book of Acts Jesus, by the Holy Spirit, was now living in every believer. Paul says, 'Now you are the body of Christ' (1 Corinthians 12:27) – he doesn't say you are *like* the body of Christ. In effect Jesus has changed bodies – instead of being in one place at one time, the presence of Jesus is spread worldwide in believers. Every believer forms part of the new body of Christ on earth.

When we moved to Chalfont St Peter in 1968 we discovered that although the new congregation was Baptist in name, it was made up of people who had their roots in many different traditions other than Baptist and some who had no roots anywhere but were drawn together by a desire to be taught and have a deeper understanding of God's word. We were all united in having hungry and thirsty hearts. On the second occasion that the church family had an away weekend, we had been focusing on relationships (through teaching on 1 John) given by a pastor whose wife had died of cancer only a few weeks before. On Sunday afternoon we met to share the Lord's Supper together. Jim had given testimony to the way in which God had applied the teaching of the first letter of John to his own life through the witness of some CMS missionaries who had been present in the East African revival. We were sitting quietly before receiving bread and wine when a lady requested that we sing 'Spirit of the living God, fall afresh on me'. We did – and He did! A restoring of relationships followed repentance. Tears were shed without any great emotional upsurge. There was such an outpouring of Calvary love among us and the sense of the presence of God was so real that no-one wanted to move out of the room. Tea was postponed twice before we finally sang a closing hymn, and a closing prayer brought a customary end. From that day on the quality of relationships described in 1 Corinthians 12 began to become a reality as men and women began to desire and to receive the supernatural gifts which were first given at Pentecost. Love was the glue that held us together.

All 'sons and daughters' have a part to play in the healthy functioning of body life. There is no place in this picture of the church for 'pew warmers'. In the human body the appendix is the only organ which does not seem to serve any useful purpose and yet it is frequently the source of pain and infection – and often has to be removed. 'Appendices' in the life of the church are commonly a source of trouble too!

Over the past thirty years women have been given a new sense of purpose in the family of God (a change of metaphor). Because of their spiritual awareness and sensitivity, these supernatural gifts have often been more in evidence in women than in men. Women have been widely used in prayer for healing and wholeness, in intercessory groups, in giving words of wisdom and knowledge that have unlocked the real cause of problems both in people and in churches. They have contributed much in the area of worship as instruments other than organ and piano are used for God's glory, and new worship songs are written. But, as in the Corinthian church, there has been a down-side in this new-found freedom. The women in the Corinthian church were taking a lead from the secular society in which many of them had been raised. They were pushing the boundaries of freedom in the Spirit to ignore the God ordained order – women today are no different!

'It was he (Jesus) who gave gifts to mankind' (Ephesians 4:11 GNB)
The letter that Paul wrote to the church at Ephesus was almost certainly a circular letter. In the first part Paul lays down doctrine and then goes on to give practical instruction on how the unity of the church is to be worked out in practice.

There are two important things to notice about this passage. The first is that these gifts (Greek *dorea*, not *charisma*) which Jesus gave (apostles, prophets, evangelists, pastors, teachers) were given to mankind (Greek *anthropos*), which means that they were given to men and women. The second thing that we need to notice is that they are gifts; and do not of themselves presuppose office. They were given to 'prepare God's people for works of service so that the body of Christ may be built up' (Ephesians 4:12). The expectation would seem to be that these gifts would be distributed throughout the family of God.

The way in which the church has evolved in all its denominational forms from the simplicity of the New Testament church has meant that these gifts which Christ gave to the church are regarded as gifts which are only in operation in those set apart for the oversight of the church (i.e. priests, vicars, ministers, elders – whatever title is relevant to particular denominations). The corollary that would be put forward by feminists is that to demonstrate any of these gifts qualifies for church oversight regardless of gender. But Paul addresses the question of oversight in the church in passages in Timothy and Titus that will be discussed later.

The attributing of these gifts only to those who are given charge over the people of God led to the pattern of church life which was the normal and expected way of ordering church government and practice in our childhood and growing up years.

What a contrast this is to our experience of church since that memorable communion service at the end of a church weekend! The change has not come about without a great deal of pain, and it is very encouraging that the New Testament describes the early church 'warts and all'. Paul's experience in his care of the early churches is mirrored today in contemporary church life, and our fellowship is no exception. But the love that God put in our hearts for one another nearly thirty years ago has brought us through in times of conflict and pain.

To illustrate the distribution of these gifts I would like to describe one of our church's ministries among women that has continued to grow and develop over many years.

This is a work amongst mothers of pre-school children. Pop-In – as it is called – began about thirty years ago as a social caring programme to give young mums, many of whom were far away from family, a break from their toddlers in a loving atmosphere. Every week about forty non-Christians were coming into the church premises. Sometimes we had talks from Christians about jobs or hobbies, but there was no real evangelistic thrust. Some of us felt that God had much more for this group. We met to pray and felt that God was telling us to be bold. We knew that we also needed to be wise. Many of the women who came were the product of the 'bra burning' feminism of the sixties. About half of them had never been inside any church – not even to Sunday School. They had no God framework in their lives. Others were rebelling against the boredom of their early Christian upbringing. Friendship evangelism had already begun. We knew from personal talks that the god that some didn't believe in was not the God of the Bible! Evangelist and pastoral care gifts were already emerging in some of our own young mums. Those of us who were in charge made a decision that we must do what we felt God was asking us to do, and so a teaching programme was begun. We were amazed that instead of numbers dropping away numbers grew.

This is still true today. Many young mums have come to a personal faith in Christ, have been discipled and cared for and have become active, loyal members of the church. They in turn have brought others – and the cycle begins again. Every Thursday morning these women listen to a forty-minute teaching slot followed by the opportunity to ask questions. These meetings have always been soaked in prayer by those responsible for organizing the group. Over the years the programme has been decided on by listening to God, not by sharing good ideas. Many husbands have also come to know the Lord through the testimony of changed attitudes of their wives, plus friendship meals and events to which they are invited.

This is a ministry that has been envisioned and carried through by women using all of the gifts that Jesus gave to the church. Evangelist and pastoral gifts are very much in evidence. Prophetic gifts have been used in listening to God and then in sharing what it is believed that God is saying. Others of us have been used in teaching about God's principles for family life; becoming whole in Jesus; facing the challenges of society's pressures today. Some who were converted through Pop-In now share in the teaching programme and also go out to share testimony and teach what they have learned. Fiona Castle was once a Pop-In mum, then she led the group for many years. She still helps to look after toddlers when she is not out as a 'sent one' (the meaning of the word apostle with a small 'a'). Much of her ministry is centred on the same family-related issues that are the main focus of this weekly meeting. One of the church elders has non-participatory oversight of the group – except that being 'retired' from his career as a university lecturer, he sets up the room and helps care for pre-school children every week!

There are many other women who use similar gifting in working alongside area elders; in being part of groups who evaluate the call of young and not-so-young people to some form of 'full-time' work for God; who care pastorally for those who have answered God's call; who form a large part of a prayer ministry team who are available at the end of every church service; who are involved in youth programmes; who are responsible for the soft-sell evangelism of our tea shop in the centre of the village; run mercy ministries to people in need – and so on!

All of this is possible because of the gifts that Jesus has given to the church.

Natural gifts

Natural gifts, like the supernatural gifts already described, are given by God even though they are passed down through a family line, e.g. music, art.

Major Ian Thomas, founder of the Capenwray Missionary Fellowship, when speaking at a large youth rally many years ago, challenged young people with guitar playing ability (the latest thing at the time!) to lay these gifts down at Jesus' feet and not to take them up again until God gave them permission to do so. Although he said this with particular reference to the growing interest among young people in the pop-music world, which he feared would be a threat to their Christian commitment, it is a good principle to be applied to every natural gift. When this is done, natural gifts such as management and administration, the ability to organize people or programmes, the ability to care for large numbers, hosting church hospitality, artistic abilities with food, flowers or décor – take on a spiritual dimension and self glory is removed from their use. Every gift and ability that has been offered to God for his use makes a big contribution to the atmosphere when the family of God comes together for worship. Those who have prepared the building, those who have arranged flowers, those who welcome people, all help to set the scene for dedicated musicians and those who have up-front responsibility to lead the congregation and to teach God's word. All have a part to play in creating an atmosphere where people find it easy to be touched by the presence of God.

Recently Sir Ronnie Flanagan, the recently retired chief constable of the RUC, speaking at a meeting in Belfast, said that everyone leaves a trace of himself or herself wherever he/she has been. What an opportunity for those congregations who worship in hired halls – especially school halls – to leave behind the fragrance of the presence of Jesus every Sunday because of the way they have worked together and cared for the premises entrusted to them. In God's eyes every gift used for him is important to him. As in our nuclear family, so also in the family of God we have an important part to play in creating the atmosphere where God can reach people.

But now we turn to the big issue.

4. God's unchanging purposes for women in the family of God

As I am writing this today a tree surgeon is at work in our garden doing a thorough job of sorting out a tangled mass of very prickly holly branches that come from four huge holly trees. These trees were growing there long before our house was built thirty years ago. When we looked out of our bedroom window this morning, all we could see was a solid mass of green through which no light could penetrate. Now it is quite apparent that there are four quite separate trees – we can see through them to the houses behind and the whole garden is visible from that same window.

This reminds me of the verse that I have already quoted, 'God made us plain and simple but we have made ourselves very complicated' (Ecclesiastes 7:29 GNB). Down through the twenty centuries that have passed since the church was born, men (intentional use of that term) have taken the simplicity of order and organization of the early church and have made out of it something that resembles our tangled mass of holly branches – complete with prickly leaves.

Different church traditions have grown out of the same soil and have ordered their structures very differently. Every tree, as it were, has divided and subdivided until we have the situation we find ourselves in today. Add to the branches the prickly leaves of the gender issue and the picture is complete!

All this is so very far removed from the day of Pentecost when the church was born. Then a band of believers, led by those men Jesus had chosen, were all filled with the Holy Spirit and were thus enabled to lead the other Spirit-filled believers forward in witnessing to the life, death and resurrection of Jesus. But when all of the complications of titles have been removed, we are left with the same basic situation – some are responsible for the leadership of others and everone is responsible to God.

God's instructions about leadership
The issue of leadership and authority in the church is a completely different issue from that of the receiving and use of spiritual gifts and abilities. The latter are distributed throughout the church. The former is a responsibility given to a few men who by maturity of life and use of gifts have shown themselves eligible for the responsibility of leading, governing and teaching God's people. This is made clear by Paul in 1 Timothy 3:1-7 and Titus 1:5-9. 'Overseer' or 'bishop' is the translation of the Greek word (*episkopoi*) used in these passages, which quite clearly points to a continuance of the responsibility given to men to

lead the people of God throughout the Old Testament. The other word that is used of the same office, is the word 'elder' (*presbuteros*), which refers to maturity of spiritual experience and is masculine in form. There is a similar word used in Titus (2:3) which refers to older women (*presbutidas*). This verse has been used to refute the fact that eldership is male. The claim is made that there were obviously women elders in the church in Crete. However, this word is not a feminine form of the word *presbuteros* but is a completely different word, used of age and not authority. The masculine form *presbutas* is used in the previous verse, which is speaking about older men. Paul has dealt with the issue of leadership in Titus 1 and in chapter 2 goes on to challenge older men and women in the church to be good role models for younger men and women.

Elders/overseers are always spoken about in the plural. No church was ever meant to have just one elder. The call upon a man's life to be an overseer in the family of God is not a call to privilege, but to responsibility. Eldership is not about status but about function. It is a call to serve, not to be served. It is a call to the kind of leadership demonstrated by Jesus himself. The elder in the church family is equivalent to the father in the nuclear family – which is the building block of the church. The same headship qualities are required.

Where does ordination come into the picture? The word 'ordain' appears in the King James version of the Bible to translate a multiplicity of Greek and Hebrew words. The word 'appoint' has been substituted for most of these words in the later translations such as the NIV. The significance of the word ordination varies in importance according to which part of the tangled mass of church order one belongs, but generally speaking the people who are ordained in the various and different forms of church life are those who hold the calling of overseer as described in 1 Timothy 3:1-7; Titus 1:6-9; 1 Peter 5. There are those who have denied the validity or necessity of such a practice, expressing the view that ordination has gained a significance that it did not have in the early church. Others take an opposite view and regard ordination as having a deep significance with its roots going back into the priesthood of the Old Testament and tracing a continuous line from the Apostles. However, for our purposes its only significance is how it relates to the position of women in the family of God.

Sampling the records of church history[19]

There is a wrong impression given by those who have campaigned for the ordination of women and/or the admission of women to offices of the church which carry with them directional leadership and teaching. The impression is that this is something that has never happened before. This is not true. By the second century AD there were certain breakaway groups that had begun to ordain women to the priesthood.

Marcion was a church leader in Asia Minor (now the part of Turkey between the Black Sea and the Mediterranean) in the second century, who gathered around him large numbers of followers. He regarded God in the Old Testament as a forbidding, punishing, woman-hating, God. He decided to dismiss the Old Testament and remove from New Testament writings any quotations or references to the Old Testament. This meant that Luke's gospel was the only one of which he approved. Galatians was his preferred epistle, which is strange since so much of it is dealing with the relationship between the faith of Abraham and the purpose of the law, but it does contain the verse that appears when taken out of context, to show Paul had changed his attitude to women (Galatians 3:28). Because of his tampering with scripture, not just because he approved of women priests, Marcion was regarded as a heretic.

Gnosticism, which also arose at this time, is a heresy that adds to orthodox belief. It probably has its roots in Greek philosophy. Paul's epistle to the Colossians is thought to be a defence against those Christians who were adding to the core of the Christian message that salvation is to be found in Christ alone. Gnostics denied the Genesis account of creation and tried to do away with any distinctions between human beings including gender. Galatians 3:28 was a key verse in their attitude to gender. There was no difference in function between men and women in their church organization.

Montanism also began in Asia Minor, with a new outpouring of the Holy Spirit. Prophecy was very much in evidence and in some groups took precedence over teaching. Two women prophets had a very powerful influence. One of them, named Priscilla, claimed that Jesus appeared to her in the form of a woman. The early Montanists did not ordain women to the priesthood, but eventually a splinter group known as the Quintellians had women priests and bishops, which they justified on the grounds that Eve had eaten of the tree of knowledge and was therefore (in spite of doing this in disobedience) qualified to be a prototype of a woman priest. Galatians 3:28 was again used as justification.

Right through to the end of the fourth century these heretical groups ordained women to priestly function. This was never true in the mainstream orthodox church and was certainly opposed on scriptural grounds by Tertullian (AD160-240) – although he was a part of the early Montanist revival; by Origen (AD185-254); and later in the fourth century by John Chrysostom, Epiphanimus Ambrose and Jerome.

Some of these men said harsh things about women, but only in the context of the quest to become priests. Chrysostom, Origen and Jerome all encouraged women in the study of theology and respected their insights and intellectual ability – yet by many they were regarded as anti-women.

It is still true today that men who speak out against women holding responsibility for positions of oversight and teaching in the life of the local church are branded as misogynist, when in fact they, like these early church fathers, are only holding fast to scripture. Throughout the Middle Ages nothing changed in church practice, although there were always those who pushed for change. Neither did the Protestant Reformation bring any change to the view held by the early church fathers. The rise of the Quaker movement (Society of Friends), founded by George Fox in the mid seventeenth century, brought a new egalitarian trend. All forms of worship and systems of church government were rejected. The Holy Spirit alone was the guide in worship and practice.

In the post-Reformation period, several new denominations emerged which put special emphasis on various church doctrines. None of them made any significant change to the traditional practice of church government and teaching. Some Methodist groups allowed women to preach in exceptional circumstances. It is interesting to note that changes began to happen as the various branches of the church became more and more caught up in liberal theology in the early and mid years of the twentieth century. In 1922 Baptists in England ordained the denomination's first woman minister. Gradually, over the second half of the twentieth century, other denominations have responded to the pressure of feminist theology. The Church of England held out until 1992.

The Salvation Army, which like the Quakers has never adhered to Biblical structures of leadership, has always allowed women to have high-ranking positions. Many branches of Pentecostalism have, since their beginnings in America early in the twentieth century, encouraged women to participate fully in all aspects of church ministry and leadership. It is interesting to compare this with the early Montanists, who gave women positions of leadership and authority because of their outstanding prophetic gifts. It would seem that whenever there is an outpouring of the Holy Spirit in renewal, women, whose gifting may have been wrongfully suppressed, are rightfully released in gifts and ministries – but this ultimately leads to a lack of understanding of the Biblical difference between the use of gifting and ability, and the unchanging rules laid down in Scripture about the responsibility given to (a few) men to lead and teach the church.

Throughout history it would seem that a redress of that balance has always come about. There are many people in every denomination who are neither sexist nor feminist who do not see the ordination of women to oversight roles as having any bearing on Scriptural truth or bringing any real benefit to either church or society. It is rather seen as a knee-jerk reaction to the increasing pressure of a secular society to conform to its ways. Modernism (which has aimed to do away with all tradition) has given way to postmodernism, which rejects the whole idea of any hierarchy, with disastrous effects on society – and no doubt on the church.

'Neither...male nor female.....' (Galatians 3:28)

This one verse of scripture has been picked out since the days of Marcion in the second century AD as the proof text for undifferentiated equality amongst the people of God. Many times over I have heard this verse quoted without any regard to the context in which it was written.

Paul wrote the letter to the Christians in Galatia to correct some false teaching that was circulating in this part of Asia Minor which said that Gentiles needed to become Jews before becoming Christians. He begins chapter 3 by going back in history to Abraham to whom God had given the promise of a distant seed (Jesus) who would bring the possibility of being put right with Him through faith. This promise was given for all human beings, not just the Jews. The law had been given as an interim help along the way to help the Jewish people to live righteous lives until the promised seed had come. 'Now that faith has come, we are no longer under the supervision of the law. You are all sons (men and women) of God through faith in Christ Jesus, for all of you (Jew and Greek, slave and freeman, man and woman) who were baptized into Christ have been clothed with Christ. There is neither Jew nor Greek, slave nor free, male nor female, for you are all one (person) in Christ Jesus' (Galatians 3:25-29). Paul uses these three groupings here as contrasts commonly seen in the society around them. Jews thought of themselves as THE people of God and consequently of higher value to God than Greeks (or any gentile for that matter); freemen were generally thought of more highly than slaves in the human scale of things; men were of more value than women. The thought of a gentile slave girl being on the same value level as a Jewish free man was unthinkable. But Paul says that in Christ such values are non-existent. Paul is not making a plea for nationality to disappear; for slavery to be abolished; or for unisex or even homosex to replace the male/female perfection of creation. He is saying that if any person is in Christ that person is an inheritor of the promise made to Abraham, which has been fulfilled in Christ regardless of who that person is.

Nowhere in this epistle are the functions of different believers in the family of God discussed. It has been suggested many times over since the days of Marcion that this verse shows that Paul had finally come to his senses and was now advocating undifferentiated equality. This would seem to be putting one scripture above other scriptures. But 'all scripture is God-breathed and is useful for teaching, rebuking, correcting and training in righteousness' (2 Timothy 3:16). In his letter to the Galatian Christians Paul was rebuking error, and correcting attitudes to other believers. He emphasizes the amazing privilege we all have to be in Christ (*en Cristo* is the phrase he so often uses). The suggestion that this verse redefines a wrong attitude to women does not bear scrutiny. The letter was written before any of the other letters written by Paul in which he speaks about male/female relationships in the home and in the church, and before he lays down the guidelines for the (few) men who are to hold responsibility for teaching and governing roles.

'I commend to you our sister Phoebe, a servant of the church at Cenchreae' This verse (Romans 16:1) is the only time in scripture that the Greek word *diakonos* is used of a woman. Phoebe is not mentioned anywhere else in scripture. She was thought to be a wealthy woman who loyally served the church in Cenchreae (a suburb of Corinth). The word *diakonos* denotes an attitude of servanthood and is used in the New Testament in contexts other than that of leadership roles in the church, e.g. the function of domestic servants who were not slaves (*doulos*) was spoken of using the word *diakonos* (John 2:5 and 9); the role of a civil ruler

(Romans 13:4); the followers of Jesus (John 12:26); relationship of the followers of Jesus to one another (Matthew 20:26); as a description of Paul and Apollos in relation to the work that they do – servants of God (1 Corinthians 3:5). These two verses (Romans 16: 1 and 2) have been used to support the argument that Phoebe had a leadership role in the church where she served because Paul used a word which he did not usually ascribe to a woman. Paul wrote these greetings about three years after he had written his stern letter to the church in Corinth (which no doubt included the church at Cenchreae), in which he clearly defines the position of women in relation to attitude and behaviour. It is likely, in addressing Phoebe in this way, he was simply giving honour where honour is due to an outstandingly faithful woman of God.

However, Paul's instructions for the appointment of deacons in a local church were given in the letter he wrote to Timothy, who had been given oversight of the church at Ephesus. The Timothy letters were probably written three or four years after the letter to the Romans. After giving his guidelines for the appointment of church overseers (or elders or bishops), he gives similar guidelines for those who are to serve the church in practical servanthood – the *diakonoi*.

Similar high standards of life and behaviour are required of the men who are to serve in this way (1 Timothy 3:8-10). When we come to verse eleven the wives are spoken of, and many believe that these instructions are for women deacons and not for the wife of a deacon. The argument used for this is firstly that no separate instruction is given for the wife of overseers – which one would think even more important. Secondly verse eleven begins with the word 'likewise', which corresponds to the instruction for male deacons. The qualifications for character are the same as those given for the male deacons. The word translated 'wives' in verse eleven is used elsewhere to denote a woman, married or unmarried. This certainly ties in with Paul's reference to Phoebe as a deacon in Romans 16:1 and 2.

In many church traditions the origin of the diaconate is traced to the verses at the beginning of Acts 6 (1-7), but in that chapter those who were to be appointed were quite specifically to be men (*aner* not *anthropos*). The word deacon is not used of these men in Acts, but the work that they were called to do was certainly described as a work of serving. Deacons were never meant to do the work of overseers. The deacon is intended to be a ministry of support to the overseers. There is a sense, however, is which every believer is committed to the work of deaconing, because we are all called to be servants.

Back to Church History

Throughout the history of the church there have been women who have demonstrated a deep spirituality. There were those older women, particularly those who were widows, who heeded the instructions passed on by Paul to Timothy. In fact widows became the first serving order of women in the church in the second and third centuries. Their ministry of care was focused on sick and socially deprived women – the earliest health visitors/social workers! But they also had responsibility for the spiritual lives of women and spent much time in prayer. In the Eastern Church (which eventually became the Orthodox branch of Christianity), an early deaconess movement probably grew out of these groups of widows. They were responsible for caring for women at the time of their baptism and discipling them afterwards, in addition to all the other things that the widows' groups had done. It would seem that in the Eastern Church at this time there was a return to the practice of separating men and women in worship. The deaconess became an intermediary between the women and the clergy.

The next development was the gathering of groups of deaconesses into convents where an abbess oversaw them. The abbess was allowed to conduct services for the women under her care in the absence of a priest. John Chrysostom's friend Olympias was one such woman (Constantinople fourth century). The early deaconess movement began to be suppressed in the fifth century because a few of these women regarded themselves as equal to the male clergy. This may have been seen by some as sexism, but others, as today, would have seen it as necessary to restore Biblical order. There were other monastic women, like Olympias, whose desire was for learning and who accepted scriptural order. One of these was the sister of St Boniface (eighth century primate of Germany) who had been trained from infancy in the rudiments of grammar and the study of the liberal arts. Her zeal for the study of the scriptures and her great wisdom earned for this woman, called Lioba, a place of respect among many prominent men of the period.

The deaconess movement was revived in Germany and in England in the nineteenth century. In Germany their main concern was the care of the sick, but in England they undertook work in the parishes of the Anglican Church. These women were theologically trained and were involved in teaching in church schools as well as working in the parish, as the early deaconesses had done. Some Baptist and Methodist churches also had deaconesses. Many Roman Catholic nuns have excelled in nursing, teaching and intercessory ministries. But as we have seen, the inevitable push for recognition as priests by some of these women has happened in the Anglican Church. So deaconing has become eldering – and women have turned their collars round.

'Then Miriam took a tambourine in her hand' (Exodus 15:20)
Miriam, the prophetess sister of Moses and Aaron, was the first of a line of women stretching through history who under the inspiration of the Holy Spirit have sung songs of praise and worship to God. Miriam also led the women in joyous dancing!

Deborah and Barak sang together after the defeat of the Canaanite King Jabin (Judges 5:2-31). Hannah uttered a prayer of worship when she left Samuel at the temple (1 Samuel 2:1-10). Mary's song of pure worship when Elizabeth had confirmed prophetically the truth of who it was that she was carrying in her womb, has echoes of Hannah's prayer. (Luke 1:46-55).

Although there is no record in scripture, it is highly likely that some of the 'hymns and spiritual songs' sung by the early church as they gathered for worship came from the lips of women.

When we come to the more recent years of church history (eighteenth century onwards), many hymns have been written by women, many of them still sung today, e.g. 'Just as I am', by Charlotte Elliott. Some women in the nineteenth century were prolific hymn writers – Frances Havergal and Fanny Crosby. It would be an interesting exercise to look through the hymn books and find out just how many have been written by women.

A former Archbishop of Canterbury, William Temple, described worship in this way. 'Worship is the submission of all our nature to God. It is the quickening of our conscience by His holiness: the nourishment of the mind with His truth; the purifying of the imagination by His beauty; the opening of the heart to His love; the surrender of the will to His purposes – and all of this is gathered up in adoration; the most selfless emotion of which our nature is capable.'[20]

In the early 1970s, Michael Harper wrote a book telling the story of an Episcopalian church in Texas called the 'Church of the Redeemer', where God was moving in power, changing the lives of many people in a run down area of Houston. The rector's wife, Betty Pulkingham – a very gifted musician – was organist and choir mistress. The renewing Holy Spirit had profoundly changed both her and her husband. Many of the people whose lives were being rescued by God from near destruction were singers and musicians – most of them women. That church far away in Texas had a profound effect on my understanding of what Archbishop Temple had said many years before. Betty Pulkingham wrote music, arranged well-known hymns, and encouraged the development of musical gifts in others. I can't remember ever seeing her up-front but her influence on worship through the choir of the Church of the Redeemer and through groups like the Fisherfolk who sprang from that church, had a profound effect on the worship in many churches, particularly in the South of England.

On many evenings when I was at home alone and the children were in bed, I used to sit in the darkness in our lounge and listen to the sung Eucharist (written by Betty Pulkingham) of that church choir, recorded as 'God's people give Thanks'. Often we both listened to it on a Saturday evening when Jim had come home from his final preparations for Sunday. God used that music to bring us into His presence in a way that we had never experienced before in our own home.

A very memorable experience for both of us was when, as part of an international, interdenominational conference in London, Jim was sharing a seminar on worship in St Margaret's Church in Westminster with some of the Fisherfolk worship group. During a time of worship at the end of the seminar the clear soprano voice of one of that group rang through that historic church in a song of pure worship. It was for us a profound moment. A tourist who had just come in to look around was converted on the spot!

Women's spiritual sensitivity, coupled with an awareness of who they are in God, the quality of humility that was in Mary, the heartfelt thankfulness that was in Hannah, and the exuberant joy that Miriam experienced, have much to contribute in helping others in the family of God to enter into His presence in worship – an expression of the priestly function of believers.

The priesthood of all believers

According to the old Covenant between God and the Jews, only the High Priest could enter into the Holy of Holies to meet with God – and that only after offering blood sacrifices for the sins of the people. A curtain covered the Holy of Holies, where the sacred Ark of the Covenant was kept. At the moment when Jesus uttered the words, 'It is finished' the curtain in the temple was split from top to bottom. The writer to the Hebrews says, 'we have confidence to enter the Most Holy Place by the blood of Jesus, by a new and living way, opened for us through the curtain which is his body' (Hebrews 10:19-20). It is because of His blood poured out on the cross that every believer has this privilege of access into the presence of God. Jesus, the High Priest of the New Covenant, is the only intermediary between us and God the Father. Every believer now assumes responsibility for a personal relationship with God and is endowed by the Holy Spirit with gifts which are given for the benefit of others. Everyone without exception has to take responsibility for the life and growth of others within the family of God.

It is interesting that although Paul gave the responsibility for the directional leading and teaching of a church to the overseers, his letters were usually addressed to the whole church – Timothy, Titus and Philemon are the exceptions. In doing this he was challenging the whole congregation to see that each one was living according to God's order – leaders and followers alike. The royal priesthood spoken of by Peter (1 Peter 2:9) (and of which we are a part) was urged to live in such a way that pagans would see their good works and glorify God. It is in this sense that every woman is a priest of the New Covenant.

Sometimes, in carrying out our responsibilities in the light of our priestly responsibilities, we can get the balance between home and family upset.

In her book '*What is a family?*' Edith Schaeffer says 'Balance must be kept between "putting the Lord first" by sufficiently putting the family first. For a family to break up – because the husband or wife or both are "putting the Lord first" in some kind of Christian work – to the extent that the children are never "first" and the marriage relationship is never 'first' is NOT 'putting the Lord first'. He has given us the responsibility of caring for continuity in oneness and family life.'[21]

The converse of this is also true. The pendulum for some young families seems to be swinging the other way to an obsession with 'parenting' that leaves the church denuded of a younger generation of leaders. Because both can't participate, it does not mean that one of the partnership can't. Wives, be willing to let your husband 'put God first' in the proper balance. By letting him respond to leadership responsibilities, be it in youth work or in senior leadership, you too will know God's blessing. God will use all of the gifts He has given you when the time is right.

'But God has called me'

God does undoubtedly call women to work at home as well as overseas. But God only calls women to work for Him in a way that is appropriate to their womanhood – i.e. to a work which does not involve directional leadership and teaching. There are two aspects to God's guidance – particular and general. Particular guidance, which comes to the individual, must never contradict the general guidance on any issue where the Bible gives clear direction.

Undifferentiated equality has been widely proclaimed from platforms and pulpits and in Christian books and magazines. To the average church member it all sounds very reasonable and right that women should be admitted to all church leadership roles. The equal opportunities legislation plus feminist pressures have meant that many more young women are taking up places at universities and colleges to study theology, and they are fully entitled to do so. However, their expectation is that they will be accepted without question into church leadership roles when they finish their studies. When this doesn't happen –and this is the reality for many – there is disappointment and frustration, which leads to accusations of sexism, without even thinking that there could be another reason. The fact is that sometimes the same thing happens to male theological graduates. A theological education and a desire to serve God are not of themselves qualifications for leading the people of God – not even for men. For many years in Scotland theological studies were normally postgraduate – not open to those leaving school. Experience of other learning disciplines or other spheres of work was seen as a necessary preparation for theological study.

When a man or woman becomes aware that God might be calling them to some kind of full-time work, those in pastoral care of that person should spend time with them determining their gifting and ascertaining that the work to which they feel a call comes within the boundaries of scripture. Those women who are called to work overseas have a wide range of opportunities open to them – being part of a church planting team, Bible translation, literacy work, medical nursing and mercy ministries. Some develop teaching and preaching gifts, which are appropriate to the situation while within Biblical guidelines. Why then should the situation at home be different? Instead of focusing on the few areas of ministry not Biblically appropriate for women, why not concentrate on the callings that are open?

But, of course, this does depend on those who have the oversight of the church realizing the need to give such opportunities in the home church setting. We live in a desperately fragmented society. We need to build up church staff teams (which carry out the vision of those who have been given the task of directional leadership) – teams that 'scratch where people itch'. It's a question of going way back to go forward. The caring and the social ministries of the early widow-deaconess groups are as needed today as they were then. Theological awareness added to nursing, social work, or legal qualifications and used in work for God and paid for by the church, combined with a woman's spiritual sensitivity and evangelism gifts, could transform a local community. Youth culture needs a radical commitment to befriending and winning the confidence of young people. This is front-line warfare against the wiles of the flesh and the devil, which are drawing young people into destructive life-styles – what could be more important than such a ministry?

When can a woman preach or teach?
When Paul wrote to Timothy at Ephesus with instructions about worship in the local church, he spoke first about the attitudes that men and women should have as they come together. Men who lift up their hands in prayer are to have right heart attitudes towards the other believers around them. Women are not to be dressed in such a way that they divert attention away from the purpose of gathering – the worship of a Holy and Righteous God. It is in this context that women are barred from teaching.

Paul relates this, once more, to the created order and then to the Fall and its consequences. He immediately goes on to give directions for the appointment of those who will oversee the church. It is in the context of the directional teaching of the local church that Paul instructs women to be silent. He is not saying that women are never to teach at any time or that women do not have teaching gifts. Most of the negative things that Paul says about women in the context of worship are about attitude and not about ability.

There are women today who exercise effective and anointed preaching/teaching ministries to women around the world. There are women who hold teaching positions in theological colleges. There are women who speak at conferences where men are also present. All these are very different from the week-to-week directional teaching which shapes the life of a congregation and builds a framework of theology to which the other teaching ministries of a local church can be attached.

It is the responsibility of every believer to weigh up against scripture what is being taught from public platforms and to discern the spirit of the one who is teaching. Unless teaching/preaching is anointed of God it is made up of vain words that God cannot honour.

There is, in the present unisex climate of society, a need for separate teaching times for men and women, so that what is meant by Godly masculinity and Godly femininity can be spelt out. Whenever a man opens his mouth on the subject of gender in the presence of women, he is in danger of being labelled as sexist if he doesn't beat the feminist drum! We have a special responsibility to our young people in this respect. They are being bombarded at school with life patterns and life origins which have no bearing on scripture. They need to know that our differing gender roles are God's idea, originating from the perfection of creation. When Paul wrote his letter to Titus he knew the climate of the society in Crete in which this young man was working – not dissimilar to our society today. It was in this context that Paul directed him to make sure that the older women were teaching and modelling Godly womanhood to young women. His concern was that they would not, in any way, detract from the power of the Gospel to change lives.

Kephale again

'I have come to believe that a case for feminism that appeals to the canon of scripture as it stands can only hesitantly be made and that a communication of it to evangelicals will have difficulty shaking off the impression of hermeneutical ventriloquism...If it is the Bible you want feminism is in trouble; if it is feminism you want the Bible stands in the way.'[22] These are the words of a theologian, Clark Pinnock, who is someone with definite egalitarian sympathies.

This Greek word *Kephale*, which means head and from which we get medical words like encephalitis (an inflammation of the brain), is the fulcrum of evangelical feminist theology. If any suggestion of hierarchy in the purposes of God can be dismissed, then and then only can a case be made for undifferentiated equality in home and church. In an earlier chapter I have already stated that wide research into the use of this word in literature which is contemporary with scripture has shown that no substantive evidence has been produced which would allow *kephale* to be translated as anything other than head – a meaning which implies authority.

I have already quoted from Dorothy Patterson at the end of the chapter on a woman in the family as mother. Here she writes not as a mother but as a theologian:

> The church has never sought to suppress gifts God has given but rather strives to ensure full and proper use of those gifts in a divinely given framework based upon natural order of creation and appropriateness of function within a master plan. One cannot accept the Bible as authoritative while rejecting its authority concerning home and church order. One cannot negate truths concerning the structure of church and home, such as the image of the relationship between God and Israel, and between

Christ and the church, just to satisfy cultural whim or to accommodate higher plateaus of education and opportunity. One cannot lift outward manifestations, such as a man's prayer posture or a woman's head covering (1 Corinthians 11) and use them to ridicule or belittle the timeless directives given to protect and edify men and women within the Kingdom. Without doubt women did have a variety of positions of service, influence and even leadership and teaching within the early church. The text of Scripture, however, bears witness that the functions that they assumed were done with modesty and order (1 Corinthians 11:2-16 and 14:10) and that they did not teach or exercise authority over men.[23]

As we go on in the next chapter to look at the place of Christian women in society, it is essential that we take God's order for home and church families seriously. Post-modern society undermines the validity of any hierarchical structures for either home or society. The reason why this Greek word is so important is that it has the potential to bring order out of the chaos of an egalitarian democracy gone mad. Neither sexist nor feminist attitudes have any place in the family of God nor in the individuals of whom it is composed.

Male domination of women is evil and a perversion of God's intention, but it does not excuse feminist retaliation by women. It is our responsibility to respond to sexist domination in another spirit, 'Your attitude should be the same as Jesus Christ' (Philippians 2:5). Disorder came into the world when the man opted out of his God-given responsibility and the woman disregarded the man's leadership. God held the man culpable then. I believe He will again hold men responsible for either abdicating responsibility or misusing responsibility. As women we will be accountable only for our own attitudes and reactions within the family, the family of God – and society.

13

A Woman in Society

'Let her works praise her at the city gate' (Proverbs 31:31). The city gate was a place of importance. It was where the elders of the city conferred and gave judgments. For a woman to be known and praised at the city gates was a great honour. Mrs Proverbs was not only a competent homemaker, a faithful wife, a caring mother, a wise and Godly woman, but also an astute business woman who was known for her works of charity and kindness. She could have become Business Woman of the Year and have won all kinds of accolades, but wisdom taught her that the fame brought by such achievements are soon forgotten. Personal glory was not at the top of her agenda.

A Panorama programme on BBC1 in January 2000 looked at the lives of several women who were trying to combine life in the high-flying business world with family life. Stress and guilt could sum up the atmosphere conveyed by all of them. One young woman, who had decided to forego marriage and motherhood in order to pursue her career, did not have much sympathy for those who wanted the best of both worlds. She didn't see why people like her should make allowances for the pressures of motherhood. This was an interesting reaction because it's the attitude usually attributed to men – who, of course, are sexist when they express such a view!

The aim of this chapter is to look in more detail at where 'our ways' have taken our society – and its women in particular – at the beginning of a new millennium, and to suggest the response Christian women can make to model 'God's ways' in that society.

The growth of woman power in the twentieth century

The way in which the presence of women has infiltrated every part of the working and sporting world in the early twenty-first century reminds me of the fable of the camel and the man who was responsible for looking after him. One cold night in the desert the camel appealed to the man to allow him to put his nose just inside the tent to keep it warm. The man somewhat reluctantly agreed. The next night the camel asked if it could just put its head inside the tent. Eventually the man agreed. The next night the camel just pushed a little bit further in without saying anything. This went on for several nights until the camel was occupying as much of the tent as the man. The camel didn't stop until it was occupying the whole tent.

The admission of women into all the professions which were traditionally the domain of men, and their political enfranchisement, were just moves in an increasingly secular democratic society – as were many of the changes in some blatantly sexist restrictions put on women by the legal system in the realms of property ownership and marriage break-up. But that wasn't enough. Equal opportunities was the goal – which eventually became equal rights. Now we hear that this is to be the century of women. Will men soon be campaigning for equal opportunity – or even just to get a nose in the tent?

Equal opportunity or equal compulsion?

In the 1950s all women could choose if and when they wanted to return to the workplace after their children started school (playgroups, nurseries and childminders – apart from grandmothers – were virtually unheard of).

In the year 2001 it is almost (but thankfully not quite) impossible for an ordinary woman whose husband is earning a reasonable salary to be a full-time wife, homemaker and mother by choice even before her children are school age because of economic pressure. Equal opportunity has moved towards equal compulsion.

It has happened subtly and gradually by changing tax laws, boosting the idea of childcare by strangers, convincing women that home is boring and unfulfilling – that real life is only to be found outside the home. By introducing the term 'working families' the Biblical provider role of the husband is undermined, and the inference is that women who choose to maintain a firm home base don't work!

In 1987, in an article in an American magazine (*US News and World Report*), President Mikhail Gorbachev of the then USSR said, 'many of our problems (in USSR) – in children's and young people's behaviour, in our morals, culture, and production are partially caused by the weakening of family ties and slack attitudes to family responsibilities. This is a paradoxical result of our sincere desire to make women equal with men in everything.'

And yet our legislators, pushed by the feminist lobby, continue to move further towards that ideal. We cannot expect anything else when many of our present MPs are young women with families who have to be left behind during the week while mum goes to Westminster to work. How can any government (regardless of political colour) be serious about upholding marriage and family life while, at the same time, taking away tax advantages from a married man who still wants to be the main provider for his family, and more or less forcing young mothers into the work place? In so doing, mothers have to pay others to do the job, which is seen to be too unfulfilling for her to do herself. Part of the reason for this is that secular feminism has succeeded in its aim to break up families and set women free from the bondage of marriage. Many of our MPs, and indeed our Cabinet Ministers, do not model marriage and traditional (no longer called Christian) family life themselves.

What's wrong with the equal opportunities ideal?
The simple answer to that question is our different hard-wiring again. Equal opportunities insists that an equal number of male

and female students are admitted to any university course. Forty-five years ago the proportion of male/female students entering the Medical Faculty of Edinburgh University was 4:1. Presumably it is now 1:1. Most doctors marry. For men this has little bearing on the course of their professional life. In spite of the best surrogate childcare provision in the world and job-sharing facilities available, it is still a fact that the working life of a wife and/or mother can never follow the same pattern as that of a husband and/or father without damage to family life. Perhaps this is the main reason that the NHS is constantly short of doctors. One hundred medical students probably produces at most seventy-five full-time medical practitioners. This is equally true for most other professions. This is the fallacy of the equal opportunities ideal. Paternity leave, maternity leave, childcare, will never change what God has built into a woman's hardwiring, whether she believes in God or not. It takes a hard woman to shut herself off from the needs of her family in order to devote herself fully to business or professional life. Those who have done it usually come to regret it.

Golda Meir, the first Prime Minister of the State of Israel when interviewed by *Newsweek* in 1973 said, 'I had to decide which came first; my duty to my husband, my home, and my child, or the kind of life I really wanted. Not for the first time – and certainly not for the last – I realized that, in a conflict between my duty and my innermost desires it was my duty that had the prior claim.' [24]

What a confusion over where duty lies! What a contrast to Mrs Proverbs who was also Jewish and was probably no less able than Golda Meir.

The gods of a secular and materialistic society
1. Education
I am very glad that I was born when I was. I was allowed to have a long and happy childhood. In spite of the inconveniences and, for me, the minor deprivations of wartime years, I learned to read and write and spell, and learned the rudiments of

arithmetic in a very gradual progression to the stage where secondary education began. This opened up the world of mathematics and science, of languages, of literature and poetry, of a wider view of history and geography, of art and music. It was all a relatively painless progression as long as one really applied oneself to the task of learning. It just seemed to happen!

One of the things that we found very different when we moved from Scotland to south-east England was the obsession that parents had with their children's education. We were certainly concerned about moving our two older children to a different system of education, but we knew that God had called Jim to lead and to pastor the congregation in Chalfont St Peter, so we had no doubt at all that if local schools were good enough for most of the children in our new community, they must certainly be good enough for our children too! Our daughter had to do something called the 11+ (at 10¼!) about a month after she started her new school. We sensed the tension and pressure that was present in parents and children alike. We weren't worried about her because she had always coped very well at school. We really couldn't understand what all the fuss was about. Needless to say she passed. For our oldest son this was a disaster area – we discovered many years later that he was dyslexic. With our third and fourth children the pressure had really got to us! The result of all these tests was that all four of our children went to different schools in different towns! Only one of these schools had a learning ethos which was, in any way, comparable to that in which we were educated. Its teachers cared more about developing the potential of each child than it did about the number of Oxbridge places gained – but it did gain Oxbridge places nevertheless.

But now pressure is being applied to children immediately they start school. Our seven-year-old grandchildren don't speak about sums and spelling and reading but about literacy and numeracy! From that tender age they are subjected to national tests and teachers and parents alike are conscious of the importance of the position of their school in national league tables.

Human knowledge is increasing at an unprecedented rate, so there is much more for children to learn. One of the definitions of education in the Oxford Reference Dictionary is 'development of character or mental powers'. It seems that only the latter part is important in today's world because it's the part that enables people to make money, possess more things and gain more power in a materialistic society. The increase of knowledge means that university degrees that used to equip graduates for a life's work are now just a foundation course for continuous further learning. Acquiring more knowledge is, for many people, a continual top priority that is put above experience of life and maturity of character.

More and more young people are being encouraged to go to universities that weren't there twenty-five years ago – or were then Colleges of Further Education. Professorships seem to be instituted in all manner of subjects that didn't even appear in university curricula in former years. In the 1950s, and for many years before and after, a relatively few school leavers went to the universities then in existence, which had been there for hundreds of years. Most school leavers (at seventeen) went into banks or civil service, nursing and commerce, where they had good prospects for advancement. Most pupils now who gain A-levels (or their equivalent) go to university to study anything from nuclear physics to leisure!

When education is seen as a privilege to be worked for, it brings benefit to society and not just to the individual. Education is now seen as a right for the individual for the benefit of the individual. For many centuries the Judaeo-Christian ethos of our society and the pursuit of knowledge were closely intertwined. Many of our older universities have their roots in monastic institutions. Glasgow University has the motto 'Via, Veritas, Vita' – the Way, the Truth, the Life. I doubt very much if many of that institution's present day students (or teachers for that matter) have any idea where these words come from or their deep significance for all human beings.

Over many generations most of us have benefited from knowledge acquired in scientific research – especially in the medical field, but King Solomon wrote, 'the fear of the Lord is the beginning of knowledge'. Sadly, for many, the pursuit of knowledge has driven them farther and farther away from its source and knowledge itself has become their god. There are a few who are sure that they will soon have found a way to create life itself – shades of a conversation in Genesis 3?

2. Leisure Pursuits

There have always been people who have enjoyed watching and participating in sport to variable degrees. The Bible would support the idea. We are meant to live balanced lives. It would seem that the people of Israel knew how to celebrate special occasions. There were times of feasting and dancing and times of fasting and praying.

However, in a matter of a few years the leisure industry has grown into big business involving enormous amounts of money. Football teams and those who play for them have become idols. The football stadium has become the place where people pay huge amounts of money to worship their heroes in action. In a lifetime professional football players have gone from earning a few pounds per week to earning thousands of pounds a week whether they play or not. Small boys have always had football heroes, but now they (and their sisters too) have to wear the same kit that their particular hero wears – at great cost to parents or grandparents.

Pumping iron has become a must to keep the body in shape. Both men and women rush from work to the gym with commitment and devotion to the fitness god. The right gear must be worn by them too!

The music industry produces new idols by the month. Some last for a year or two and others disappear from view in months. Lyrics have become more and more blatantly sexual in content.

Children as well as teenagers are caught up in a frenzy of adulation. Music has become a big part of young people's lives. Homework is no longer done in silence. They must have music booming in their ears. Peer pressure to conform is enormous. Clubbing has become the leisure pursuit of many thousands of young adults – no weekend is complete without the buzz it brings.

3. Material Possessions

Have you ever wondered what is in all those gigantic vehicles that clog our motorways? Some tell us clearly, but others don't. It strkes me that they are all full of things – things which are regarded as necessary in today's increasingly materialistic climate, things that fill the empty void left when a nation debunks God. But they don't fill that empty void for long, and the manufacturers oblige by producing a newer, better, shinier, more complicated model. Children have always wanted things. I can remember wanting to have a new bicycle. All my friends (nothing changes) had new bicycles. I never actually had a new one, but I did always have a bicycle which served the same purpose as the one I always dreamed of having. My parents weren't being mean. They couldn't afford to buy me a new one. They had other priorities in their provision for me. But it seems that children never grow up these days as far as possessions are concerned! The toys are much bigger and more complicated though – not bought because of need but because of a desire for the biggest and the latest. The shopping mall has become a kind of cathedral to the god of possessions.

4. Sex, Sex, Sex

In the 1960s it was as though a Pandora's Box of promiscuity was opened as legislation brought what was termed as sexual 'freedom' to women. The contraceptive pill became available on student campuses. Pregnancy was no longer a risk factor in promiscuity, but even if a young woman became pregnant she could abort her baby. The right to choose was not about saying 'no' to promiscuity but 'yes' to destroying babies! Wherever unisex is promoted, homosexuality is not far away. I am not so naïve as to believe that premarital, extra-marital and same sex relationships were not there before laws were passed and repealed. It's all been there since the forbidden fruit was eaten and human beings decided that they knew better than God.

It has happened again and again through history in every civilization when people have turned away from the moral law put in their hearts by God. Until the 1960s our laws protected the Judaeo-Christian morality of Britain. I was a fifth year medical student doing a course in psychiatry before I knew that homosexual and lesbian relationships existed. Now our younger grandchildren are in danger of being taught that it is perfectly acceptable for one of their classmates to have two mummies and no daddy or two daddies and no mummy! When we first had TV there were programmes that we could watch as a family and enjoy. Family-viewing evening programmes are now almost nonexistent – at least ones without unnecessary sexual content and immoral relationships. But the sad thing is that these programmes reflect where it's at in our society and so fail to shock people, as they would have done only a few years ago. They aren't the far-fetched seedy musings of some scriptwriter. The majority of the viewing public regard these relationships as normal. One well-known soap, in a recent episode, had the local vicar sleeping with the local pub licensee with whom he was besotted; a lesbian vet living with her female HGV driver partner; a farmer's wife having an adulterous relationship with her young lodger – all this was happening against a background of bitterness of spirit and flagrant lawbreaking. In the whole set up there was one young woman, portrayed as being naïve and simple (in current language 'sad') for refusing to sleep with her boyfriend before they were married. All this was shown in the early evening, long before bedtime for most children.

But we are told that:
— As long as a relationship is stable and loving it doesn't matter whether the people are married or whether they are heterosexual or homosexual.

— As long as teenagers use condoms it's normal that
    they should explore their sexuality.
— Marriage will soon be history so it's OK to have as
    many partners as you like.
— Everyone must be free to do what feels right for
    self. It doesn't matter how much emotional stress
    and hurt it causes others in the process – children
    are very adaptable.

How long can people go on believing such nonsense? Many of
the ideals of the extreme feminists of the 1960s have been realized
– equality (or is it female supremacy?) in everything, sexual
freedom for women released from the bondage of marriage and
domesticity. Money, sex, power (political, economic, intellectual)
have always been at the heart of the decline and fall of great
civilizations. They bring destruction because they are all false
gods that occupy the spirits of Godless people – gods whose
idols are everywhere.

Is this what we women 'really, really want', - or do we want to
find ways in which God could use us to change things? Could
we learn how to rebuild womanhood in a way that would be
relevant to our society at the start of a new millennium of
opportunity? Could we give woman-power a meaning that would
initiate the rebuilding rather than the demolition of society?

Women in the building industry?
The book of Nehemiah came, once more, to the forefront of my
mind as I was pondering how to write this chapter.

When Nehemiah's brother arrived in Susa (where Nehemiah
was still living in exile) to tell him about the sorry state of the
walls of Jerusalem, Nehemiah could have expressed his horror
and sorrow, wept with his brother, promised to pray – and then
have done nothing.

Many of the people of Judah (now known as the Jews) had
returned from the seventy-year exile in Babylon and the temple
had been rebuilt. The walls, however, had been left broken down

and crumbling. The temple was exposed to further attack and the beauty of the city of Jerusalem was spoiled. Nehemiah did pray – but his prayer led to action. In answer to his prayer he was given permission to return to Jerusalem and was provided with materials for rebuilding. When he got there he motivated others to join him and together they saw the miracle of the beautiful walls rebuilt and the gates securely in place. Jerusalem was secure once more. This happened in a very short time because 'the people had a mind to work' (AV) or 'for the people worked with all their heart'. (Nehemiah 4:6 NIV)

It would be hard for anyone to deny that some pretty drastic repair work is needed to the protecting walls of our nation today. There are no political solutions. Each party in opposition has wonderful solutions to offer, but in power they are as helpless as their predecessors.

I believe that if women had 'a mind to work', the walls could begin to be rebuilt. There is an old saying, 'The hand that rocks the cradle rules the world'. This has nothing to do with the egalitarian woman-power of today but with the fact that women have always played a large part in creating a stable society by being a secure anchor for husband and children in the home; by being available to help, encourage and care for others as neighbours; or by working through voluntary organizations which are church or community based. This is the ethos in which many people of my generation grew up. Was this such a bad scene? Contrary to what we are led to believe, these women did not live unfulfilled lives. Is it a coincidence that it has been in the years since the bra-burning feminists of the sixties stepped up their crusade for equal everything and women began to become obsessed with being male clones that the whole stability of home and family life has disintegrated? Laws that brought so-called sexual freedom have encouraged promiscuity in all its forms and have robbed children of stable home lives. Men have responded to the demand for equality by opting out of accepting responsibility for the children they have fathered and seem to feel little guilt for moving on to start another family. Women are at least 50 per cent to blame for the havoc that rootless youngsters are causing in some city areas.

We need to get out of the demolition business and into the building business.

We need to start by rebuilding the true picture of Biblical womanhood, which has nothing to do with being uneducated, cowed, shrinking violets but has everything to do with taking every opportunity to learn and be prepared to be of service to others, whether it be in the home as a wife and mother or out in the professional or business world where single women have a unique opportunity to make their presence felt for good. Womanhood needs to be restored. Personhood has no Biblical basis. Womanhood has.

Building in the Home

Stop being 'only a housewife' or 'only a mother'. Stability will never return to our society until women realize how we have been duped by feminist ideals.

Don't be ashamed of enjoying homemaking. 'Home' is a word that has brought tears to the eyes of the hardest men who have been separated from it by war or circumstances – and they are not thinking of bricks and mortar, but rather of a mother's care. Homes are building blocks that can be used to build new, strong walls around our society. Homes are also brick factories for the next generation of home builders. Homes need to be used for the benefit of others. Their doors need to be ever open so that others can come and go – always open to the possibility of 'entertaining angels unawares'.

Building in the professions

When the time comes in family life where it seems right to re-enter a profession, it is absolutely essential that what we commit ourselves to is compatible with our prime responsibilities (already chosen by marrying and having children), otherwise we will be demolishing one while trying to build in another area, the one cancelling out the other. Women professionals, whether married or single, need to be there as women, not as male clones. It is possible for a woman to be in a superior professional position to a man and yet to affirm him in his manhood. Part of the rebuilding of walls by women must include encouraging men to be real men – not macho bullies or wimps. It is important to react to male chauvinism in a non-retaliatory manner. If we know that we are where God wants us, he will give wisdom in every situation. The fact that we are women will sometimes cause us to approach things differently, but we reach the same conclusions in the end and are not less able.

1. As Teachers

As a mother of four children who had varying experiences of education I know what a hard and often thankless job teaching can be. But that awkward, overactive child may be one of tomorrow's national leaders! Even in the same family with the same parents the response to the challenge of being educated is unique. Response to the same teacher by different members of the same family is not always the same.

Teachers, like parents, are involved in shaping the material for building the next generation. Teachers have an incredibly difficult job to do in an atmosphere of near anarchy in some schools. This is a job of national importance. Satan does not want young people to grow into stable trustworthy adults. In a nation where there is loss of respect for those in authority, teachers need Christian parents to pray for them and for the pupils for whom they are responsible. For Christian women, teaching is a calling to a tough mission field. This is true for nursery teachers right through to those who teach at university level.

Recently, at a conference, a professor of chemistry from Moscow, who became a Christian in a remarkable way while studying in Italy, said that he had come to the conclusion that the woman who had taught him English at school way back in the days of the Cold War may well have been a secret believer. She couldn't say anything, but she portrayed something which eventually made sense to this young man. As it becomes more difficult to say much to young people at school today the silent witness of caring attitudes and actions can convey a great deal.

How important it is for teachers to keep their eyes on the task of creating solid, dependable building blocks, even when they are knee deep in rubble!

2. In Caring Professions

This heading represents a wide spectrum of jobs, all of which are concerned with the physical health and general well-being of people from cradle to grave. What a challenge there is for Christian women in this whole field today! When a woman allows her femininity to express itself, she models compassion, gentleness (i.e. controlled strength), warmth, consideration, perception and a host of other attributes. Anyone who has been a patient in hospital will know how important these qualities are in the practical caring of sick people. Of course, knowledge, training, efficiency, ability to make decisions, are all part of the picture too. But a woman who has children knows the anxiety that a sick baby can induce – even when the mother is a doctor! A woman is often much more in tune with the molehills of everyday living which can become like mountains when sickness comes unexpectedly.

Hospitals are now very different places from the ones in which I trained and worked. Everyone gives the impression of being overworked and fraught. People have always worked long and hard in the care of sick people, but now no-one seems to have time for the care that was once given by the young probationer nurse, and the junior nurses whose clinical skills and knowledge were still every limited. Battleaxe sisters had their place I have discovered – not that they were the favourite people of junior nurses, medical students and junior doctors. This comment is gleaned from personal experience of being a patient, and from the experiences of friends, taken from several different hospitals in recent months. It mirrors the attitude of the world around us. Professional proficiency and success leads to higher financial rewards. Careerism has taken over from a sense of vocation in many of those involved in the NHS today. The opportunities for Christian women, however busy, to display a different attitude and to bring a new devotion to patient care in every aspect of hospital life is enormous. When patients are aware that they are not just John in bed 1, or Mary in bed 20, but a person with needs other than four hourly pills or a drip that needs changing, it can make a great difference to their progress. If they were given back the respect of being Mr John Smith or Miss/Mrs Mary Jones, that might help too! Doctors, nurses, physiotherapists, radiographers, occupational therapists, speech therapists – in fact any one who works in a hospital – can all demonstrate Jesus' love in a unique way. We also have the advantage over unbelieving staff that God has promised to renew our strength when it seems that we have no more to give.

The same is true for those who do similar jobs in the community. One of the great advantages that I have had in not being employed in the NHS is that I have had time to listen to people, time to weigh up where the real problem lies (often not a physical one at all), to advise people to go to see their GP, what to say when they get there, and to allay the unnecessary but real fears of others. This is a luxury that GPs don't have in these highly time pressurized days. Community nurses have a great advantage over GPs. They see people in their home setting that can add valuable information to a case file.

Increasingly pharmacists are having more people contact. I know of one pharmacist who has had wonderful opportunities to show care and concern to people in the course of her work. People everywhere and of all ages are looking for people who care. Most neighbours are out all day. There is no-one to turn to. Anyone who has had any training in the 'caring professions' can find plenty to do, whether in paid posts or not.

Some years ago we used to sing a prophetic song from the heart of God – 'Tell my people I love them, tell my people I care, when they feel far away from me, tell my people I am there'. There is an application of these words to every human being for whom Christ died.

3. In the world of business

Many people in the business world have seen their businesses prosper because they have set out to apply principles of Godly honesty and Godly integrity in all that they do. Whether at boardroom level, as employer or employee, as PA or receptionist, as office girl or tea maker, there is always an opportunity to demonstrate a different spirit from those round about in the cut and thrust of the business world. Integrity can be costly, as a friend of ours discovered some years ago:

'As a fairly new Christian I was working as a graduate PA in a firm of heating consultants. We hit a period of recession and they began to get into debt. The firm started to be pushed by creditors who would ring up demanding settlement of their bills. Although there was no money available, to fend them off my boss would instruct me to tell them that there was a cheque in the post. He would also instruct me to tell them that he was out, even although he was sitting at the desk next to mine when the calls came through. I was caught in the dilemma of obeying my boss or betraying God's principles of honesty and integrity. Being a single parent the job was really necessary to me but, in the end, I had to take a step of faith and hand in my notice stating why I was doing so.' She found another job almost immediately. Her old firm went out of business soon after she left.

Women in business can produce building blocks of honesty, integrity and dependability – all of which are much needed in the business world today, whether on the bottom rung of the ladder, the top, or halfway up. If the latter, you might run the risk of not rising any higher!

4. In the service industry

A large number of women today help to eke out family finances by working part time in supermarkets and other shops, in catering and in helping people in their homes. Every job matters to God. Wherever you are, you are salt and light in that situation. Courtesy, helpfulness and a genuine desire to be of service can bring encouragement to those with whom you come in contact. Everyone of us knows what a difference the attitude of the person at the checkout, the shop assistant who is helpful, the waitress who finds pleasure in serving food, can make to someone who is having a bad day, or who is weighed down with family concerns.

There are many who work in schools as classroom assistants or dinner ladies. Children know those who care about them – even a smiling lollipop lady can cheer a child's drooping spirits after a hard day.

Courtesy, helpfulness and a genuine desire to serve are the building blocks of those in so many seemingly humdrum jobs.

5. In Voluntary Work

There is still plenty to do in the area of voluntary work. Mothers of school-age children and those who have retired have more time on their hands because of our automated houses. Many young mothers are far away from their mothers or else their mothers are working full time. Surrogate mothers and aunties can mean a great deal – I know from personal experience. There are many older people who don't want to give up their own homes but need help with heavy chores, or in getting to the shops, or church. There are many church and community day-centres for elderly people. There are mother and toddler groups that need extra help. There is never any need for any woman to be bored or unemployed.

Working alongside those in education on school governing bodies is a vital role to play, especially for those who have had hands-on experience in education. Whatever gifting we have can be used – writing to people in authority about things that we care about – not the usual kind of self-assertive and aggressive opinions, but the voice of women who want to be women.

There is no end to the way in which we women could make a difference in being builders of broken walls.

What Motivated Nehemiah?

It would have been very easy for Nehemiah to remain in Susa and continue to be the king's cupbearer. But he knew how important Jerusalem was in the spiritual life of the Jewish people. He was motivated by a much deeper concern than building stone on stone. The broken walls of Jerusalem were the result of the disobedience and carelessness of God's people that had caused them to be devastated by an enemy. Because Nehemiah was willing to shoulder the responsibility of the hard practical work, people came together to get on with the job instead of looking around and bemoaning their plight. He not only built the walls, but he prepared the way for the prophet Ezra to come and focus the hearts of the men, women and children of this remnant of God's chosen people back on the One who had chosen them, delivered them from exile and brought them home once more. This is what motivated Nehemiah – not a self-centred desire for praise and adulation.

If careerism and personal prestige is at the heart of what we are doing, then there is no hope of society being changed by women. If we are more concerned with what we get out of what we do rather than what we put into what we do, the resulting satisfaction will be fleeting no matter how high we rise or how highly we are thought of by those in the world around us.

Right through the Bible it seems that part of being a woman is a positive willingness to sacrifice self for the benefit of others. Mary, the mother of Jesus, is the supreme example of this. This is what feminism has destroyed because it is regarded as weakness (the doormat syndrome). Self-assertion has replaced submission (yielding in love). Aggression has replaced gentleness (controlled strength). Women who earn the right to speak by their demeanour are listened to when they do speak. We are constantly being bombarded by the importance of self-image, self-esteem, and self-worth. The irony is that these words can never become a reality as long as they are prefixed by 'self'. It's as we begin to believe what God says about us, it's as we assimilate into our being what these two words '*en Cristo*' – in Christ – mean that the importance of self is struck a deathblow.

> Lord bend this proud and stiff-necked I,
> Help me to bow the head and die,
> Beholding Him on Calvary
> Who bowed His head for me.

If we really want to build for the future then we need to find our security in God – and that is what I pray the final chapter will help us to do.

Post-logue – Who am I?

The vast majority of people today have no answer to that question in terms of anyone or anything outside of themselves or their own family line. Someone wrote these lines –

> If you are convinced that there is no God – you are an accident
> you are an accident out of chaos.
> You have no meaning, no reason for being here,
> You are worth nothing unless you perform a use or meet a need.
> People may choose to value you for what you do because they need you –
> Or because they want you to value them in return.
> You have no inherent value.
> You are a human doing and not a human being
> Your birthplace was accidental
> You have no purpose for living except the one you give yourself.
> Your only achievement will be to reproduce, which is meaningless.
> Your personality is the result of parents, friends and heroes.
> You are nothing special unless you are famous.
> You must earn love unless you choose to love yourself unconditionally – no one else will.
> If you die tomorrow that would be your end – if you are convinced there is no God.'   (author unknown)

Although many people would declare that they believe in a god, the god they believe in bears little resemblance to the God who created them. Most people are convinced (because they have been told it so often) that they are creatures who have somehow evolved from 'the primordial soup' (but where did that come from?). Without belief in a Creator God there is no alternative but to look for one's worth and esteem within self. St Augustine once said, 'Thou has made us for Thyself and our hearts are restless until they find their rest in Thee.'

Those of us who have come to know the God of the Bible know that our whole being is rooted in the perfection God of creation and that's where we begin to answer the question 'Who am I?'

Created by God

The psalmist says 'for you created my inmost being, you put me together in my mother's womb' (Ps 139:13). Each one of us was conceived by God's say-so (that's why no child can be labelled illegitimate). It wasn't just the result of the sexual passion of a man and a woman. It was because God chose to unite that sperm with that ovum to create a totally unique human being. I am a woman, endowed with all the attributes of femininity because God chose to create a woman. It was God who put me together in my mother's womb. It was God who put you together in your mother's womb. He chose to make us women and not men. It is beyond our ability to comprehend the fact that God knew each one of us before we were born. He has always known our entire genetic make up and our DNA. He made us the women he wanted us to be. From that moment our intrinsic worth in him was sealed, because we were created by him and for him. Many women all over the world have been robbed of that knowledge because they have been raised in societies that put a higher value on male babies than on female babies. It still happens in countries that have been Christianized. It has even been true in Britain. This attitude has led to many women being unable to appreciate their intrinsic worth in God and has sown seeds of resentment and rebellion in others.

If any reader has any doubts about her intrinsic worth in God, then meditate on Psalm 139. Put your own name into it. 'God created (your name)'s inmost being, he put me together in my mother's womb.' Give thanks to God for the wonderful truths about him and about you expressed by King David in Psalm 139.

Loved by God

'The steadfast love of the Lord never ceases...'
   (Lamentations 3:22, RSV)
'How great is the love that the Father has lavished on us
   that we should be called the children of God.' (1 John 3:1)
'For God so loved the world....' (John 3:16)

God loves us because God loves us because God is love. We do not need to earn God's love (indeed we cannot earn God's love), because it is his nature to love. He doesn't love us because of... He loves us in spite of... His love is unconditional. The whole of the Old and New Testaments are records of God's undying love for people – the crown of his creation.

The Old Testament is the record of his love for a people to whom he chose to relate in a special way in order that all people everywhere would eventually come to know him. In spite of all their sin and rebellion, he says through the prophet Malachi, 'I have (always) loved you.'

In the New Testament God showed his love in the supreme way by giving his son to die for our sins in order that the relationship broken by the man's disobedience and the woman's rebellion in Genesis 3 might be fully restored.

Condemned by sin to judgment

God hates sin – but he still loves sinners. God loves righteousness even more. The consequence of sin is judgment. 'For all have sinned and fall short of the glory of God' Romans 3:23 (NIV).

Sin is a taboo word today – a word that our society has tried to eliminate from our vocabulary. It is regarded as an old-fashioned word associated with the religious language of a bygone age. It has no place in the enlightened secular and all inclusive society to which we now belong – a society where tolerance of everything and everyone is the prime virtue. As in the days of the Judges of the Old Testament, ' everyone does what is right in their own eyes' (Judges 21:25) – there is nothing new about existentialist philosophy. Once the parameters of behaviour set by God are debunked, people have to create a more amenable god – the god of self. The worth and the image, was a reflection of God, now become a reflection of self – my worth, my image, my rights.

Someone has said that sin defines itself. It has I at the centre! But my worth, as we have noted before, does not depend on what I have achieved, or how highly I think I am regarded or how happy I am with me. It's only when I is stripped away and I acknowledge the reality of my sInful nature that, paradoxically the way is prepared for me to find my true worth which is intrinsic to my humanity, which has been obscured by my fallen nature's bias towards sin. Sin is anything which opposes the righteousness of God.

In his book *Spiritual Depression – its causes and its cure* Martyn Lloyd Jones says: 'In response to the question "Are you going to preach to us about sin, are you going to preach to us about conviction of sin, surely that is going to make us still more unhappy? Are you deliberately trying to make us miserable and wretched?" – To which the simple reply is, "Yes!..It may sound paradoxical – the term does not matter – but beyond any question that is the rule, and there are no exceptions. You must be made miserable before you can know true Christian joy. Indeed the real trouble with the miserable Christian is that he (she) has never been truly made miserable because of conviction of sin. He (she) has bypassed the essential preliminary to joy, and has been assuming something he/she has no right to assume...ultimately the only thing which is going to drive a man (woman) to Christ and make him (her) rely upon Christ alone is a true conviction of sin."'

'All have sinned,' is God's verdict – no exceptions – apart of course from the One who rescued us.

Rescued by God

'You see, just at the right time, when we were still powerless Christ died for the ungodly. Very rarely will anyone die for a righteous man though for a good man someone might possibly dare to die. But God demonstrates his own love for us in this, while we were yet sinners Christ died for us.' (Romans 5:6-8)

It took the death of his own Son on the cross to restore the fellowship between God and man and woman to be restored. The Jews had been offering the sacrifices that God had required by the shedding of the blood of animals that were placed on the altar. The shedding of Jesus' blood was the final sacrifice for sin.

Our personal rescue is sealed by our personal repentance and our personal belief in Christ as Lord and Saviour.

What is repentance? Repentance is not just saying sorry, but it is:

1.   Recognizing sin in the head, i.e. calling sin, sin – not my little weakness.
2.   Feeling sorrow in the heart.
3.   Confession with the lips.
4.   Turning away from sin as an act of the will.
5.   Making restitution where possible.

'If we confess our sins he is faithful and just and will forgive our sins and purify us from all unrighteousness' (1 John 1:9).

Personal cleansing and forgiveness follow personal repentance. We are made acceptable to God. Personal profession of belief in Christ seals restored relationships with God. We have entered into a new life in Christ.

Accepted by God

Therefore if anyone is in Christ he/she is a new creation; the old has gone the new has come! All this is from God who reconciled us to himself through Christ.

(2 Corinthians 5:17-18)

This means that it is as though everything that happened from Genesis 3 to Good Friday has been blotted out. God's relationship with the crown of his creation has been restored. Each one of us has the possibility of living in fellowship with God as he intended when he created the first woman from the first man. Our worth in God, marred by sin, has been totally restored. We will never be more acceptable to God than we are when we stand before him cleansed from each and every sin. 'There is now no condemnation for those who are in Christ Jesus' (Romans 8:1).

It is not difficult to acknowledge that we are sinners in God's eyes. What is more difficult is the acknowledgment of each and every sin in an ongoing way after we have entered into our new life in Christ.

'The blood of Jesus goes on cleansing' 1 John 1

I remember watching a TV programme (many years ago) where two young detectives, one male and one female, had made a real mess of the case in which they had been involved and which had resulted in innocent people being accused. In the closing scene of the programme they were walking past a large Catholic church. The young woman said something to the effect of, 'I'm going in to make my confession, are you coming with me?' 'Oh no', replied the young man, 'I'm a (naming a Protestant denomination) we don't confess our sins we just brood over them.'

My baptismal hymn was:

> Just as I am, young, strong and free,
> To be the best that I can be,
> For truth and righteousness, and Thee,
> O Jesus Christ, I come.

That bred in me a feeling that it was up to me now. It was a challenge to be a good person, a truthful person, a hard-working person – it was all striving to keep up to my promise. To admit

failure in any area was to let God down. When I heard the
statement of that young actor on TV I could identify with what
he was saying. Until the time in the 1960s when the Holy Spirit,
through the testimony of others, convicted me of self-pity and
pride and criticism (and all my other 'little weaknesses') I had
never known the release of confession and repentance as an
ongoing reality in my life as a Christian. I had learned to wear a
mask so that no one knew what I was really like. Passages like
1 John 1 had never really hit home as applying to believers. Basilea
Schlink of the Sisters of Mary at Darmstadt in Germany wrote
a book in the 1970s which was worth buying for its title alone –
Repentance – The Joy-Filled Life. When God brought me back to
the cross in repentance in the 1960s there were two immediate
reactions. First of all, I discovered that I was a much worse person
than I thought I was but, on the other hand I had a much deeper
awareness of what Jesus had done for me when he took my sin
on Calvary – and I experienced in a deeper way than ever before
the joy and the reality of peace when God is ruling in the heart.
The tense of the Greek verb in 1 John 1:7 means that 'the blood
of Jesus, his son, goes on cleansing'. It is a continuous process
throughout our lives.

Equipped to become disciples
* Created and loved
* Condemned by sin but rescued from judgment
* Accepted as a brand new person
* Equipped for service by the Holy Spirit

Realizing and personally acknowledging all of these truths bring
us into the experience of being truly born of the Spirit of God.
I was badly born. What do I mean? Perhaps as you've read my
testimony spread through previous chapters you don't need to
ask that question! It took me about twenty years to go through
the whole process of understanding and entering into all that
God had prepared for me. That was certainly not what God
intended. I have no doubt that I was a Christian but I wasn't a

well-grounded one. There are many people who struggle their way through their Christian life because, like me, they had been badly born. Perhaps new life began by 'asking Jesus into your heart' at the end of an evangelistic meeting or even by your own bedside as a child. God hears such prayers and knows what is in a person's heart. There is no doubt that something real has happened but there is no understanding of all that has happened in the experience of new birth – on God's side or ours.

In the process of pastoral counselling I have met many women who have never entered into the wholeness which being in Christ brings because they have never heard the full story. Even although they profess to be Christians they are totally absorbed into the world's view on image, esteem and worth. Life is split into three distinct compartments marked home, church, society which have little relevance the one to the other. Many have never grasped the immensity of all that God has done to make us brand new people. We don't need to live our lives dogged by past failures and experiences. Jesus dealt with all these things on the Cross. We, as believers, have Christ living in us by the Holy Spirit, and we are now living in Christ. We have the power to choose to live righteous lives in a fallen world. Satan will oppose us at every turn but he can only gain ground in our lives if we allow him to do so. If we insist on thinking about ourselves or other people the way we did before we became Christians then we are giving Satan ground in our minds. All negative thoughts come from him. If we do the same wrong things that we did before we became Christians then we are giving Satan ground in our emotions and our bodies. This is why it is so important to deal with all the self-centred sins that ruled over our lives before. It is also why we need to be quick to respond to the gentle but persistent convicting power of the Holy Spirit when he challenges us about wrong words spoken, wrong attitudes held, or wrong actions done. But we need to refuse to listen to Satan's negative whisperings in our ears which bring us under condemnation when he says, 'You've really blown it this time. You surely don't believe that God will forgive you again.' When God hears our confession and knows that our hearts are repentant, there is no such thing as 'again'. When God forgives he forgets – unlike Satan or us. Satan cannot forgive, he only condemns. Satan doesn't allow us to forget. We say we have forgiven others but we keep on remembering what they have said or done.

In his first letter Peter speaks about believers as a 'peculiar' people (AV translation). This word has developed another meaning from the one it had in Elizabethan English. In modern translations it is translated as 'chosen' or 'different'. It means that we should stand out in a crowd, not because we are continually awkward or negative but because we have a totally different raison d'être. Peter goes on to say, 'Your conduct among the heathen should be so good that, when they accuse you of being evil-doers, they will recognize your good (i.e. clean, upright, straight) deeds and so praise God in the Day of his coming.' (1 Peter 2:12 GNB)

The final equipping for discipleship (if this has not already taken place) is to be baptized in water and to become an active living member of the new Body of Christ on earth – the local church. There is no such thing as a detached Christian – when a limb is detached from the human body it dies. The same is true in the spiritual realm.

Some years ago Colin Urquhart wrote *In Christ Jesus*, a book which had a profound effect on my thinking about myself and others. One chapter is entitled 'Your portrait in Jesus' in which he lists about three hundred positive scriptural statements about those who live in Christ. It is a portrait of our true image in Jesus, where we find true esteem, and why we can rejoice in our worth. We need to learn, day by day, to apply Biblical truths to our lives in such a way that we are not swayed by the standards and pronouncements of a secular society.

Finally – The best of times? Or the worst of times?

To those of us who are older, who have lived through a World War, who have watched the Judaeo/Christian foundations of our heritage crumbling away to accommodate a multi-faith society; who remember the times of national crisis when our leaders called us to national days of repentance and prayer – for us perhaps this would seem to be the worst of times. But those days are gone. It may be that those of us who were brought up by Christian parents in secure Christian homes need to repent of taking our Christian heritage for granted. Perhaps future generations will regard us as the people who stood by and watched while the nation came under the control of unbelieving people. Evangelical Christians, unlike those of earlier years, had cut themselves off from the real world where our Lord lived out his earthly life and where he directed us to be salt and light.

But Christians all over the world are living in societies which are hostile to their beliefs, where their lives are constantly in danger. The fact is that it is in these countries that the church is growing and not declining. Someone has said that we need to turn our setbacks into springboards. We need to look forward and not back, to look up and not down, to look outwards and not inwards. We may not understand the information super highway or what postmodernity is all about but we need not be afraid of these things. We can use our ageless information super highway which we call prayer to reach any person, at any place, at any time via the One who is the Creator of everything! One of the strongest prayer strongholds in our church family is centred in our home for elderly people where a group of women (average age 70+, some very 70+) meet to pray for our nation, for local, national and world wide mission. There is no age limit in serving God. We need to look forward with certain hope to see God move again in our nation as those who are younger take up the challenge and go forward. They need our encouragement and not our criticism. We may not like the way things are done now, but that does not necessarily mean that God doesn't like them! We need to pray that those who are younger and more physically able will hold fast to the central unchanging scriptural truths which are God's ways for all time, while being relevant to contemporary society in mode of presentation. Young women have enormous pressures on them today which we never had to face. Remember that we all need to be building blocks and not stumbling blocks.

To those who are in middle age and younger years – your whole lives have been lived against a background of constant change. Your education has taken place against a strong feminist agenda. Many of the things which cause perplexity to those of us who are older are not a problem to you. The greater part of your life lies before you with all its challenges.

Don't dismiss the history of the years of the twentieth century – learn from all that as happened – good and bad. Accept the challenge to build anew where those of us who are older have allowed the enemy to demolish and destroy. Build on strong foundations of Biblical truth. Use every natural and spiritual gift which God has given you. Use them for his glory and not your own. Use them always in ways which are appropriate to your womanhood. Don't run ahead of God's purposes for your life and don't lag behind. His timing is always perfect. Young or old, when our lives are ordered by God – and not by a Godless society – any time can surely be 'the best of times'.

References

1. Dickens, Charles. *A Tale of Two Cities* (London:Penguin Classics)
2. All historical details and dates gleaned from *Chronicle of the 20th Century* (London: Longman Group Ltd, 1988)
3. Statistics are from 'Abortion, the personal dilemma' written by RFR Gardner ordained minister and (at the time of the passing of the Act) Consultant Gynaecologist, published by (Paternoster Press 1972.)
4. *Matters of Life and Death*, John Wyatt, p128, (Leicester: IVP, 1998)
5. *Social Focus on Women* published in 1997
6. Jill Lawson, Sevenoaks, Kent (used with permission)
7. Information on Edith Pechey from Edinburgh University magazine, Edit Summer 20007.
8. Oswald Chambers *My Utmost for His Highest* – June 13 (London: Marshall Morgan and Scott, 1963)
9. *The Inevitability of Patriarchy* by S G Goldberg, p44
10. Nicholas Davidson *The Failure of Feminism* (Buffalo,USA: Prometheus, 1988)
11. Roy Hession *The Calvary Road* (London: CLC, 1950)
12. Elisabeth Elliot *Passion and Purity* (London: Hodder Christian Paperbacks, 1985)
13. Wayne Grudem, *Recovering Biblical Manhood and Womanhood* (Wheaton, Illinois: Crossway Books, 1991)
14. Elisabeth Elliot, *Let me be a Woman* (Wheaton, Illinois: Tyndale House, 1986)
15. ibid.
16. William Barclay, *Daily Study Bible* (Edinburgh: St Andrews Press, 1981)
17. Weldon Hardenbrook, 'Where's Dad?' in *Recovering Biblical Manhood and Womanhood,*
18. Elisabeth Elliot, 'Virginity' Elisabeth Elliot Newsletter 1990
19. Historical records mainly gleaned from Wm Weinrich, Professor of Early Church History, Concordia Theological Seminary, Fort Wayne USA. 'Women in the History of the Church'. *Recovering Biblical Manhood and Womanhood* Chapter 15.
20. Archbishop Wm Temple, *Readings in John's Gospel* (London: Macmillan, 1968)
21. Edith Schaeffer *What is a family?* (Hodder Christian Paperbacks, 1975)

22. Clark H Pinnock *Women, Authority and the Bible,* (Downers Grove, Illinois: IVP 1986)
23. Dorothy Patterson, 'Why I believe Southern Baptist Church should not ordain women' Baptist History and Heritage July 1988
24. Golda Meir *Newsweek* November 1975

Christian Focus Publications publishes biblically-accurate books for adults and children. The books in the adult range are published in three imprints.

Christian Heritage contains classic writings from the past.

Christian Focus contains popular works including biographies, commentaries, doctrine, and Christian living.

Mentor focuses on books written at a level suitable for Bible College and seminary students, pastors, and others; the imprint includes commentaries, doctrinal studies, examination of current issues, and church history.

For a free catalogue of all our titles, please write to:

Christian Focus Publications, Ltd
Geanies House, Fearn, Tain,
Ross-shire, IV20 1TW, Great Britain

For details of our titles visit us on our web site

http://www.christianfocus.com